SPECIAL OPERATIONS EXECUTED

SPECIAL OPERATIONS EXECUTED
In Serbia and Italy

MICHAEL LEES

WILLIAM KIMBER · LONDON

First published in 1986 by
WILLIAM KIMBER & CO. LIMITED
100 Jermyn Street, London SW1Y 6EE

© Michael Lees, 1986
ISBN 0-7183-0629-5

This book is copyright. No part of it may be reproduced in any form without permission in writing from the publishers except by a reviewer who wishes to quote brief passages in connection with a review written for inclusion in a newspaper, magazine, radio or television broadcast.

Typeset by Print Co-ordination,
Macclesfield, Cheshire.
Printed and bound in Great Britain by
The Garden City Press Limited
Letchworth, Hertfordshire SG6 1JS.

To the memory of the late Corporal Bert Farrimond, miner, poacher, entrepreneur and dedicated radio operator. Tough, unswervingly loyal and, like his Boss, outspokenly intolerant and contemptuous of poseurs. He never once in any way let me down.

Also to those many Italians in the ranks of the Resistance and to those civilians, to whom I owe my escape and my life.

Contents

		Page
	Acknowledgements	11
	Foreword	13
	Prologue	15
I	M04 Cairo: 'The Tweed Cap Boys'	17
II	Briefing for Yugoslavia	27
III	Arrival in Serbia	36
IV	The Bulgar Massacre	51
V	The Morava Valley Reconnaissance	68
VI	Četnik Internecine Strife	81
VII	Sabotage Operations Commence	94
VIII	Deal with Partisans Fails	109
IX	We Carry War to the Enemy	123
X	Ally Dumped	138
XI	Back to the Fleshpots	149
XII	Journey to Pino	159
XIII	Journey from Pino	188
XIV	Fleshpots Revisited	211
XV	Arrival in Emilia: Fools' Paradise	217
XVI	The Reggiani Regroup	230
XVII	Sizing up Botteghe/Albinea	245
XVIII	The Grand Finale: Down to Earth with a Bump	259
	Index	275

List of Illustrations

	Facing page
An SIS man with Major Radislav Djurić	48
The author with Čikabuda	48
The author with Major John Sehmer	48
Joško's wedding	49
Peasant girls	49
A delivery of slivović	49
'Collaboration' meeting	64
Captain Jovo Stefanović	64
Group of Četniks with Stefanović	64
Pesić, Lt Andrejević and Četniks	65
Winter quarters	65
Lt Tomlinson, Sgt Harry Lesar and the author	65
Lees on Hitler	112
Lees with the horses	112
Winter quarters with packhorses	112
Sgt Faithful and Peter Solly-Flood	113
Major Peter Solly-Flood	113
Winter quarters	113
Captain Boon with Peter Solly-Flood	128
Peter resting on the way back from the railway	128
Bringing home the bacon	128
Captain Robert Purvis	129
British group prior to evacuation	129
On the way out to evacuation	129
The wedding of Mike and Gwen Lees	164
Wedding group	164
Secchio village, Mission HQ	165
Scalabrini	165
Secchia valley	165
Major Wilcockson, the author, Corporal Farrimond and Don Carlo	180
The author's Mission	181
The barn near Albinea where the author lay wounded	181

	Facing page
Dr Chiesi at the 1949 Italian celebrations	240
Glauco Monducci and the author in the bullock cart *Laurence Lewis*	240
With Gordon Lett in front of the Villa Rossi	240
The Villa Rossi	240
The entrance gates of the Villa Rossi	241
Gianni Farri with Glauco Monducci *Laurence Lewis*	241
The 1985 celebrations in Albinea	256
Mike and Gwen Lees revisit the mountains	257

Illustrations in the Text

	Page
Area of operations in Yugoslavia	52
North Italy. The route from Prea to Mentone	195
Emilia	226
The approach route for the attack on the Villa Rossi and the Villa Calvi	261
Pictorial illustration of the approach	262
Plan of the Villa Rossi and the Villa Calvi	263

Acknowledgements

My thanks are due to Basil Davidson for his witty and vivid account in his book *Special Operations Europe* of almost unbelievable shenanigans in M04 (SOE Cairo HQ) in 1943, which explained a lot which has puzzled me for years. It was also thanks to his review of Nora Beloff's intriguing book about Tito that I learned from that charming lady of David Martin's work *Patriot or Traitor* – The case of General Mihailović (Hoover Archival Documentaries). This report of the Committee for a Fair Trial of Draja Mihailović is a must for anyone interested in Yugoslavia and I have to thank David Martin for his tireless work in opening Pandora's box by locating extensive files dealing with SOE in Yugoslavia in the Public Record office which I suspect got there by oversight since the master SOE files have never been released under the Thirty Year Rule. Re-reading my own official report and those of colleagues encouraged me to resuscitate my faded manuscript.

Laurence Lewis was to blame for awakening long dormant memories of the Italian episodes and my thanks are due to him for numerous kindnesses. Peter Lee, Chairman of the Historical subcommittee of the Special Forces Club, has to bear responsibility for drawing the attention of Kimber to the MS which I had actually sent to him for the Club archives. I owe him thanks for much help and encouragement since.

I also owe thanks to Stevan Pavlowitch of the History Department of Southampton University for help with names and maps.

In particular I wish to express my very sincere appreciation of the work done by the Director, teachers and students of the Scuola Media Statale L. Ariosto of *Albinea* in preparing delightful illustrated pamphlets in 1965 and again in 1985 commemorating the Villa Rossi action and for permission to use their work.

My acknowledgement is due to D.J. Costello (Publishers) Ltd. for permission to use material from *Echoes of Resistance* (Costello 1985).

MICHAEL LEES
1986

Foreword

In March 1949 I was invited by the Council of Reggio Emilia to become a Freeman of their beautiful city in the Emilian plains. Prior to the ceremony in the main square of the city a Mass was celebrated in the private chapel of the Villa Rossi at Albinea, the scene of the raid on the German Army HQ, the story of which is related in this book. The Mass was celebrated by Don Carlo, the Green Flames Brigade commander, and I sat with my wife in the front row of the chapel together with General Roveda, Eros, the political commissar, and a number of other leading Communist members of the three Garibaldini Brigades of the Reggio Emilian Division of the Italian partisan movement. The celebrations were organised by the Communist Party of Reggio Emilia, and paid for by the Christian Democrats, and the whole occasion symbolised the cooperation between all political parties in the liberation movement when Italy found her soul, which cooperation was total in my area during the period when I was the British Liaison Officer there.

After the Mass we moved the few paces to the Villa Rossi where a plaque was unveiled in memory of Lieutenant Riccomini, Sergeant Guscott and Corporal Bolden of the 2nd SAS who fell in the battle inside the HQ.

All this took place at a time of acute political tension in Italy and the Italian Army were posted in force in the side streets of Reggio where we later moved. It was hardly conceivable in the then existing situation that a celebration involving some thousands in the main square, and particularly one organised by the Communist party, would pass off without trouble. Nevertheless it did. There had been a gentleman's agreement between the parties to eschew politics and the only digression occurred when Eros, the political commissar of the Reggiani Division, unable to contain himself in an otherwise apolitical speech, invited me to ask the British Government to stop being beastly to Communists in Malaya. Major Gordon Lett, previously British Liaison Officer in the Rossano Valley and in 1949 British Consul in Bologna, who was sharing the occasion and the honours with me, looked enigmatic and the moment passed. Sadly, Eros was killed shortly thereafter whilst trying to escape to Yugoslavia. Eros and at least two other leading figures at the ceremony were actually outlaws at that time. Such was Italy in 1949.

Soon after, my injuries incurred in the Villa Rossi attack caught up with me and I was hospitalised for some months. I used this time to write this book, in which I tried to portray the life of an ordinary adventurous youngster, brought up in the military tradition like so many of my generation, who joined the Special Operations Executive seeking action, and who got caught up in a world of politics and intrigue.

The resulting manuscript ended up in an old tin box and I got on with making a living. It stayed in that box till Laurence Lewis, researching for his thoughtful book about the Italian Partisan movement (*Echoes of Resistance*, Costello 1985), started to dig into the past. Then I was invited to another very touching fortieth anniversary ceremony in Albinea and shortly thereafter the launching of Laurence Lewis's book brought me into contact with Peter Lee, chairman of the historical sub-committee of the Special Forces Club, and we got talking about the need to put the record a bit straighter about what really happened in Yugoslavia in 1943 and 1944. All this led me to dig out the frayed and faded manuscript which I myself had not read through since I first put it away.

This book was written when I was thirty-five years younger and at a time when there were little or no research facilities, particularly in respect of places like Yugoslavia under Communist control. The book is a true account of my adventures and experiences but, being a simple fighting soldier, I had obeyed orders and kept no diary. Thus, even in 1950, I had to rely on six-year-old memory for the names of people and places. Furthermore, to protect them, I changed many of the names and only now after forty years am I trying to get them right. I must apologise to those I have wronged by getting the odd names mixed up but I stand by the events recorded. They took place as recounted, each and every one.

I am making no endeavour to modernise the text. It is presented as it was written by an unsophisticated young man who loved action, in the hope that it will interest and entertain the new adventurous younger generation.

MICHAEL LEES
1986

Prologue

I walked to the door of the cowshed and looked outside. The sun was setting in a blaze of golden glory behind the distant mountains to the west. The peaks stood out clear with their white snow caps broken by fierce grey rock. A thousand feet lower stretched the tree line, the first few groups of stone houses where live the hardy mountain folk, then the lower hills spotted with larger villages, the land showing more signs of cultivation, until my eyes settled on the immediate vista of rolling hills, olive groves, rough roads, and large gaunt farm buildings which characterised the Italian plains. I looked for a moment longer, drinking in the beauty of the scene. Then, as the sun slipped behind the hills, I shook myself and turned back to the shed.

Inside, the men were still sleeping, crowded into three small stands their arms and ammunition piled in the mangers. Two guards, drowsy from the atmosphere of warm dung, peered sleepily at me...

'Find Gordon, Modena and Gianni. Tell them to call in the guards, have a meal and be ready to move in an hour's time. Conference for all commanders in twenty minutes.'

I walked across to the farmhouse and went upstairs. Roy was sleeping soundly in the double bed which we had taken over for the day. I woke him up...

'I've ordered parade at eight and final orders in twenty minutes time. Get up and we'll see if we can get the farmer to give us some milk and eggs for supper.'

Roy, the SAS commander, opened one eye...

'You bloody pest; I was just dreaming of dining at the Berkeley.'

When we had eaten, the section commanders came in; they sat down and called for more wine. They were a mixed collection, the pick of five races. The SAS officers, two young subalterns, well disciplined and capable-looking were noticeable for their clean scrubbed appearance.

Roy and his men had dropped to us expressly for this job. They had been with us some three weeks only and their uniforms were still tidy and well pressed. The others bore the marks of a long time in the mountains. Gordon, Commander of my special bodyguard and sabotage squad, was a young Italian officer, tall, well-built and very good looking, dressed in torn ski trousers and battle dress jacket many sizes too small. Modena, the Russian, intriguing by virtue of his reactionary leanings, wore peasant trousers and a leather jacket. Jimmy, the Frenchman, was dressed in shorts and ski-jacket and Hans, a German deserter employed as my orderly, in full German uniform. They were indeed a motley crowd, but less so than the men under their command. In addition to Roy's SAS parachutists, our force comprised Russians – deserters from two armies – French, one Spaniard, a Yugoslav and of course, Italian partisans, the pick of the fifteen hundred men in the Reggiani partisan division.

The orders were given by Roy, slowly and singly and translated as necessary, Italian being the lingua franca. Occasionally it was necessary to put a sentence into French or Yugoslav, which Modena understood, to be sure that all was clear.

'And remember, the Corps HQ which we are attacking tonight controls the whole front from Bologna to the coast. The destruction of this HQ will save thousands of Allied lives in the push which is just starting. Two German generals live in the Villa Rossi. They must be captured or killed. If we cannot get into the Villa Rossi or Villa Calvi we will surround them, burn them down and see that nobody escapes. If we are challenged en route Hans will answer in German and, if we meet a patrol or the alarm is given, move straight in and attack. The job must be completed within a quarter of an hour of the first shot. Is that understood?'

'*Capito.*'

The men formed up in three columns outside; their faces blacked, their arms wrapped in flannel and every man carried an automatic weapon. I checked that all understood.

'Gordon, *pronto?*'

'*Pronto, Capitano.*'

'Modena, *je 'l'ste gotovi?*'

'*Da, Gospodine Kapitan.*'

'*Êtes-vous prêt,* Jimmie?'

'*Oui, monsieur le capitaine.*'

We moved off into the night.

CHAPTER ONE

M04 Cairo: 'The Tweed Cap Boys'

It was in Shepheards Bar in Cairo in early 1943 that I first heard of the activities of the 'tweed cap boys'. My informant, a gentleman of cheerful mien with an inferiority complex and a glamorous blonde, was making a gallant attempt to impress his bored companion with an exceedingly detailed account of his recently acquired position on the staff of a certain highly secret department of General Headquarters in Cairo. I always find other people's conversation fascinating and, as they had chosen to sit at my table, I felt no compunction in listening to graphic tales of the activities of various secret agents controlled, I was led to understand, by this cheerful but somewhat insecure reveller.

By the time Joe, the bartender, had dispensed his last 'suffering bastards' and tactfully suggested that the bar must now close, I had succeeded in persuading the, by now almost recumbent, staff officer, that we had certainly been at school together and that in the absence of his girl friend, who had long since departed in fury, I was a sufficiently appreciative audience for an account of the no doubt admirable work he was doing in aid of the Allied war effort. Eventually I put him to bed.

Though I suppose I should have done so, I did not report his careless talk. He was probably overworked and certainly tight and, as I was to discover later, almost everyone stationed in Cairo already knew everything he had told me. It seemed unkind to get a man into trouble who had done me a good turn.

I was enjoying a week's leave from my unit, a Parachute battalion stationed in the Canal Zone. I had been with this unit for nine months and I wanted a change. Although I loved the hard life, plentiful exercise and, in particular, the parachuting with all its trappings, I was by nature not very amenable to discipline instilled by others and I consequently loathed the routine of a unit in training. I was restless, as were most who had seen no action and who felt that the war would pass them by, and I had been looking around for some time for another job.

That casual meeting made a deep impression upon my unsettled mind. Although, at first, I listened from amusement tempered with curiosity, I later found myself memorising all that my informant said and pressing him for further details. It seemed that the pseudonym 'tweed cap boys' was used by initiates to denote members of a special organisation which was designed to despatch agents to various parts of enemy-occupied Europe, in particular the Balkans. Some were civilians of alien nationality, dropped to keep us informed of enemy activities; they were of little interest to me but I was amazed to hear that others were parachuting into Europe too. English officers, sometimes in uniform, without special language qualifications, whose job it appeared was not solely to report on the enemy but to contact and advise the various guerilla groups which, it was whispered, were springing up all over Europe. It had never occurred to me that there might be room in Europe for both the Germans and myself.

As he talked bemusedly on, he disclosed a tale which was as fascinating as it was disjointed and, as yet to me, obscure. Though two years later such tales were commonplace, they were original and stirring then and I feel that I may be forgiven for devouring it all. I decided to discover all there was to know of this secret organisation and, if it were at all possible, force my way into it, although I had only the sketchiest idea of what that would imply.

But to have airy ambitions was one thing; to fulfil them was a very different matter. Persistent enquiry in the course of the next few days and subsequent observation of the activities of various officials who had been pointed out to me as involved in this work showed me where the headquarters were located. From there it was but a short step to discover the system of recruitment and it was this which appeared to constitute an insurmountable obstacle. I was told that any stranger visiting these headquarters would find little to distinguish it from any other military office. The floor would be dirty, tin mugs lying around the passages, windows, shelves and doors would be covered with the usual military hieroglythics. One could imagine what would happen to anyone daring to walk in and ask for a job. He would be greeted with raised eyebrows and denial of any special work or vacancies and advised to consult his commanding officer if he wished to join the staff. It is possible that no one ever dared. Recruitment, I learned, was carried out by personal introduction only and, at that time, any other approach would undoubtedly render the applicant highly suspicious. My leave finished on this discouraging note.

I was in Palestine some days later, when a friend asked me to take a letter to his cousin in Cairo, when I passed through on my way back to the unit the following day.

'John will be delighted to see you,' added Richard. 'He's a full colonel, poor fellow, but don't let that worry you. He has a very dull job chained to a desk, and he's always glad to see people and hear what's going on outside.'

He went on to mention that his cousin was a keen horseman and would probably ask me out to dinner if I talked about horses with him. He handed me an envelope addressed in his firm upright handwriting.

The address was strangely familiar.

*

I paid off my taxi and walked into the building. A pleasant-looking lance corporal in battle dress sat at a barrier.

'Good evening, I've come to see Colonel Lonsdale.'

'Have you an appointment, sir?'

'No, but he knows I'm coming.'

'Right, sir, do you mind waiting a minute.' He picked up the telephone.

'Is that Colonel Lonsdale's secretary? There's an officer to see him . . . right I'll send him up. . . Do you mind filling in this ticket and getting it initialled before you come down? Harry, show the officer up to Room 59.'

We went up a flight of stairs, along a corridor and into a sparsely furnished office. A nice looking girl in a thin flowery frock got up from a table equipped with a typewriter and three or four full trays.

'Good evening, Colonel Lonsdale is waiting for you, will you come with me?'

We went through an intercommunicating door into another office. Behind a bare table sat Richard's cousin. He was a man of about forty, well built, with thick black hair and a great twinkle in his eye. I introduced myself and handed him the letter.

'Come in and sit down. I'm very glad to see you, you must tell me all about Richard and what he's doing. Mary, tell anyone who calls that I'm out. Hope you didn't have any trouble getting in, I think they've got pretty slack recently. You're stationed in the Canal Zone, aren't you?'

'Yes, but I've just come down from Palestine.'

'Oh, you've been up there have you. What were you doing there?'

I was glad of this opportunity to draw him out...

'I've been on a course... in the intervals of hunting Jack with the Ramleh Vale.'

His eyes glistened and I could see that we were well set. To confirm this, he pressed his bell and ordered two large whiskies from the orderly who came in.

'I'd ask you out to dinner but I'm most infernally busy and I've got to see God at seven and God knows when I'll be free.' He laughed heartily at his blasphemy, explaining, 'God's what we call our chief, you know! I'm going away on Tuesday for a long time. We older people have to do training courses sometimes too,' he added rather unconvincingly.

Seizing this as my cue, I attempted to work the conversation round to the work he was doing. I tried hard to give him the impression that Richard had told me all about it but he immediately became evasive, and a few minutes later he looked pointedly at his watch. Realising that I would achieve nothing here, I thanked him for the drink and left.

My feelings were mixed as I walked back to the hotel. My first approach had failed but I now knew my way in and a definite plan was forming in my mind. Lonsdale was going away, out of touch perhaps. Had he not said 'Tell Richard to write to me but he probably won't get an answer'. All the better – if I used his name for an introduction no one would realise how little he knew me. They'd only know that I'd spent an hour or so talking to him in his office, apparently as old friends. Underhand maybe but the end justified the means.

It was three long weeks before I was able to visit Cairo again and during this time my curiosity had hardened into an absolute determination, out of which had sprung a definite plan. I resolved to waste no more time, but stake everything on a bold bluff.

All depended on Lonsdale having gone away as he had intended. At the time I imagined that there was little risk in assuming that he would have done so. When I later discovered how people going on operations were often delayed for weeks, even months, I realised how lucky I was that Lonsdale kept to his schedule.

'Have you a pass, sir?' asked the warden at the door.

'No, I'll fill one in. I want to see Colonel Lonsdale.'

The warden scanned his list...

'I'm afraid he's not in, sir.'

Thank God, I murmured to myself. At least there was a chance that events would now work out as I had planned. I sounded annoyed.

'Oh damn; it's really rather important. When will he be back?'

'Well, sir, I don't know.'

'I'd better see his second in command.'

The warden looked suspicious, but he picked up the telephone.

'There's an officer here come to see Colonel Lonsdale. Would the major see him, miss?' A pause: 'Right, miss.'

'Will you go up and wait, sir. The major is busy now, but he'll see you in ten minutes.'

I walked slowly upstairs. On the landing a staff officer, dressed in a kilt, was talking to a man in torn battledress without unit markings or badges of rank. The latter's hair hung low over his shoulders and his dark eyes gleamed out of a brown face covered with a mass of stubble. He talked English with a marked accent. They appeared to be discussing some action in which the wild looking foreigner had taken part and, as they saw me, the officer in the kilt signed to the other to be quiet, drawing him into an office and shutting the door behind them. I passed on to the secretary's office.

'Hullo, I'm sorry Colonel Lonsdale is not here. Didn't he tell you he'd be away?'

This, with a pleasant smile, from the girl in the flowery frock. It was just what I had expected and my lie was ready.

'He did say something about it but he didn't tell me when, of course. He asked me to come back on Monday last but I couldn't get up to Cairo then, so I came today; I had hoped that he would still be here.'

She hardly heeded what I said and moved into the next room, shutting the door behind her. I sat down on the edge of the table, fiddling with my cap and trying to read the files which lay on her desk. I found myself feeling more and more nervous as the minutes ticked by and the possible consequences of my misrepresentation occurred vividly to me. When she came back silently into the room, it was all I could do to prevent myself turning and running from the building.

'Will you come in now, please.'

The kilted officer I had seen in the corridor got up from a table. His greeting was cold and businesslike.

'Good evening. I'm sorry the colonel is away. What can I do for you?'

I found myself stuttering, 'I'm afraid it's all rather involved. The colonel is an old friend of mine and I came to see him a couple of Saturdays ago. We talked things over and he suggested I might like to join this organisation. He told me to come back on Monday to discuss it further but I couldn't get up to Cairo. Of course, he couldn't tell me which day he was going away and I'd hoped to find him here tonight.'

His right eyebrow rose dubiously . . .

'Colonel Lonsdale never told me anything about it.'

I was warming to my rehearsed part and I lied more glibly this time . . .

'He was expecting to see me on Monday evening: probably with the rush and everything he forgot about it.'

'Yes, very probably.' The major thought for a moment before he went on: 'Well, I think the best thing I can do is to send him a signal about you. Do you know if he wanted you to go to join him?'

My heart sank. This was not what I wanted at all. If he sent a signal, Lonsdale would either have forgotten my name completely or would signal back to say that he had never suggested such a thing. In either case, I'd be in a hopeless position.

'Oh no, I don't think he particularly wanted me to join him,' I protested, adding lamely: 'He just suggested that I might be suitable for this organisation.'

It was obvious that the major regarded my story as a very dubious one; on the other hand, he could not openly discredit it. He decided to hedge:

'Well, I'm afraid there aren't any vacancies in our branch just now. We're more or less closing down. I don't know about the others. You'd better come back in about two weeks' time.'

I went out rather crestfallen. Two weeks would be ample time to check up on me if he cared to do so and to expose my bogus story. However, there was always a chance that he would forget completely about me, in which case I might be able to bluff him into something on my next visit. I knew little more about the organisation to which I was trying so hard to sell myself than I had on overhearing that conversation at Shepheards, but opposition had made me even more determined to join than before and I never questioned trying again.

A few days later I was back at the door for a third time. The warden recognised me and handed me a card to fill in. I wrote my own name and the major's on it.

The warden read it.

'I'm sorry – the major is away.'

After a few moments' consideration, my first sensation of

disappointment gave way to relief. At least I would not have to tackle that 'hard nut' again.

'Who is standing in for him?' I asked.

The warden mentioned the name of a captain. 'You'll find him a very nice gentleman, sir,' he added confidentially.

I was shown up into a different waiting room, on the ground floor this time. After about ten minutes a young solid-looking staff captain with a pleasant smile came in . . .

'Good evening, did you want to see me?'

I told my story and finished by outlining my interview with his boss. I went so far as to say, however, that the latter had been very keen to see me again. The captain swallowed it all.

'I'm afraid he's away for a bit. Would you be able to come back in a few days' time?'

It was clear that if I was ever to get anywhere, this was my chance. I sounded annoyed:

'I'm a common soldier, and I can't get leave whenever I like.'

He thought for a moment.

'Well, you'd better come up and see the Recruiting Officer. If both Lonsdale and his number two know you, you ought to be all right. I'll take you up now.'

I thanked him more profusely than I felt he expected.

Walking upstairs I tried to look casual but that was far from what I felt. My bluff had come off and now everything depended on the impression I made at the interview. Even if I was turned down, at least I could feel I had had a chance. I quickly banished the disturbing thought that I still knew nothing of the organisation I was joining, as I relied on passing off my ignorance under the veil of secrecy which dominated everyone in the building. The captain knocked on a door.

'Hullo here's a possible recruit for you, his name is Lees and he's a friend of Lonsdale.'

I followed him into the office where another major, a giant of a man, sat at a table in one corner. Behind another table was a tall elegant captain, wearing the uniform of the Scots Guards. I saluted and smiled gratefully at my companion as he went out, closing the door.

'Take a pew,' said the major. 'Now why do you want to join this organisation?'

I was prepared for this.

'Because, from the little I know of it, it's an interesting and exciting life and because I consider myself an individualist.'

This appeared to satisfy him.

'Do you know any foreign languages?'

'I speak French fairly well and I used to speak some German. It would not take me long to learn any foreign languages necessary.'

Part of this statement was not wholly true but I was confident that I would not be tested and, although they questioned me searchingly, I had the feeling that this was formality. What mattered was that my 'sponsor' knew me well and was prepared to answer for me.

When he had finished the major handed me a dull-looking form which demanded particulars more or less similar to those which he had already asked about. As I read it through he asked casually:

'By the way, how old are you?'

'Twenty-one,' I replied ingenuously.

The moment I said it, I knew that I had made a gaffe for the two exchanged glances and the major explained:

'You're very young. We usually never take people under twenty-five, and you have no special qualifications.'

He played with his pencil, doodling on the blotter, and then he picked up the telephone.

'We'd better see if Davidson could use you.' He turned to his companion. 'Will you take him down?'

We wandered around a labyrinth of corridors, down some stairs and along more corridors. Typewriters clacked from behind closed doors and the sound of deep voices and female laughter came from some of the rooms. Turning a corner we nearly bumped into an orderly carrying a trayful of glasses; cocktail time it seemed! We stopped at a door and the captain went in leaving me in the passage. After a short time he came out and led me into a brightly lit office. There was a small desk by the window, comfortable armchairs dotted the room and the walls were hung with large scale maps of the Balkans.

The man who rose from behind the desk was tall, good-looking and carried himself well and I was immediately struck by his charismatic personality. He wore the badges of a major with parachute wings on his arm. After shaking hands he gave me a seat, proffered a cigarette and smiled disarmingly.

'The people upstairs have offered me your services; they've told me nothing about you, so I'd better find out for myself.'

Davidson asked me much the same questions as I had been asked previously, but with the difference that he studied the answers carefully and was obviously sizing me up.

'What are you doing at the moment?'

'I'm with a Parachute battalion,' I answered.

'Have you asked them if they are willing to let you go?'

I replied that I had not done so, adding that I thought it unlikely that they would take very kindly to such an application. I felt that this would give a good impression, and in fact it was the truth, though I was probably the least essential link in my unit. There was a definite policy of refusing all applications for transfer and my previous attempts had already been turned down. I went on to say that I had hoped that an organisation such as this might have the power to demand all whom they required. Davidson's reply was non-committal, but his next question raised my hopes:

'Do you speak any Balkan languages?'

'I'm afraid not,' I replied.

Davidson took a book from a drawer and handed it to me across the desk.

'You had better start studying this,' he advised.

I looked at the cheap brown paper cover. It was a Serbo-Croat Grammar.

*

The following day I was required to endure a seemingly interminable series of interviews. Davidson apologetically steered me through security, intelligence, administration, finance, many degrees of commanding officers and finally the head of the organisation, Lonsdale's 'God'.[1] Everybody was charming and helpful, but I felt that any enemy agent attempting to penetrate this organisation would certainly have broken down long before the stage I finally reached that day. It needed truly British stoicism to answer the same questions, put in the same way, by remarkably similar people, in identical offices, during a hot Cairo afternoon.

Two weeks later saw me over all the fences and preparing for the future. Once past that seemingly impregnable first barrier, my recruitment was a matter of straightforward routine. I saw my brigadier[2] who, once he had assured himself that I understood what I was intending to do, allowed me to leave my unit with no

---

[1] Lord Glenconner.
[2] General Sir John Hackett.

recriminations for having gone behind his back. I went quietly, making no farewells, and for secrecy's sake I told brother officers that I was going to take up a staff appointment at GHQ. I don't think many believed me, my loathing of any routine was too well known, but I had to use some cover story which would allow for a temporary stay in Cairo. Only one man knew exactly what I was to do, and he made a remark that I was to remember often in later months.

I was in my tent packing when Micky Thomas came in. He was a nice person, intelligent and sympathetic:

'Hullo, Mike, I hear you are leaving us.'

'Yes, I'm becoming a staff officer in Cairo,' I confessed.

'No, you're not,' said Micky grinning, 'You needn't try your cover stories on me!'

I tried to look astonished and spluttered a protest. He silenced me:

'I was in Davidson's office myself just after you left on Saturday; he asked me what sort of chap you were.'

'Oh, and what did you say?'

'Well, if you want to get yourself killed, that's your own business and I wouldn't stand in your way. I gave you a good chit.'

'Thanks, Micky, but what were you doing there?'

'I was negotiating for a job myself but I turned it down. I'm a regular soldier and that sort of thing won't help my career much; besides, I don't think they would let me go from here.'

'Don't spread it around, will you?'

'Good God, no, but I'll give you just one word of warning before you sign on irrevocably. Remember this; don't cry if you're let down. Those people have a very bad reputation for doing that if it suits them.'

I was only twenty-one and wildly enthusiastic about my new job. Is it to be wondered at that I paid little heed to Micky's warning.

CHAPTER TWO

Briefing for Yugoslavia
First Lesson in Balkan Politics

Comfortably ensconced in a flat on Gezira Island I applied myself wholeheartedly to studying the language, taking advantage of the excellent arrangements made by Davidson. My tutor, a Yugoslav refugee, spoke excellent English and as at that time I was his only pupil, I benefited from the individual attention he was able to give me. The privacy of our lessons too afforded me the opportunity to draw him out to relate his experiences during the German advance into Yugoslavia and to comment on current Yugoslav affairs.

Joško was a young Serb intellectual from Belgrade. In civilian life he had trained as a lawyer, although like many other Balkan law students he had never practised his profession and had taken law examinations merely as a preparation for a political career. In spite of this, he never divulged his leanings to me and when three years later his true position was disclosed, it came as a very great surprise to me.

Joško was tall, dark and good-looking, but one could not fail to observe his love of good living, which was expressed in the soft white skin of his hands and, in spite of his comparative youth, the definite bulge under his waistcoat. Later I was to discover that the Serbs, who are a robust hard-living race, when transferred to the unaccustomed luxury of the town, rapidly grow fat, soft and decadent; many become obese.

Whatever his political and physical failings however, Joško had a clear, keen brain and the ability to seize upon essentials. As with all Serbs, narration came naturally to him and he built up for me a clear picture of what was happening in Yugoslavia, clarifying the tangled web of events since the last war which had sabotaged the Yugoslav experiment.

Joško went on to speak of the mutual distrust of the Serbs and Croats and explained how until the last war Croatia had constituted an integral part of the Austro-Hungarian empire, taking the side of her Austrian masters, whilst the Serbs fought gallantly with the Allies, enduring a defeat which ended with a terrible winter retreat across the mountains of Albania, a retreat in which but one man in three got through. He spoke of how, while these bitter memories were still alive in their minds, the Allies had created the Jugoslav or Southern Slav State, comprising Serbia, the mountain kingdom of Montenegro, Dalmatia, the coastal strip previously dominated by Italy, Bosnia and Herzegovnia, mountain territories inhabited by people of mixed religions and races, many of them Moslems since the days of Turkish domination, Macedonia, Croatia and Slovena.

All these smaller states were united under a central government in Belgrade. The Serbs, being in numerical majority, controlled the government and used their dominance unscrupulously to discriminate against the Croats. The Croats in their turn refused to recognise this government, and for years their deputies never took their seats. The dynasty was Serbian and the Serbian orthodox and Croatian Catholic faiths clashed continually whilst, to complicate the issue, over two million Moslems were scattered throughout the land. Apart from their common Slav origin which was but a loose tie, there was no sound basis on which to build a united nation.

Joško went on to tell the story of the German ultimatum to Prince Paul, Regent of Yugoslavia, in March 1941; of the acceptance of the terms by Paul's government; of the bloodless coup d'état by the elements of the army led by a nationalistic clique of Serbian Guards Officers who overthrew the Government in a night, placed the country under martial law, deposed Prince Paul, putting young King Peter on the throne and announced to the world that if the frontiers were crossed they would fight. It was a brave stirring tale over which Joško lingered proudly.

'The coup d'état took place on 27th March 1941. On that day, as your Mr Churchill said, "Yugoslavia found her soul". The officers, who had seized the reins of government, proclaimed martial law, mobilised the army and prepared to defend the country against any attack. I was attached to the General Staff at the time. The General realised that with only twenty-odd badly equipped divisions he would be powerless, when the attack came, to hold the frontier bordering Italy, Austria, Hungary, Rumania and Bulgaria to Greece. He would have liked to withdraw his army at once into the mountain fastness but unfortunately the nation was divided against itself. Many Croats resented the coup d'état, officered as it was by Serbs, and others openly declared their pro-Austrian leanings. Those who remained loyal were loyal not to Yugoslavia but to Croatia, and they would therefore never have accepted orders to withdraw from their homeland without resistance, to defend that of their rivals. Many of the units were officered by Croats and the General knew well that such an order would never be obeyed.

'On April 16th, the Germans bombed Belgrade without warning and on the same day they crossed the frontiers. War was never declared.'

'And then?' I asked.

'And then, my dear Lees, we stood no chance. The Germans attacked with their many armoured divisions through Hungary from the north. The Bulgars over-ran Macedonia in the south and marched into Serbia. The Allies gave us no support. They could not. King Peter left with his government for Cairo and eleven days after the first bombing we had to capitulate.'

'But resistance to the enemy never died down?'

'To understand truly about our resistance you must go to my country and know the people. We Serbs have been fighting for eight hundred years. We have been dominated many times by other nations and many times we have thrown off the yoke. Our people are born to be outlaws and to fight against the oppressor; no tyrant has ever subdued the Serbs.'

I was later to discover that eloquent speeches about his country are part of every Serb's make-up. They are intensely nationalistic and proud.

'But you ask about the resistance. When the army capitulated, rather than surrender their units into enemy hands, many officers ordered their men to make their own way home across the mountains. These men carried their arms with them and heavier weapons that could not be carried away were hidden in secret caches known only to the most trusted peasants in the locality. The spirit was there, the arms were there, it only needed the man, the leader.'

'General Mihailović,' I interrupted, having already read a little about Yugoslav affairs. His was a name recurring in many reports.

'Yes, as you say, Mihailović, but he was then only a colonel, an officer of the Staff HQ. When the army capitulated Mihailović never surrendered. He took to the mountains in peasant clothing and hid for a few weeks until things settled down, when he sent messengers all over Serbia inviting loyal friends to join him. Simultaneously in remote parts of the Serbian and Montenegrin mountains other resistance groups started to form. Many ex-soldiers returning from the war, finding their homes burnt and their wives and families killed, had no choice but to work for the enemy or take to the hills. Others more fortunate found their homes intact but a price on their heads; they went too. Eventually these men formed themselves into organised bands under local leaders and liaison sprung up between units until a core of resistance spread over large areas of the country.

'The imperative need of these isolated companies was some central command to co-ordinate and dictate a unified policy and Mihailović recognised this need. By then his own band had grown into an army and many veteran officers had flocked to his standard. He sent out these men, each as his representative for a specified area, and through them he endeavoured to bring the mountains under his own control. He also sent officers disguised in various ways to territory in Croatia and Slovenia which did not yet harbour guerilla bands, and to the plains and towns to start underground movements there. Within a few months his net of intelligence communications and command spread throughout the country.'

Once warmed to his subject, Joško would talk for hours but I was a willing audience and loth to interrupt him; his accounts were fascinating and I could learn from his verbal account far more than I could from any files.

'You ask how the British first came into the picture. That is a fascinating story. Mihailović realised that, to strengthen his movement sufficiently to be of any use to the war effort, he must get in touch with the outside world and solicit both benevolent propaganda and material support. At his mountain headquarters were a number of radio experts who had lately been technicians in the army. These men were ordered to make a wireless transmitter from whatever materials were available to them. They scoured the countryside for parts, raided stores, and eventually constructed a very crude station from which they sent out signals at various times each day, calling on Allied stations to reply. This was a highly dangerous activity, of course, for their transmission could be equally well picked up by enemy detectors. Three long months dragged by and no answer came; the technicians feared that their signals were too weak to reach the outside world and they advised that they close down.

'Then, when their patience was almost exhausted, they were heard by a British destroyer at sea in the Mediterranean and contact was established. The signals were relayed to Malta and codes were established by methods which are still secret. Shortly afterwards the guerillas were recognized by the British as regular forces of the Yugoslav army, and Mihailović was appointed by King Peter as Commander-in-Chief and Minister for War.'

Another evening Joško talked about the existing puppet government set up by the enemy occupiers of Yugoslavia. After the capitulation the Germans, having annexed whole provinces around the Yugoslav border, doled out slices of territory to their loyal allies the Italians, the Albanians and the Bulgars. The Bulgars, who had joined in the fray at the eleventh hour, did disproportionately well out of the share-out, acquiring most of Macedonia and large areas of southern Serbia for their pains, thereby repeating their jackal-like behaviour in the last war. However, they were not the only lucky ones, for the Hungarians acquired a rich province, the Bačka, along the banks of the Danube, as the price of allowing German troops to violate their neutrality.

What remained of the country was divided into two: Serbia and the neighbouring territories not annexed to Bulgaria, Albania and Hungary remaining under mixed Axis occupation whilst in Croatia the pro-Axis nationalists were allowed to form an independent State of their own.

To administer the occupied territories the Germans formed a puppet government in Belgrade under the Serbian General Nedić, an elderly army officer. This government and its leader resembled in many ways the Vichy administration in France. Nedić who, though very weak, was certainly no Nazi by conviction, nevertheless acceded to all the German demands, hoping thus to save his compatriots from excessive reprisals. The mass of the people were indifferent to him. They regarded him as a collaborator but realised that, in his own way, he was doing his best for them and they felt themselves to be better off administered by his government than under direct German rule.

In the Independent State of Croatia on the other hand Ante Pavelić backed by Mussolini had established a fully fledged Fascist State. Pavelić, who as an outlaw had been implicated in the murder of King Alexander in 1934 at Marseilles but was never brought to justice, was the leader of the notorious Croatian Ustaša movement which was a terrorist organisation whose ideals were violently nationalistic.

The Ustaša, which was comprised of the very worst Croatian elements, many of whom like Pavelić had returned from enforced exile, were embodied in the political and military police force in Croatia. Adopting the very worst Nazi methods, they opened concentration camps and carried out the most appalling atrocities, their victims being in particular the Serbian minority living in Croatia. It is believed that, adopting a practical policy of complete extermination, they murdered over a hundred thousand Serbs within the first few weeks of power, throwing the bodies into the Danube

until, so the Serbs have it, the river ran red with blood. However true or exaggerated that may be, it is certain that some tens of thousands of
Serbs returned to their fatherland floating down the river towards Belgrade, their corpses disfigured by the torture they had undergone before death.

Nedić's forces were of a very different calibre, consisting of a military police force and frontier guards; they resembled the pre-war Serbian Gendarmerie and, in fact, included the bulk of the latter who had carried on in accordance with the normal police tradition. In the early days of the occupation the Nedić police were used in drives against Mihailović's growing army but the Germans soon discontinued this practice when they ascertained that, rather than apprehending the outlaws, the Serbian troops were assisting them in every possible way.

It was in the course of this discussion that Joško first mentioned the Partisans.

'The Partisans are another guerilla organisation whose ideal is resistance to the Germans now but with all their activities directed to seizing power and bringing about a complete social revolution after the war. They are led by fanatical communists but they include many ordinary people who have either been conscripted or who have joined their forces through propaganda. For the first few months they worked together with Mihailović, but trouble soon arose between them and now it is rumoured that they are fighting each other in the mountains.

'When Mihailović was appointed Minister of War by King Peter and the exiled Yugoslav government in London, he called upon the Partisans to place themselves under his command; they refused to do so. Mihailović is fighting for the King and a normal democratic way of life after the war. The Partisans are fighting for social revolution and the establishment of a communist state. It is not surprising that they fight each other, when the Partisans have openly denounced the Dynasty.'

To my simple mind, this appeared a fantastic situation.

'But why do they fight amongst themselves now? Can't they wait till the Germans are defeated and then settle their differences peacefully?' I asked.

Joško smiled. 'When you go to Yugoslavia, my dear Lees, you may understand why.'

*

Some days later I received my marching orders and the general plan for my mission was outlined to me. My ultimate destination was a group of mountains south of Skoplje in Macedonia in the territory annexed by Bulgaria in 1941. Headquarters had for some time been aware that a resistance group of Yugoslavs was forming in that area. They had no detail concerning its strength or how it fared. It was only known that its leader was a Serb called Trbić. This was a particularly vital area for it covered the main railway line from Skoplje to Salonika which carried the bulk of the supplies for the enemy forces in Greece and railway maps showed that there were a number of large bridges on this stretch which were particularly suitable for attack. If one or more of those bridges could be destroyed, this main artery in the enemy's communication system might be paralysed for some time and, at the proper moment, this might constitute a considerable contribution to the war effort.

A British officer had been dropped into this area about a week previously. He was a mining engineer by profession, and he had spent some years in charge of mines in the Skoplje area and spoke the language fluently. In view of his intimate knowledge of that territory, he had been dropped 'blind'. That is, he had been parachuted somewhere into the vicinity of where the guerillas were purported to be, trusting to his local knowledge to carry him through until he could link up with them. This risky course had been forced upon him because they had no communication with the outside world and it was therefore impossible to warn them of his arrival. This officer had taken a wireless set with him and a special watch had been kept on his wavelength night and day since his departure. Not a signal had been heard and Headquarters were forced to the conclusion that he had been killed or captured.

As this plan had failed, it had been proposed to send my mission to Trbić via the nearest guerilla unit which had communication with Cairo. This unit, commanded by a Major Djurić, already had a British officer, Sehmer, with them, who had dropped in about a month previously. He was instructed to arrange our reception and to despatch a courier to Trbić telling him to send an escort to accompany us to his headquarters. At this time Sehmer was reported to be operating on a mountain called the Kapaonik in occupied Yugoslavia about a hundred and fifty miles through the mountains from Trbić's territory.

In view of this long march, it was decided that I should take no supplies with me and only the minimum of wireless equipment, as we should be unable to carry anything but the barest necessities. Once established with Trbić I would be able to arrange 'parachutage' and I was promised immediate delivery of six plane loads of material.

This plan appeared the most satisfactory in spite of the long march which it entailed. At least our arrival should be secure, as it had been reported by Sehmer that Djurić was very powerful and had liberated whole areas of the mountains. I hoped that he would be able to give us concrete help to reach our destination.

A few days later a signal was received from Sehmer expressing his approval of the plan and reporting that he had despatched a plain clothes courier to Skoplje by train with a message for Trbić, asking him to come personally. In the course of this signal, Sehmer pointed out that, though Djurić and his forces were firmly allied behind Mihailović, he was not at all clear where Trbić's allegiance lay, and that he had heard rumours that there were Partisans operating in his vicinity. I mentioned this to Davidson and asked for instructions. His instructions were very clear.

'Your job is to help the Yugoslavs to fight the enemy and not to take part in their civil war and, if it should come your way, you must do everything in your power to stop it. The Partisans are getting stronger and, though the plan at present is to support Mihailović in Serbia, you may find that this is no longer possible and that you have to change sides. At all costs keep an open mind.'

'Of course,' I replied, 'I've no ambition to become a Balkan politician.'

Davidson laughed shortly. 'If you succeed in avoiding doing so, it won't be through lack of temptation.'

I was introduced to my party the following day. 2nd Lieutenants Tomlinson and Smith, the engineers, were regular sappers of about eight years' service. They had both been sergeants until recently, had seen action in the desert and had been promoted for this mission. The wireless operator, Leading Aircraftman Thompson, had done two years ground service in the RAF and, becoming bored by his base job, he had answered a call for volunteers for special service. He was sturdy, a boxer of some repute and an excellent operator; he seemed just the type I needed.

We spent that week collecting our equipment and making last minute arrangements. Everyone was charming, helpful and ready to show interest in any points raised, the organisation priding itself on always equipping 'Joes' with whatever personal arms and equipment that they might demand, however odd were their requirements. If particular stores were not available from the Quartermaster, an officer would be sent out to buy them. If not available in Cairo then special manufacture would be arranged. One of my acquaintances, an officer with a romantic turn of mind, once asked for a forged steel bow and arrow with which to murder sentries and a rubber stamp imprinted with a black hawk to mark his victims. Another wanted a specially constructed catapult with luminous sights to serve up poisonous meat to barking dogs! Both demands were satisfied within a few days.

Unfortunately each member of the staff had his own pet essential store and, when I came to review the collection which had been forced upon me, I was faced by an enormous stack of absolutely 'straight from the horse's mouth' necessities, all of which would have to be carried on my back. I am a fairly strong man but a mule could not have carried that mountain of ammunition and toothpaste, stabbing knives and chewing gum, anti-louse powder – I had seventeen tins, boxes, packets and cartons of this delectable, pepper-like, insecticide. I took one large tin with me but soon discarded it on finding lice preferable to chronic hay fever.

CHAPTER THREE

Arrival in Serbia

The aerodrome at Derna, recaptured some four months before, had changed hands many times during the war. The relics of burnt-out aeroplanes littered the ground between the runways; Messerschmitts, Hurricanes, Junkers, Blenheims and the twisted steel skeletons of hangars pointed towards the sky. Across the road which bounded the landing strip a squadron of dummy Warhawks perfect in every detail looked genuine even from the ground. Where the field finished to the north the ground sloped away to the sea. On the south side lay the flying control and the yellow-tented living quarters near which a squadron of Liberator bombers was dispersed on the edges of the field. A battered old Halifax, her once black paint bleached grey by the sun, stood near flying control under tattered camouflaged netting; beneath her belly men fussed about lifting packages and fixing parachutes to the heavy metal containers locked in the bomb racks.

We had fitted our parachutes and packed our kit for the last time. I had jettisoned the greater part of my equipment, taking only a haversack, a light sleeping bag, a sten gun and ammunition, a spare shirt, underclothes, washing kit and, that great necessity of life, a roll of toilet paper. These fitted snugly into a container with a roll of maps and the wireless set. I marked the container so that I should recognise it on landing and surrendered it to the ground crew.

We were to take off at six. It was then about half past three. Having nothing more to do I wandered into the Mess which was housed in a large marquee, comfortably furnished with a long bar at one end. It was for the use of the despatching officers, whose job it was to organise our departure in liaison with the RAF, and by all members of parties going on operations, irrespective of their rank. At that time we were the only party in transit and Tomlinson and Smith were there already. They were drinking beer, as they talked to Sergeant Carter.

Sergeant Carter was a remarkable person. A man of some thirty-five years of age, plump and jovial, he had joined a Yeomanry Regiment at the start of the war, seeing service with them in the desert when he had been badly shell-shocked. Found unfit for further active service, he became employed as Mess Sergeant at this station. His job was a thankless one normally but he took his responsibilities seriously. They were large enough too, for his was the task of keeping the 'Joes' cheerful and happy while they waited to go on their journey to enemy-occupied territory. They comprised men of all nationalities, some emotional and highly strung, already regretting their decision and debating whether they dared back out or not. Many, though outwardly calm, were inwardly shaking, as they waited weeks for suitable flying weather or returned with the aircraft because the dropping zone could not be located. For the latter the time was particularly trying and they, even more than the others, saw in Carter and his bar the last outpost of truly British territory before the great unknown.

Carter was a psychologist; he would jolly us along, cracking jokes with the despondent, talking of home with the homesick, calming the excited. His bar was open all day and drinks were free to all awaiting operations but few were drunk before leaving. He had one other great attribute, an infallible memory for faces. Those of us who came back might walk into his bar months, perhaps years, later but he could always greet us by name and recall small incidents which had occurred. To Carter must go a great part of the credit in averting last minute refusals. He kept a cardboard top from a case of canned beer, which all outgoing 'Joes' were required to sign; those who returned countersigned. When I signed there were some twenty names on the list but no counter-signatures. In all I signed that card five times; on the last occasion it was covered with some hundreds of signatures.

I had barely time to order myself a drink before the officer in charge of the station came in carrying a sealed bag. He thrust it into my hands.

'Here's your money and your identity cards. The Met report is good so you should get off tonight.'

The cards he handed us bore a photograph, name and number and 'the bearer is a British officer, entitled to treatment as such' stamped in three languages on the back.

'What about the money? Do you want to count it? There's five hundred sovereigns, four million dinar and two million leva.'

I broke the seal, taking out a full haversack and a smaller bag tied with twine. It was full of sovereigns and the haversack contained notes. It would take all night to count.

'I'll count the sovereigns and take your word for the rest, but where the devil am I going to carry it?'

'God knows,' replied the station commander. 'That's your worry. Here's the receipt, will you sign it?'

Tying up the sovereigns in a handkerchief I put them into an ammunition holster in my belt and dividing the notes I gave some to each of my companions. I stuffed the remainder into the pockets of my battle dress till they bulged like a dowager's bosom.

It suddenly struck me how ludicrous was this scene. My pay would be dribbling into the bank, about thirty pounds a month, no more; yet here in a bar I was casually signing a receipt for thousands of pounds. Why sign the receipt? If I lost it I could never repay it. If I cared to steal it nobody could prove that I had. Crazy indeed. But what else was to be done? An accountant could not be sent round to check my books; I doubted whether I should be able to keep any books. This job must be important if the Treasury, notoriously so thrifty, were prepared to risk so much; but what was a thousand pounds, two thousand, ten thousand? A mere fleabite compared to the fifteen millions a day the war was costing our country alone. And yet before the war a unit commander had to fight the paymaster for twopence to buy a sheet of blotting paper. Guns, tanks and aeroplanes were in short supply because they were too expensive. While Parliament talked of averting wars, they voted down the Services Estimates. Now we were at war; now, because earlier we had saved thousands, we were spending millions. A few thousand pounds thrust casually into my hands to use as I thought fit to help the war. Ridiculous, but true.

I watched my three companions standing alongside the bar. Tomlinson was gazing silently into his beer while the other two talked to Sergeant Carter. They joked boisterously, laughed rather heartily, then they started to sing the parachutists' song:

> Bless em all, bless em all,
> The long and the short and the tall, ...
> You'll get no promotion, if your chute doesn't open,
> So cheer up my lads ... bless em all.

'Morbid?' I wondered. 'No, it's not that. They're singing that song because it's not the jump that they fear. We've all done our training jumps and we know that the parachute only fails to open once in a thousand times. It's safer than crossing Piccadilly in the traffic. What is it that we are all feeling; afraid? That's the wrong word, we're not afraid. We know that parachuting is straightforward and we're not afraid of being killed in battle or being shot by the enemy – that's too remote at present. That possibility is only one day nearer than it was yesterday and yesterday we were behaving naturally. Yesterday we didn't talk too loudly, laugh too raucously. Perhaps it's because we're doing something we've never done before – we've never talked to anyone else who could tell us first hand what to expect. It isn't fear; fear is something much more physical. If I was afraid of going to Yugoslavia I would not want to go. I would only go because I ought to, because in default I'd be a coward. But I want to go. More than that, I'm desperate to go and if anything were to happen to put it off I should be miserable.

'Uncertainty, that might be, but then all life is uncertain. I don't know what will happen tomorrow but then six months ago I did not know what would happen the following day and then I behaved naturally. Do we feel different because other people expect us to do so? Perhaps they expect us to show some signs of fear and subconsciously they are influencing us, willing us to behave oddly.

'Is it that Sergeant Carter, whilst trying to entertain us, is thinking that we are nervous and is transmitting that thought to us? Do we realise subconsciously what he thinks and feel compelled to show our cheerfulness? I don't know. I'm not afraid . . I'm sure of that. But I'm holding myself in and watching what I do; that's not natural, therefore it's not normal. Perhaps I'll understand why tonight; perhaps I'll never know.'

'Dinner is served, gentlemen.'

A huge meal had been prepared, 'Eat, drink and be merry . . . no, it's commonsense to have a good meal now; we may not get another for a long time.' It was only half past five, and we lunched well, but I tried to eat heartily. I hated to disappoint the cook after he'd prepared such a repast and 'If I don't do justice to the meal, people will think me nervous'. The meal dragged painfully to a close and as I got up to leave I felt completely natural again. What nonsense, I asked myself, had I been thinking half an hour before – I felt perfectly normal, I *was* perfectly normal. I was convinced then that I had never felt any different, that I had never debated whether or not I was afraid.

We dressed quickly putting on underclothes and battle dress; far too hot for a sticky evening in the desert in the late spring. Then came our equipment, binoculars, compass, revolver, fighting knife, medical kit and water bottle and, on top of everything, a thick woollen flying jacket covered by a zip fastened overall made without buttons or tags which might catch in the parachute harness: the sweat trickled down my back and I felt like a Christmas tree.

The Halifax loomed like a gaunt black monster against the setting sun. The sky was clear and a faint breeze whispered over the field. The aircrew were already there and introduced themselves to us. They were a truly cosmopolitan crew: a Canadian captain, a New Zealander, two British and an Australian rear gunner, who promised us a spell in his turret to try the guns.

We shook hands all round and for a moment that tension came back into the air.

'Goodbye, best of luck to you all.'

'Goodbye and thanks for all your help.'

We climbed into the aircraft through the parachute exit and settled ourselves in the fuselage. Flasks of coffee and some sandwiches were passed up to us. The crew climbed in and the pilot started the motors, testing each in turn. He opened the throttle and released the brakes, the aircraft throbbed and rattled as he roared his motors turning into the wind and gaining speed staggered heavily into the air.

Feeling a hand on my shoulder, I shook myself and wiped the sleep from my eyes. The despatcher shouted at me:

'We're due over the target in twenty minutes, better get your parachute on.'

A faint blue light illuminated the fuselage of the Halifax; a mass of packages attached to parachutes were stacked along the floor. The others lay sleeping; Tommy and Smith on the bunks in the rear of the pilot's cockpit, Thompson on the rough wooden hatch covering the parachute exit. The despatcher stood beside me wearing oxygen apparatus. He took off his mask.

'We're flying up the course of the Morava; we passed Pristina just now. The blackout is none too good there; we turn off to the east soon. It's about another fifty miles.'

Feeling weak and drowsy I pulled myself to my feet and went forward to rouse the others. The aircraft had been flying at 16,000 feet and we gasped for breath as we struggled into our parachutes.

The despatcher put on his earphones and plugged into the intercom. We waited, tensed up, imagining all that could go wrong... Would the pilot find the dropping zone?... the fires might not be laid out properly... the recognition signal might be wrong.

The rear gunner appeared through the door of his turret and took up position by the hatch cover; the despatcher jerked his thumb, the gunner raised and locked the hatch; the hole gaped open and a current of icy wind shot into the fuselage.

'He's found the fires; we're circling.'

The engines throbbed and roared alternately and I felt my belly swing over as we banked into a stiff turn.

'Action stations!'

I slipped into position at the rear of the hole, on the edge facing forward with my feet dangling into space. Tomlinson stationed himself opposite me, and Smith and Thompson sat one on each side behind us, ready to swing in. The despatcher bent down and yelled:

'Skipper's compliments, sir. Good luck and happy landings.'

I felt the aircraft straighten out; she shuddered and the engines dropped to a murmur as the pilot throttled back. In a bracket on the side of the fuselage a tiny red light flickered into being. Time stood still. The red turned to green. I jerked myself to attention and Tommy's boots shot upwards past my face. My feet were already in the slipstream when I heard the shout:

'*Go.*'

*

As the parachute jerked open I collected my senses. My eyes searched for something to see, my ears for something to hear but there was nothing but perfect peace of the night air wrapped like a felt blanket around my head. I looked down but could not yet make out anything there and, for a moment, I was as one completely detached from the world. That illusion shattered as the wind swung my parachute around and I saw the target below. Ten small flickering fires formed the letter W and from one side of the pattern a torch flashed intermittently, dash, dot, dash. Then the fires swung out of sight and all was dark again below.

The pilot had promised to drop us from a height of 1,500 feet. That would give us some forty seconds in the air. I settled myself to sit comfortably in the harness, bent my knees and slid my hands up the webbing straps fixed to my shoulders to grip the buckles above my head. Thirty seconds to go; I looked around for the other members of the party. I could see nothing and looked down again to complete darkness. Ten seconds to go. I tensed my legs for the shock; five seconds ... three ... two ... time. I still drifted down. We must have jumped higher than planned. I still could see nothing below and the fires seemed to have disappeared.

At last I made out a line of trees a short distance in front and below me. They came level, then rose until I could see them above my head. The ground followed them up from below and passed above; then came more trees. A sudden ridiculous qualm: 'I'm falling down a well', was shattered as my feet hit the ground. I rolled over, slipped out of my harness and got up to find myself standing on a narrow pathway near the bottom of a precipitously-sided ravine. Fifty feet below a river roared over rocks and boulders; above, a steep slope, covered with stunted oak and brushwood, stood out against the sky.

It was clear that it had only just stopped raining. The grass was wet and a glorious smell of fresh green vegetation assailed my nostrils. The warm, wet night, the perfumed air, the green grass, the roaring river, glistening phosphorescently as it tumbled down below, were balm to my senses. I remembered only five hours back, the hot, dusty desert smell, the hard-baked, yellow ground, the dirty water. That was yesterday, this was the present and the future, this was Life. I looked at my watch; half past ten Cairo time, half an hour after midnight local time. Tomorrow was today. Intoxicated by the natural beauty of the place and elated at my safe arrival, I hummed as I rolled up my parachute, by habit plaiting the silken rigging lines and pushed the bundle into the bag on the harness slinging it across my back. I called 'Tommy', quietly. He should have been somewhere near as he had jumped just behind me. The river roared on but there was no answer. I took out a whistle, blowing two short blasts, and a reply came at once from the creek below. I followed the path along the valley till I came to a place where the ground flattened out into open meadows. The river, swollen by rain, rushed down in a mass of foam. Thompson stood by the river, revolver in hand.

'*Stoy*, who's there?'

'All right, it's me, don't wave that blunderbuss in this direction. Have you seen the others?'

'No sir, but there are some chaps over the other side of the river; the fires are further down the valley.'

'Well, we'd better close on the fires.'

We started off through a maize field and had gone but a short way when we heard the sound of voices. Whispering to Thompson to follow suit, I dropped on one knee behind a boulder to listen. The voices came nearer, chattering excitedly, and it was clear long before they reached us that they were no regular troops. As they came into view I stood up and flashed my torch onto the leader.

He was a short stocky creature dressed in a broadly cut jacket and knickerbocker breeches of heavy dark cloth; his feet were bare and his body was festooned with cross belts stuffed with ammunition. Three grenades and a murderous looking knife were suspended from his belt, another knife hung under his arm, and he carried an ancient rifle some five feet long slung over one shoulder. The whole lot was surmounted by a thick mass of whiskers, with a soft cap perched on top. This apparition rushed up to me, flung his arms around my neck and kissed me passionately, while a flood of unintelligible talk flowed through the bristles. Letting me go, he turned to vent his emotion on Thompson. By now a crowd had collected and we endured countless close embraces from other hairy warriors. Falteringly, I asked them to conduct us to the fires. They were overjoyed at my few words of their language and all started talking to me at once. Someone took my parachute and we set off.

As the procession moved down the valley, I staggered along in the centre surrounded by a crowd of jabbering, gesticulating guerillas. They talked far too fast for me to understand what they said but it appeared that we enjoyed adequate goodwill. To all their questions, I answered: '*Da*', (yes), or '*Dobro*', (good), which seemed to satisfy them and stimulate further discussion. The fires were smouldering on a slight rise across the river and, as we approached the water, I heard a voice asking in halting Serb with an English accent, whether we had been located. A moment later the owner of the voice, a goblin-like man, appeared. He wore well-cut riding breeches, a service jacket and a peasant cap. I noticed that he too was festooned with weapons and he carried a long alpenstock. He greeted me effusively and for a moment I thought that he too would embrace me. 'You must be Lees. I'm Sehmer.'

'How do you do. This is Thompson, the W/T operator. There should be two other bodies around somewhere.'

'Yes, they're up by the fires. One of them fell in a tree and hurt his back a bit but it's nothing serious. You'd better come up and be introduced to Djurić.'

As I moved to wade the water, he caught my arm,

'No, don't get wet; one of the chaps will carry you across.'

A young Serb, little more than a boy, came up. He rolled his breeches over his knees and bent down so that I might climb onto his back. I looked down at him uncertainly; in my flying kit I felt enormous and must have weighed over 17 stone; my porter was lightly built and could have been no more than nine stone but he picked me up as easily as though he were carrying a small sack of corn, walked rapidly over the pebbled bed of the fast running river and put me down on the other side. He turned back to make further journeys for the others.

'That chap's no weakling,' I remarked.

'You'll find they're all as strong as mules,' replied Sehmer. 'They can carry very heavy loads all day without tiring. They're bred to it in these mountains.'

As we climbed the rise from the river, a fascinating sight met my eyes: the fires, now barely smouldering, had been built in a clearing above the river, which was now a hive of activity. A small group, who were clearly officers, stood in the centre directing operations. At their feet was a pile of stores which had been dropped by the aircraft. Soldiers and peasants staggered in singly carrying packages and parachutes, others came in groups of four with the heavy metal containers and, dumping their loads, scuttled off for more. While the men brought the stores into the clearing numerous bullock carts, some driven by women, arrived to reload them and, as soon as they were filled, rumbled off into the darkness. I noticed that, where the fires had been kindled, a square of turf was cut out and carefully laid aside. Men were now destroying all traces of the night's activities by stamping out the embers and replacing the sods. Covering these operations were three well sited machine guns, and a spirit of haste pervaded the scene; Sehmer explained why:

'We're in a hurry to get the stuff cleared tonight; the bullock carts are taking it all to a clearing in the forest about five miles away, where we'll sort and distribute it tomorrow. We've used this dropping ground a bit too often and there are rumours of Bulgar troop concentrations about two hours away. If they've heard the plane tonight, they'll be here by dawn.'

Djurić, the commander of the formation to which Sehmer was attached, was a tall well-built, middle-aged man. He wore a walrus moustache, stained yellow by smoking but, unlike the majority of his men, he was clean-shaven. He had Asiatic features with high cheekbones and slanting brown eyes and I noticed that those eyes were shifty. He was dressed in a British battledress tunic, grey Serbian army breeches and a fine pair of German jackboots. Djurić was surrounded by a group of his officers. Most were dressed or partly dressed in British uniform but I noticed that they all carried the German Schmeiser sub-machine gun. I was to discover later that this was a question less of utility than of prestige – it is a pretty gun. To one side of the group stood a soldier holding a sturdy mountain pony.

Sehmer made the necessary introductions and for some minutes I wrestled with my few words of their language. Djurić spoke German of which I understood a little but spoke none. He also understood French but I had decided to start as I must go on and to learn their language by always using it.

Shortly afterwards Tomlinson and Smith arrived on the scene. The former was limping slightly but he hastened to assure me that all was well and that he was suffering from nothing worse than a few bruises. We were all tired and I breathed a sigh of relief when Sehmer explained that he had arranged for us to spend the night in a house in the immediate vicinity. He assured us there was nothing we could do until the morning, when the stores would be opened and sorted, and he suggested that we come to the rendezvous soon after dawn. He gave me the excellent news that Trbić himself had come up from Macedonia to meet us and escort us south.

Panting under our heavy clothing, we moved off slowly, recrossing the river and starting through the woods. The path, after the rain, was slippery under our rubber boots and it was hard going as we climbed for some ten minutes before coming to open ground on the slopes above the river. Cultivated fields lay on either side and dimly in the darkness we saw the outline of a small one storey building in front of us. We walked through a gate and across a muddy yard. In the squat buildings on the right, animals could be heard moving around in their stalls, a faint chink of light came through a crack in the door of the house and from its kennel a dog barked fiercely at us.

As we reached the door, it was opened from inside and an old woman came out onto the threshold. She wore a full peasant skirt to the ankles, a brightly coloured blouse made from parachute silk and a kerchief of similar material tied around her head and under her chin. Signing to us to enter, she held up an oil lamp to show the way through the outer room.

This room was bare of furniture save for a heavy oak table, the floor was of packed mud, there was no ceiling and the moon shone through chinks in the tiled roof. From the heavy beams which supported the rafters hung dried red peppers and strips of biltong and clusters of garlic were nailed to the walls. The wood smoke from a large open hearth filtered away through the roof and a huge pot hung by a chain from a rack over the fire. There were only two rooms; in the other a heavy iron cooking stove stood on one side discharging fumes through a metal pipe to the tiny chimney in the roof. Two rough wooden beds piled with straw and covered by heavy home spun blankets were placed on each side of the stove. A dresser, a round table some eighteen inches high and four or five three legged stools a foot square and about nine inches tall comprised the rest of the furniture.

Three or four peasants squatting on the stools by the fire rose immediately we entered the room; they offered us stools and we balanced ourselves uncomfortably around the table. An old peasant, who appeared to be the owner of the house, made a great show of hospitality and got his wife to hasten our dinner. Two or three dishes were already cooking on the stove and a pleasant aroma from the oven reached my nostrils.

Meanwhile our host had departed to reappear a few minutes later carrying a bottle in one hand and a wineglass in the other. He filled the glass with a colourless liquid, crossed himself, removed his hat and went into a long rigmarole. As he spoke fast and chanted his words I failed to catch the gist of what he said but I did understand an occasional word. '*Bog*' . . . constantly repeated, '*da savesnići dodje skoro*' ('that the Allies come soon'), and his final words '*zdrav si*' ('Good health'). Finishing he crossed himself three times, raised the glass with one quick movement and drained it. He poured another offering it to Sehmer who signed to him to give it to me. Following his example I exclaimed '*zdravsi*' and drained it at one gulp.

The fierce liquid rushed down my throat, my gullet burned and I felt the heat from the raw spirit spreading through my body. Loth to appear a weak drinker I struggled, red in the face and gasping, to nod appreciation of the drink.

My action met with great approval. Heads were nodded and knowing smiles passed around the circle and as he addressed me I gathered, rather from his gestures than his words, that my host was delighted at my fluency of language and intrepid drinking. The rigmarole continued, each in turn drinking from the same glass, first Sehmer, then my three companions. The latter, having diagnosed my discomfort, sipped carefully to get the taste and I noticed that Tomlinson surreptitiously poured his share down his sleeve. Sehmer explained that the speeches asked God's help that the crops would be good, the weather clement and that the war would finish with an imminent Allied landing in Yugoslavia. The toast was in the nature of a prayer.

I was later to discover that alcohol played an integral part in all religious ceremonies and equally religion had its share in alcoholic ones. I never discovered why one glass alone was used, whether it was due to the paucity of glasses or to delay the process of getting drunk, though the Serbs suffered from no inhibitions in the latter respect, an evening being considered ill-spent if any member of the party retired in his proper senses.

The bottle contained the universal Serbian drink – *rakija*. *Rakija* is the general name for the spirit. In the mountains it is normally made from plums, the specific name being *slivović*; in the plains from grapes, giving *klekovačka*. Some peasants prepare a pear brandy, *kruskovačka*, but in all cases the method of manufacture is the same. The raw fruit is picked, crushed and distilled in a vat; the steam passes through a pipe immersed in a tank of water, and the finished product condenses out.

In Serbia, every peasant has his own still; distillation taking place during the autumn some two months after the fruit is collected. This is a very happy time: the harvest is in, all is prepared for the winter hibernation and the manufacture commences. The fires are stocked, the vats filled and, as the raw liquid drips out, it is drunk at once till all present collapse into a stupor. Miraculously, as all lie sleeping, a large open barrel appears under the still to collect the spirit. Some hours later the workmen awake to find the fires cold, the vat empty save of residue, an indigestible substance used as jam, and the barrel full of *rakija*. This is stored away and the process repeated daily until all the fruit is consumed and the winter supply of elixir lies safely in the podroom.

That night we were drinking the plum variety. Spending most of my time in the mountains, I was to come to know this very well and recognise it as a true friend but on this first occasion I was so concerned with its strength that I had little chance to analyse the taste. The ability to enjoy *rakija* must be acquired by practice. In strength and effect it is not unlike vodka and the grape variety, *klekovačka*, is very similar to Italian *grappa*.

Two plates stood on the table. One contained chunks of rancid goat's milk cheese. The other, sliced liver, kidneys and intestines, roasted on the embers of the fire. These were served in all but the poorest houses as an apéritif and I always found them so appetising, particularly the cheese eaten without bread, that I often exhausted my appetite by the time the meal proper arrived.

The supper consisted of bread and a communal bowl of soup made from beans boiled in water, one or two slices of potato and a very small portion of meat floating in the dish. There were eight of us at the table, the soup provided being in quantity and quality about the equivalent to that number of portions served in the average English railway restaurant and I wondered how these very robust people ever consumed enough nourishment. Then watching our host sitting on my left, I understood. While in his right hand he held a spoon, his left tore off great hunks of bread and stuffed them into his mouth. During the meal he must have eaten the equivalent of half an English cottage loaf, the small share of soup he succeeded in scooping from the bowl, being used to wash the bread down. An Englishman can happily exist for an indefinite period without bread. To a Yugoslav peasant bread is the only absolute necessity of life and he firmly believes that his digestion will not function with other foods alone. However good a meal you offer him he will be dissatisfied without an adequate quantity of bread as well.

The meal finished when we scraped the bowl empty. We were all drowsy by now from the effects of the *rakija*, hot food and the close atmosphere of the smoke-filled room. The great events of the day caught up with me and suddenly I was very tired. Sehmer noticed this.

'You'll be needing to get some sleep. You can stay with our outpost here, the men sleep in the barn and they'll be back as soon as the dropping ground is clear. Our quartermaster will be coming up later and, if there's an alarm, he will show you where to go. I must go off and supervise the transfer of kit to the rendezvous which is about four miles away through the woods. It will take you about an hour and a half to get there, so if you set off at dawn you should arrive by 8.30. That will allow you time enough to separate your stuff before we unpack the containers and distribute the stores. Don't worry about your wireless. I am going off now to see that it has all been found.'

He paused: 'By the way, it's ridiculous us calling each other by our surnames, what do people call you?'

'Mike.'

'Well, I'm John.'

Imagination flickered. John Peel with his almost grey coat, his little bow legs encased in riding breeches, and his odd peasant cap, running over the mountains which might so easily have been Wales... Sehmer slipped deftly into his ammunition-filled braces, slung his rifle over his shoulder and bustled off into the darkness. I wandered back into the room to find the party engaged in graphic if blasphemous accounts of their individual descents from the Halifax, while the peasants sat spellbound listening to every word, understanding none.

An extraordinary reaction this; on training and operations I have done in all twenty-nine parachute jumps and on every occasion I have

(Above left) An SIS man with Major Radislav Djurić

(Above right) The author with Čikabuda (Uncle Buda), quartermaster of Djurić's forces

(Right) The author, a Polish officer and Major John Sehmer

Joško's wedding

(Left) Zigorka and Milunka, peasant girls *(Right)* Serbian peasant delivering slivović

been filled with an unaccountable exhilaration and have felt an urge to accost complete strangers and describe every detail of my performance. This effect seems to be general and lasts for some hours after the jump. I think that many of the rumours of German parachutists in Crete taking Benzedrine or similar drugs arose solely as a result of their exuberant enthusiasm and self-confidence caused by a successful descent.

'Come on . . . time for sleep.'

The host made us free of his two beds. Where he and his wife slept that night I do not know. I imagine that they squatted by the fire in the outer room. Automatically I stripped off all my clothes, throwing them carelessly on the floor. Little did I realise that this would be the last night for twelve months when I would sleep fully undressed in bed. On this occasion I acted without thinking; later I learned to take the elementary precautions subconsciously by sheer force of habit and I could never sleep unless my boots were ready beside where I lay.

Thompson and I shared one bed, Smith amd Tomlinson, the other, and snores soon reverberated to the rafters. I found the events of the day coming back to me and, though physically exhausted, my mind engrossed in these events was too active to let me sleep. The previous night I had slept in pyjamas and sheets on the aerodrome, safe in British territory. Now I lay in a peasant's hut a thousand miles away in enemy country with all routes of escape sealed. That was the crux of the matter, if an avenue of retreat had lain open then I would still have felt that uncertainty which came to me in the bar for those few minutes during the afternoon. But now that, for better or worse, the decision was irrevocable, I felt completely at ease and confident. I had no idea how long I would be there and I didn't care. However long it might be, it could not be short. Therefore I must learn, and learn quickly, the rules of survival, so that I might remain in these mountains alive and free, by virtue of my own wits and not be dependent on others for guidance.

I was pondering this resolution when the door rattled open. In the light of the burning lamp I saw a large figure move ponderously into the room.

'*Dobro veče Kapetan.*' ('Good evening, Captain.')

'*Dobro veće.*'

'*Jesam Čikabuda.*' (I am Čikabuda.)

Sehmer had already told me about Čikabuda the quartermaster, who I gathered was a truly remarkable character, notorious and beloved. He was a big man, some five feet eleven inches, which is tall for a Serb, and he was broad with a large rounded paunch. His Slav features had filled out with good living and his large twinkling eyes were deeply sunk into his head. They were blue grey and he wore gold-rimmed spectacles. He was dressed in good peasant costume and he carried no arms, his only concession to his military standing gbeing a pair of buff-coloured army boots. His whole personalit radiated goodwill; the name of Čikabuda translated means Uncle Buda, and I could see at once that he had been aptly named.

He repeated his statement. '*Je sam Čikabuda.*'

Twenty-four hours later I realised the significance of this ponderous self-introduction. Over an area of half the size of Wales, everyone knew, or knew of, Čikabuda. He was a rogue, but a pleasant, kindly rogue, and well respected. I talked to him as best I could and found him easy to understand. He talked slowly and carefully, discovering which words I knew and working them into his sentences. In the period before I became fluent in the language, he was the only Slav I met who bothered to talk slowly so that I might understand better. Conversely, I found that talking fast and ungrammatically, I was far more often understood than when I formed and pronounced my words carefully.

Čikabuda informed me that the dropping ground was now clear of stores and that he had come here to sleep. He was shocked, he declared, to find that his bed was already occupied but, as he liked the English and as I must be tired, as a special favour he would sleep on the floor! I must realise however that this was a special favour and a special concession which would not be repeated. Mumbling benignly he lay down by the fire and two minutes later the house shook to the rumble of his snores.

CHAPTER FOUR

The Bulgar Massacre

It was five o'clock and still dark when I awakened but, as we were to start at dawn, I aroused the others. Tommy complained that his back was very painful; he appeared to have strained the muscles and sleeping on a hard bed had stiffened them up. Čikabuda explained that the outpost would be remaining, so, ordering Tommy to stay in bed, I dressed and prepared to leave. Unfortunately just as we were starting, our host rushed in with a bottle; he protested that we couldn't possibly leave without breakfasting and he insisted on us drinking some *ljuta*, the strongest form of *rakija*.

Ljuta is *slivović* twice distilled and its alcoholic content is greatly in excess of whisky. It was some time before I became accustomed to the Serbian habit of always starting the day with strong drink but it is a necessary stimulant because the first meal is not eaten until around 10.30 a.m. and, as one rises with the dawn, the hardest work is completed before this meal. The British soldier demands his breakfast if he is to work or fight well in the morning; similarly, the Serb demands a glass or two of *ljuta* which is an excellent substitute.

After drinking one glass I slipped away but the bottle was still circulating. The sun was just coming up as I looked out on Yugoslavia for the first time. That impression is with me still.

The house, which was marked on the map as about 3,000 feet above sea level, stood alone in an open space at the top of a steep slope. To the east a series of ridges rose like a divine staircase to a snow capped mountain peak; northwards, the ridge on which we stood continued for about two miles, then descended to a plain, across which lay a high mountain with an apparently perpendicular face; to the south and west was broken country, rocky hills covered with oak and beech, interlaced by rushing watercourses which emptied into the river in the valley below.

The pure white snow on the higher mountains outlined against the fresh green of the trees in full leaf was balm to my sand-sore eyes and this beauty was perfected by the absence of roads or any other mark of modern ways. Only a single winding bullock track struggling across

Area of Operations in Yugoslavia

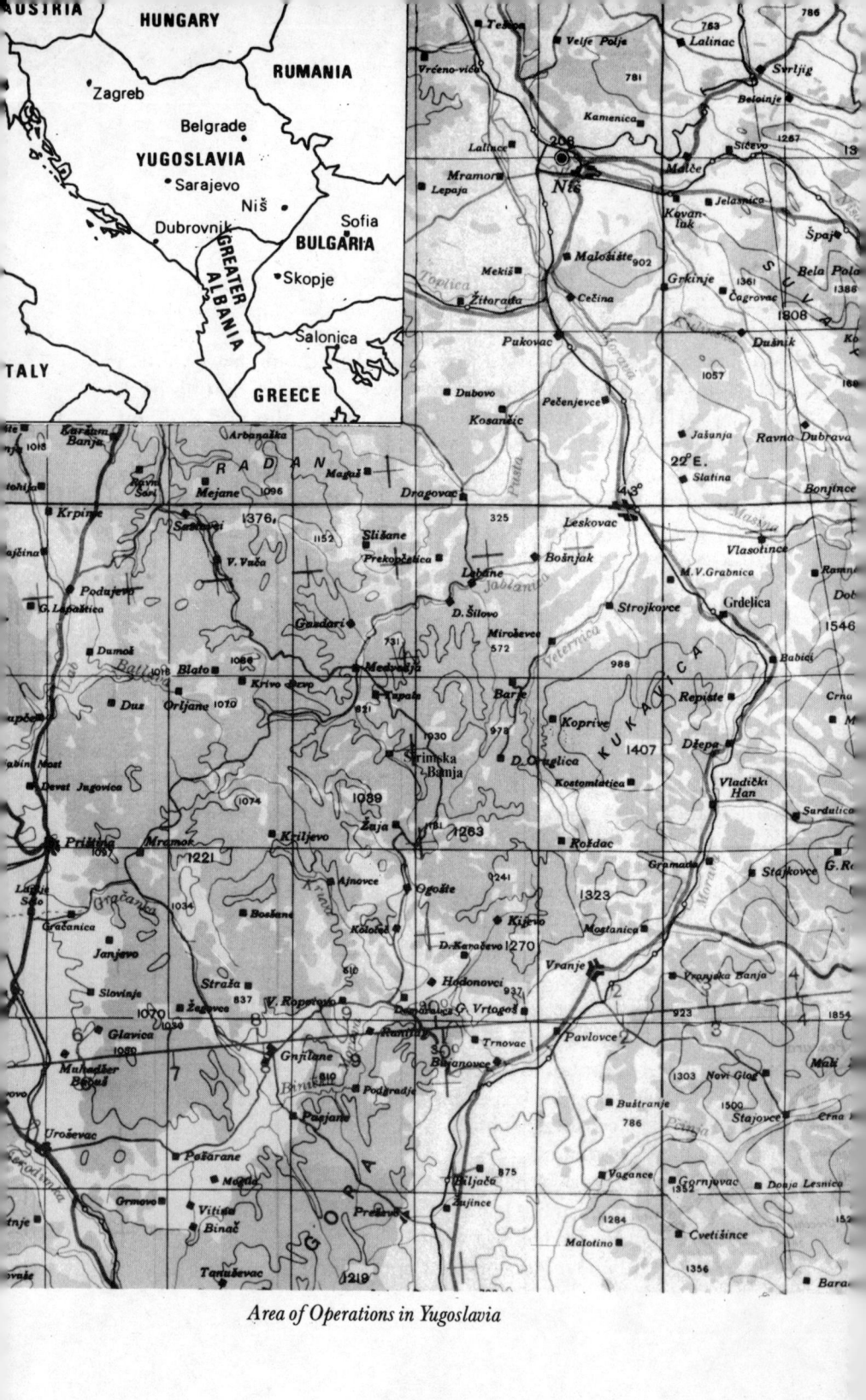

and around the broken contours of the hills showed that the inhabitants of this Garden of Eden were not entirely cut off from the outer world. The hills were dotted with little homesteads, the buildings placed singly or in pairs, but I could see no groups large enough to be called a village. The houses were of one storey, whitewashed with red tiled roofs, generally surrounded by outhouses, and mostly half a mile to a mile distant from one another. Although cattle were grazing around each homestead, there were no fences except those enclosing the actual yards and buildings. They were unnecessary, for the nature of the ground and steep slopes prevented stock from roaming.

It was an enchanting scene and I was sorry to turn away as Čikabuda came out with Smith and Thompson. We set off together descending the muddy path to the valley and following the course of the river upstream. The air was still and the leafy carpet underfoot muffled our footsteps. Apart from the faint song of the river, there was no sound. It occurred to me that, except for the inevitable farmhouse sparrows, I had seen no birds.

'*Nema li tice nigde?*' (Are there no birds here?) I asked Čikabuda.

He explained that all wild life was rare. At one time there had been much feather but most had been trapped or killed for food. Apart from the sparrows, an occasional hoody crow and wild-duck or geese flying high in passage, no birds are seen in that part of the mountains. Fur is represented only by wolves, which make an appearance in midwinter. Though the song of birds was missing, the wild flowers were lovely beyond compare. Primroses, crocuses and countless rock plants were in abundance and their scent was heavy on the air.

We walked in complete freedom, as the area was supposedly controlled by Djurić's irregulars. Soldiers were hurrying back and forth along the path and we overtook a group of men carrying a heavy package dropped the night before, which had been missed in the darkness and found after daylight that morning. Those whom we met wished us good-day and called jocularly to Buda. All stared at us curiously. After following the course of the river for some way, we turned up a track into the forest and shortly afterwards we reached the rendezvous. This was in a clearing some thirty yards square, where the grass was trampled down and deep ruts from bullock carts interlaced the muddy ground. A pile of stores sorted into the various categories lay in the centre of the clearing; twelve heavy metal tubular containers, some half dozen rectangular felt-covered packages and numerous small parcels, which had been dropped free. The parachutes were stacked separately; multi-coloured silk from the heavier loads, plain white canvas from the felt parcels. The cords had already been removed from each. A large crowd of men bustled around the place, sorting and stacking stores as they were brought in. This was my first chance to study these soldiers of Mihailović. The average height seemed around five foot nine, with few who varied from that standard. I am around six feet two and I have never met a Serb as tall as myself; seldom did I meet one approaching that height. Similarly Sehmer, at five foot three, was always the shortest man present in any group. They were all stockily, some strongly, built, with huge feet and hands, dark hair, brown eyes and slightly Asiatic features. Their dress varied by stages from peasant attire to full British uniform. In Serbia all clothes are made at home by women; the thread is spun from sheepswool and the yarn for the shirts and underclothes prepared from a crude flax, which is beaten out with heavy sticks. The cloth is made up into knickerbocker breeches and a broadly cut jacket, generally of a chocolate brown colour and often decorated with an interlacing silken pattern on the lapels. A plain white shirt is worn without collar or tie. Footwear is homemade from untanned hide, cut into a pattern to wrap around the feet with about four pairs of strongly knitted socks. The national headgear, the sikaca, is a peakless cap of grey colour, in shape not unlike an RAF side cap, worn opened out and square on the head.

Djurić's full-time troops were distinguishable from the peasants in that most wore some articles of English clothing, either jacket, trousers or shirt. I noticed that in spite of the heat of the day, some wore as many as two or three shirts, one above the other. Their arms too were of every conceivable type and pattern; German, Italian, Yugoslav and Bulgarian rifles of varying shapes, sizes and calibres; Brno, Czechoslovak light machine guns, MG34, Spandau, Bren and Sten. It was clear why each man carried such a prodigious amount of ammunition; with such a diversity of weapons, there could be no central supply. A section of ten men might need ten different calibres of ammunition.

Sehmer, who was supervising the unpacking of a wireless set, greeted us:

'We've found most of the stores. If you'll separate your kit we'll get on with distributing the rest. I've got you a horse to help with your set and batteries as far as the place where your escort is staying. Before you start worrying about that, come and meet the rest of my crowd.'

John's mission consisted of two New Zealand sergeants, demolition experts, a British wireless operator and a Slovene interpreter. The latter, an ex-pilot of the Yugoslav Air Force, was also trained in wireless work. They were a carefree bunch, enjoying their odd existence, but were hungry for news of Cairo and home. I left Smith and Thompson talking to them and went with John to meet Trbić.

Trbić, who before the capitulation had been a regular artillery officer, was dressed in peasant clothes. He explained as I already knew that he had no wireless set in his area and had therefore received no supplies. Consequently he was extremely glad we had come to join him and wished us to start work as soon as possible. We accordingly set to discussing our journey, deciding to start two days later and that I should go with him that evening to make further preparations. In view of the long march ahead of us, we agreed to reduce our equipment to the minimum. Apart from our arms and personal haversacks, we were to take one wireless set fitted into a suitcase, weighing forty pounds, a battery of about fifty pounds weight and a small hand generator for charging it. This kit, inadequate as it was for a proper wireless station working daily schedules, was as much as we could possibly hope to carry on the long route south.

The rest of the plane's load was being distributed and I watched with interest; I was not unduly impressed. When the containers had been unpacked and the explosives, arms and clothing counted, Djurić, seated on a rock like any Caesar, allocated shares to his commanders who, in turn, distributed the stores amongst their men. Angry voices arose, as all claimed more than their share or declined the allotment if it were some heavy, undesirable weapon such as the Boyes anti-tank rifle. I was astonished to see officers striking and kicking men who displeased them and to observe unwelcome orders becoming the subject of long discussions which often terminated in a flood of invective from all sides. While the distribution continued amidst these wrangles, Sehmer and I betook ourselves to the quiet of the forest to talk things over.

When we had settled ourselves out of earshot, I gave him his mail from home, which I had packed in my kit, and a further supply of maps and codes for which he had asked. Then I asked him to tell me about the people and what pitfalls to avoid.

'I like the Četniks,' stated Sehmer.

I asked him to explain exactly whom he included under this heading...

'Četnik,' replied Sehmer, 'is the name now used to describe all men who recognise Mihailović as their leader. It comes from the word *ceta*, a company or band. Četniks have existed for over half a century. Originally they were a form of Home Guard in which all the peasants banded together under a leader in each area. Before the last war they staged the great uprising against the Turks and later fought the Bulgars under their leader, Kosta Pećanac. In this war, after the capitulation when the enemy started to suffer from the attacks of Mihailović, to save keeping huge forces ready all over the country, they decided to form a Home Guard and use it alongside the Nedić forces to police the mountains.

With their true Teutonic simplicity they were both astonished and gratified at the number who agreed to serve. The intention was that the Germans would supply these peasants with arms and delegate a trustworthy leader to each area to call them out when necessary. In effect what happened was that the peasants took the arms, returned to the mountains and, at the first opportunity, deserted to Mihailović. In this particular province the delegate was Germanophile, so they cut his throat. This error cost the Germans dear and gave a huge impetus to the strength of Mihailović's forces. Because so many of his men were Četniks originally, the name has stuck and it also serves to distinguish them from the Communists, who are more politely known as the Partisans.'

As he paused for breath I asked:

'Are you people fighting the Partisans yet?'

Sehmer shook his head. 'There aren't any Partisans around here. As you know, the Serbs are all loyal to the King so they side with Mihailović and in Serbia there are very few Communists indeed. As a matter of fact there is a group of about twenty who appear now and again but as Djurić has five thousand men altogether in his area, apart from armed peasants who could be called on if necessary, they don't make much odds and at present they keep out of his way; if they were to become strong, I've no doubt there would be really bloody warfare between them and the Četniks.'

I told him about the warning I had received that the Partisans might become stronger and we must be prepared to change sides; Sehmer was appalled at the suggestion:

'Well, honestly, I'm dumbfounded. I can't conceive that they could ever be stronger than the Četniks. Of course the Partisans always go round saying that the Četniks are fascists and collaborators but people here just laugh at them, as they would at any other soap box orator. Personally, I would refuse to change sides. These men are my friends now. They've given up everything to come into the mountains and I couldn't desert them.'

When we went on to discuss the effects of the atrocities carried out by the enemy reprisals, more terrible in Serbia probably than anywhere else in Europe, Sehmer again showed that he was very much in sympathy with the Četniks' policy:

'Of course, many people ask why Mihailović with his huge forces isn't doing more. Living here as I do, it's easy to understand. He realises that the invasion, which they all believe will come through the Balkans, can't be started for another year at least. If he attacks and takes a town, as he easily can do now, the Germans return two days later with tanks and flame throwers. They burn down the town and kill all the inhabitants and the people come to hate Mihailović for bringing this trouble upon them, as the capture and loss of a town helps the war in no way.

'That is what happened at Kraljivo in 1941. It was taken by Mihailović, recaptured, and 5000 people were shot in reprisal. Mihailović is liked by the people now and, if he is to survive, he must keep their good will. He plans to build up a huge army in the mountains, meanwhile carrying out only 'undercover' sabotage on railways and so on. He argues that the mere presence of his dormant forces is sufficient to pin down enemy divisions in this country and thus help the war and he hopes in this way to protect the mountain folk, who will feed his men till the balloon goes up, when he is strong enough to sweep the Germans from the country. It's sound reasoning.'

Remembering Davidson's advice, I protested at this seemingly biased view: 'Of course it all depends what the Allies want.'

Sehmer ignored my interruption: 'The Communists who, unlike the Četniks, are townsfolk operating in areas away from their homes, follow an opposite policy. They are out for quick Allied recognition to support their political ideals. Personally, I believe that if they got the whip hand they'd be less use to the war effort than these men who are such ardent nationalists and out for nothing but to save their country from the Germans and to live in their own way under the King.'

At that moment Sehmer was interrupted by a soldier who requested us to return to the clearing at once. Djurić came across and talked rapidly to Sehmer in German. I noticed that the men were sorting out their kit as fast as they could and that the empty containers were being placed on bullock carts and rushed off into the forest. Peasants followed with spades. As Djurić finished Sehmer translated:

'Scouts have just reported that they have seen a battalion of Bulgars moving towards the dropping ground. They'll be there by now; we must get all the stuff clear and stand by to move.'

As he talked, a horseman galloped up on a sweating pony, slid quickly to the ground and reported to Djurić. It transpired that another force, this time Germans, was approaching from the opposite direction.

Djurić called a hurried meeting. When he had finished his officers collected their men together and departed in different directions through the forest. I asked Sehmer what the policy was to be.

'Djurić has sent each group back to its own area. If the enemy are only patrolling they will stay in position. But if it's an organised clean up, as seems probable from the reports of Germans as well as Bulgars, we won't have a chance if we try to hold out; each group must slip individually out of the ring.'

Borrowing Sehmer's interpreter I found Trbić, who was busily engaged filling sten magazines and asked him whether we could go ahead with our original plan, only leaving right away.

'Not a hope', he replied. 'We'll have to wait until this trouble quietens down a bit. We have to cross the Bulgarian frontier at the start of our journey and if this is a major offensive the line will be double-manned. At best it's a tricky place and, carrying all this wireless equipment, it'd be impossible to get across unobserved.'

'Then what do you suggest?' I asked

'I've only got five men with me and we're all in civilian clothes. We've got identity cards, in fact we came here by train. Alone we can pass the Germans; with three British it would be impossible. I'll take the wireless with me back to the house where we are billeted, hide it there and leave one man to keep an eye on it. You stay with Djurić and the other English for the moment. I'll scout around and, if I can see an opportunity for us to slip through, I'll send for you; otherwise, we'll join up as soon as the land's clear. The way should be clear within a few days.'

That seemed good enough. I wanted to get communication established to base as soon as possible, but Thompson could do that using his own crystals on Sehmer's set. The wireless would certainly be safer with Trbić and unhampered by us he could pass as a harmless peasant and move around looking for a chance to slip through to the south.

'All right, you go ahead, but don't forget to keep in touch with me. We want to leave for your part of the country as soon as possible.'

At that moment Tomlinson appeared with the men from the house above the dropping ground. He was excited and gave us a detailed account of how he had watched the Bulgars moving along the river valley. From his report, it seemed fairly clear that this was no routine patrol.

We sat in the clearing with our packs on and ready to move. Every few minutes couriers came running in with news and others departed to seek fresh information.

Having collected my sten gun, I passed the time filling spare magazines with ammunition and distributing them about my body. I had recovered the bulk of the money distributed amongst my party the previous evening and I packed it into a haversack, leaving the equivalent of about £30 each with Thompson and Tomlinson in case we were forced to separate. It had been decided that when I went south with Trbić, Tomlinson would accompany me and Smith remain with Sehmer as his second-in-command.

A fresh influx of couriers brought the disturbing news that Bulgars were approaching from two directions and the spearhead of one group was only half an hour away. Djurić came over to us:

'We'd better move off. Are you ready?'

As he spoke the staccato barking of a light machine gun came from the valley which we had followed that morning. We picked up our guns, hurriedly forming a loose column of the nine members of our two British Missions. The twenty Serbs, members of Djurić's HQ staff and his bodyguard, moved ahead and through the woods on the flanks.

As we slowly filed out of the clearing, a group of ten Četniks appeared. In the middle of the group were three civilians, stumbling along blindfolded with their hands bound. The leader of the newcomers rushed up to Djurić and broke into rapid speech illustrating his story with a galaxy of gestures. I asked Leban, Sehmer's interpreter, what it was all about.

'Those chaps are spies', he replied. 'They were caught wandering around the woods. The peasants report that they were asking our whereabouts. They are Croats from Zagreb and have Bulgarian passes. We've been trying to catch them for a long time.'

'What will they do with them?' I asked.

'It depends on how hard we are pressed, whether we can keep them with us or not.'

We marched in single file along a narrow path through the forest, the prisoners and escort travelling behind our column. In the middle a shaggy pony, heavily laden with wireless equipment, picked its way daintily. As we marched, scouts continued to arrive, report and depart again, and occasionally we passed single men, ostensibly cutting wood, actually links in a very thorough information service.

Later on, I was to be astonished by the amazing co-operation of the peasants, in rendering information about enemy movements. On spotting any military formation, they would at once down tools and rush off to tell their nearest neighbours, who would in turn set out to tell someone else. As they always travelled at a good four miles in the hour over the worst possible country, the news reached us far in advance of the enemy's arrival in our territory. Unfortunately though, if the news had any distance to travel before reaching headquarters, it would be relayed some dozen times and the report each time lost nothing in the telling. The Serbs have no equal in their powers of exaggeration: sections became battalions; platoons, army corps, till there was confusion in the extreme.

After some time I learnt two very good rules: when asking a Serb the time necessary to march from one place to another always multiply the answer by two; on receiving a report of enemy troop concentrations divide by the distance in terms of hours marching from the place where the report originated to the place it was received. The result, halved for good measure, should provide an answer which, if not accurate, would be nearer to the truth than the original figure.

It was past mid-day. We had been marching some two hours when, turning off the track into a little dell in the woods, we sat down and waited to see what the enemy held in store for us. Information arriving left us in no doubt about the magnitude of the attack. Indeed, in Tommy's words it was to be a real 'Bustard'.

As the spearhead was reported to be close, Djurić had given orders for silence and we sat alone with our thoughts. It started to rain, my groundsheet was in my pack but, not liking to remove my equipment at this juncture, I remained still, muttering curses as the water trickled down my back. It was noticeable that the reassuring smiles and grins, which had previously passed amongst the English members of the party, were now gone. Thirty still figures, thirty despondent faces, waited in the woods in the rain.

Sometime later I noticed that the three prisoners were no longer with us; I leant over to Leban who was sitting nearby, and whispered:

'What's happened to our Croat friends?'

'They're dead,' he answered laconically.

'But I never heard a shot. I didn't even see them being taken away.' Leban raised one finger and drew it across his throat.

*

From the time of my jump until Leban made that gesture, I had lived as in a glorious dream. The beautiful scenery, the quaint surroundings, the guerillas dressed as true bandits out of an adventure novel, had all seemed part of some exciting game. At that moment I awoke fully to the grim realities of the life. This was no playing at war, this was serious and harsh, when three human beings, spies perhaps, but still human beings, could be taken off quietly into the woods and killed without trial, because it was expedient that they should die; butchered with a knife, because a shot would draw attention to us. For a second I felt sick as I imagined their feelings, sharing for a moment their agony of terror as, thrown onto the ground, their heads pulled back by the hair, they suffered that final excruciating moment when the knife drove into one side of the neck and grated out across and through the jugular vein.

Today I know that it was good that I learned of the fate of those three men. It shocked me deeply but it prepared me to take worse in my stride.

We remained in hiding till nightfall when we set out to march to a village reputed to be clear of the enemy where we intended to stop for the night. We took a tortuous route out of the forest, following the course of the valley for some distance and then climbing a seemingly never-ending slope. At each building we passed, watch dogs set up a fearful clamour which was promptly echoed by other dogs in neighbouring compounds, until the night was made hideous with their incessant barking, which served as a clear indication of the direction of our retreat. We hurried along, hoping to by-pass the clamour, and we reached our destination, a group of houses set on the side of a valley, shortly before midnight. Indoors a warm welcome awaited us and we were soon seated by the fire sampling our host's *rakija*.

During the journey that evening I had found the bag of gold sovereigns a heavy load to carry and Djurić had offered to put the haversack into a metal strong box tied to his saddle, which he used for money and secret papers. I had agreed readily. Before settling down I noticed this box placed under a pile of equipment in the corner of the room. I thought nothing more of it at the time and wrapping myself in a blanket I lay down by the fire and was soon asleep.

I awoke with a start as the door burst open. The first light of dawn was filtering through the window and a wild-eyed peasant woman stood wailing on the threshold:
'*Ide Brzo, Bulgari su tu, Brzo Brzo.*'
'What's that she's saying?'
'The Bulgars are here.'
'Where?'
'Here, go quickly, quickly, hurry.'

Pandemonium reigned as men leapt up, still buckling their equipment as they rushed through the doorway past the weeping woman. I seized my boots, laced them up and turned to find my equipment and sten gun.
'*Ide, Brzo, Brzo.*'
'Where are the others, John?'
'They've gone on ahead with the Serbs. Hurry up – it seems serious. Make for the forest below.'

John disappeared through the open doorway. A pile of abandoned equipment littered the room and I suddenly remembered: '*My God, the money.*'

As I turned back to search for the strong box, a machine gun barked outside. The box lay where I had seen it the night before. It seemed that Djurić valued his skin highly. I lifted it but found it far too heavy to carry, and there was no time to waste.

The machine gun settled down to a steady rattle, rat tat tat. I shot out the lock of the box and seizing the precious haversack ran to the door. Keeping my body under cover, I looked outside.

On the hillock opposite the house a machine gun was mounted in action and a second was already placed in position. A group of brown uniformed soldiers tended the guns and I could see others climbing into position on the further side. There was no sign of the Četniks or of other members of the British party.

Bullets spattered the ground in front of the house and I ducked back inside; impossible to leave by the front now; one would be a sitting shot at point blank range. I ran to the room I had just left but as I stopped to look around a burst pierced the wall beside me. I rushed across the room to the back window and, flinging it open, dropped to the ground.

The others had made for the forest; I must do likewise but it seemed impossible to cover that open ground past two machine guns mounted at point blank range. How the devil did the Bulgars get into that position unnoticed? The God-damned sentries must have gone to sleep. When the alarm came, they all b-d off like a lot of rabbits. I swore that when I found them I would have plenty to say to them but pulled myself up as I realised that I would have little chance of doing anything if I stayed cursing behind that house; the enemy would close in soon, and I was alone. Looking hurriedly around I noticed that a small fold in the ground covered in thick undergrowth led from the back of the house halfway across the open field and bending double I followed this cover till it finished then I crouched down and turned to look at the enemy.

The machine gun had stopped firing and its crew lay alongside. A section of infantry was advancing cautiously in my direction and another was making towards the house I had just left. It appeared that though they were only a few yards away they had not yet seen me crouching behind the bushes.

'Well, there's nothing for it, I'll have to go or they'll catch me sitting here,' I murmured as I looked first at the trees thirty yards distant and then to the right at the muzzle of the machine gun. It was so close that I recognised its make; it was an Austrian-made Schwartzlosser. Three weeks ago in Palestine the instructor, Stan, had described that weapon as outdated and too heavy. It looked pretty deadly to me now!

'Come on, just three seconds and you're there.'

I leapt to my feet, sprinting to the cover of the woods. As I ran I saw in front of me the body of a Serb. He lay on his face, arms sprawled out in a pool of blood, within a yard of the forest sanctuary. Five yards to go ... four ... as I reached the outskirts of the wood the machine gun fired a burst and bullets whistled close by but I was already out of sight as, diving over the body of the dead Četnik, I fell amongst the trees. Getting up, I made off downhill, and after about a hundred yards I ran into Sehmer who was crawling through the bushes.

'Where's everyone gone?' I asked, panting.

'Djurić is just ahead; Harvey, Leban and about six Serbs are with him.'

'And the others?'

'They left before us. Djurić says they're with Vlada, his Adjutant. He seemed pretty sure.'

'Pray God they are. It's impossible to search for them if we've no idea which route they followed.'

John was hopeful: 'We'll link up again soon, probably tonight.'

We hurried down to the valley where Djurić was regrouping his men to move off. Calling Leban to translate, I asked him:

'Where are the other members of my Mission?'
'They're with Vlada; they've taken a different route,' he replied.
'How do you know?'

A sullen look came over his face and his eyes shifted craftily. He answered too glibly: 'A peasant escaping from the village told me.'

I was tormented by doubt. When I had last seen him Djurić was travelling too fast to stop and talk with peasants. Had my men got away or not? I knew Djurić didn't know; he was lying to save his face.

But what could we do? No use going back; the Bulgars were certainly in possession by now and, even if the six men with Djurić could be persuaded to return, I knew that to be impossible. We should stand no chance against those machine guns. No, we'd have to go on and hope for the best. As we moved off my fears increased. Everybody had got away from the house, of that I was sure, but that machine gun had fired for a long time. They must have been firing at something. That dead Serb I had seen lying at the edge of the tree, perhaps he was not alone.

We made off in the direction of the dropping ground. The enemy, conducting a drive through the whole area, had passed through here and it seemed unlikely that they would return by the same route. We travelled slowly as two of the Serbs had been wounded, one of them, an officer, through the foot; he was in great pain and needed assistance to keep going.

We reached a hiding place two hours later. It was a cave at the top of an almost perpendicular slope surrounded by thick scrub. Djurić decided to remain here until the trouble blew over.

Joško, the wounded officer, cut off his boot and asked me for bandages. On examining the wound I found that a bullet had passed through his ankle, splintering the bone, leaving jagged ends visible amongst a mass of blood congealed around the gaping exit wound. How he could have borne placing his foot on the ground let alone marching across difficult country was a wonder to me; but he appeared quite indifferent to pain and never winced when we cleaned the wound and applied a dressing.

The Serbs have a capacity to withstand physical suffering far in excess of our own. In the mountains there are no doctors, so when men fall sick they must die or recover unaided. It seems that nature has equipped these people with tremendous vitality and resuscitative ability and I am inclined to believe that this natural strength explains, if not excuses, many of the callous practices which appear barbarous to us but which, in the Balkans, are accepted as the

(Left) 'Collaboration' meeting between local commander Nedić guards, the author and Jovo Stefanović *(Right)* Captain Jovo Stefanović, a true gentleman

Group of Četniks with Jovo Stefanović. Yugoslav buffs please note: no beards or bandoliers. The fighting Četniks worried less about adornments.

(Left) Pesić, Lt Mile Andrejević and Četniks

(Below) Winter quarters

Lt Tomlinson, Sgt Harry Lesar and the author at winter quarters

normal mode of life.

The misfortunes of that day followed quickly one upon the others. At noon five Četniks, members of our party, rejoined us. They had no news of the missing Englishmen but stated definitely that four Serbs had been killed that morning. That left three Serbs and five English to be accounted for. As we sat quietly smoking, Sehmer and I glanced covertly at each other from time to time, each hating to voice the terrible conclusion which we knew the other had reached.

Why did it have to be those boys? Three of them had arrived only the night before and were still completely bewildered by the unfamiliar surroundings. Thompson, in particular, was a grand person. Not content with a safe but useful job with the RAF, he had come in search of action and in a cruel manner fate had granted his wish. Unwarned, unprepared, caught like a rat in a trap, mown down by a machine gun, he had found that action achieving nothing for the loss of his valuable life.

When the peasant woman entered the cave, it needed only one glance at her face to confirm our fears; her story was as simple as it was stark. Two British lay dead at the outskirts of the village and another, by her description Smith, had crawled to the valley below, where she had found him. Seriously wounded, he was now hidden in a miller's hut. She had no news of the remainder, but informed us that the Bulgars had burnt the village and departed.

As she was talking a Četnik arrived carrying news of Blackmore, Sehmer's operator. He had been wounded but had eluded capture by feigning death. After the enemy left he was carried into the forest by the peasants, where two of them were looking after him as best they could. As dusk was falling I set out at once with an escort of three to look for him. A peasant was sent to summon a doctor from the nearest town ten hours march away and John accompanied the woman to attend to Smith.

When I arrived Blackmore was unconscious, and it was indeed a miracle that he was not already dead, for no less than four bullets had entered his body under the left armpit, just above the heart, passing through his chest and emerging on the right side below the waist. We dressed his wounds, made a rough stretcher and carried him to the cave and soon afterwards Sehmer returned with Smith on a bullock cart. He was conscious and in great pain. From one shattered leg the foot hung limply and a huge wound, black with congealed blood, gaped in his shoulder above the heart. He talked deliriously and groaned as we tried to check the bleeding from his wounds which had been reopened by the jolting of the cart.

Two dead, one missing. These two without medical attention were sure to die; the day had surely cost us dear. For a moment I lost control of myself and, turning on Djurić, burst out at him in French:

'You knew all this this morning, yet you kept silent because you were afraid we'd ask you to go back.'

Sehmer caught at my arm. 'Shut up, Mike, it won't help.'

He was right; we too were to blame, I suppose.

Under morphia Smith became coherent and we managed to piece together the story of what had happened. He had slept with the others and, on being awakened by the alarm, they had looked around for their belongings and discovered that, seizing this God-sent opportunity, some Cetniks had stolen Thompson's boots. The search for these boots delayed them somewhat and, as they came out of the house by the front door, they saw the last of Djurić's group disappearing into the woods below. They tried to follow but at that very moment the first Bulgar machine gun opened fire and, catching them bunched together outside the house, had mowed them down. In the first long burst Thompson was killed outright and Blackmore, Smith and one of the New Zealand sergeants from Sehmer's party were hit, the latter two only in the legs.

From where they lay Smith had seen me come to the door of the house and turn back, but he had been unable to make his voice heard above the general uproar. He reiterated again and again that a group of four Serbs had seen them and passed by offering no assistance. Unable to move, they had remained on the ground till the Bulgars advanced towards the houses. Expecting to be taken prisoner, Smith and Lindstrom, the New Zealander, had taken their identity cards out of their wallets so that they could point to the stamp in Bulgar stating 'the bearer is a British officer'.

The niceties of war, however, were lost upon the Bulgars. Rushing upon the wounded men they ransacked their pockets and tore off their boots. Smith's leg had been broken by a bullet and, when they tugged at his foot, he fainted with the pain. He came to a few seconds later to find a sergeant leaning over him. As he opened his eyes he heard two single shots followed by a rattling groan from Lindstrom lying just behind him. Before he could open his mouth to say a word the Bulgar reached down and, taking his automatic from his pocket, spat in his face and fired a shot at his heart. After that Smith could remember nothing else.

Smith's story was the plain truth. Contrary to all the rules of war, the Bulgars had murdered our men in cold blood as they lay wounded. They had not bothered to take them prisoner to question them or perhaps torture them to reveal the many secrets that they knew. As we were to discover later, they had even left secret codes and papers lying beside the bodies of the victims, taking only their money, boots and other articles of use. Two wireless sets complete with crystals and signal plans had been abandoned by Djurić's men in their panic. We found them later; their cases had been slit open with a bayonet but the sets were still intact and fit for our use.

This act of the Bulgars was that of uncivilised savages and bestiality of this kind could help their cause in no way. Had they been guided even by common sense, let alone human decency, they could have brought in a pretty haul when they returned to base to report to their German masters. But they had let their blood lust overcome their reasoning, murdering in cold blood with less thought than they gave to squashing the lice from the lining of their shirts.

Across the valley the mountains were obscured by a bank of cloud. In the evening gloom the Balkan scene was harsh and unrelenting, hard as were the people forged under the shadow of its peaks. Occasional lightning flashes shot to the ground from out the massed clouds and thunder rumbled intermittently in the distance. As the sun sank below the horizon Sehmer came out of the cave to tell me that Smith was dead.

CHAPTER FIVE

The Morava Valley Reconnaissance

I sat on a rock beside the path, occupied in the very necessary task of disinfesting my only shirt. Sehmer squatted beside me, cursing and swearing as he hacked away vainly trying to remove a week's growth of stiff, gingery stubble.

The enemy had finished their work and departed and we were back in the house where I had spent that first congenial evening after my arrival in Serbia. It was fitting that I should have returned there. For the last two weeks we had suffered tribulation after tribulation. Now, with our losses accepted and our plans altered, we could start again from the same place, as if the last two weeks were nothing but a grim nightmare from which, at great cost, we had gained experience to protect ourselves from a similar disaster in the future. After showing signs of improvement Blackmore had died quite suddenly from delayed shock, while the missing Tomlinson had been located with a bullet wound in his right arm; we left him hidden in a forest hut, cared for by a charcoal burner's wife, a motherly old soul. He was improving daily, and hoped to be fit within a month.

With Blackmore and Thompson dead, our essential lifeline, wireless communication with base, had been imperilled. To make matters worse Sehmer's equipment had been destroyed on the morning of the massacre and there was only my set left, one small battery and a hand generator which Trbić had hidden away. To work it we only had Leban, the interpreter, who was half trained, temperamental and unaccustomed to our specialised equipment. For three days and nights we had cranked the stiff handle of the generator, till our arms ached, blisters formed on our hands and the sweat dripped from our foreheads; then thrice each day we watched Leban, with his key, dissipating our labours to the unresponsive ether; then back to that heart-breaking work, till time came for him to try again. On the third morning a faint answer came but before he could transmit a message the battery expired. We set to cranking with a will and six hours later Cairo received the story of our predicament.

It was some days later before we received fresh orders and, when we did, it was clear that, having lost over half of the effective strength of the combined missions, base were loath to risk any more losses for the moment, lest our contact in that area be completely wiped out. Sehmer was ordered to remain with Djurić and await reinforcements, including another wireless operator in place of Blackmore. It was hoped that these would arrive within a few days.

My orders were to cancel my journey to Skoplje and to proceed to an area in the mountains about fifty miles to the south, which commanded the main road and railway between Niš and Skoplje. I was to contact the groups there and prepare to attack enemy communications.

John finished his painful task. Having lost our packs we had only one razor, a bar of ersatz soap and a threadbare toothbrush to serve Harvey, the New Zealand sergeant, Sehmer and myself. The razor, for which we had no spare blades, served to enhance our self-respect but made little difference to our appearances. Having removed his dentures preparatory to his turn with the toothbrush, Harvey had been outvoted by two to one from using that article of equipment.

It had already been agreed that Harvey and Leban should come with me, the former to replace Tomlinson, who would not be fit to march for some time and who would be safer hiding in Djurić's more remote area; Leban was to act as my wireless operator until I too could get a reinforcement.

Two days' march brought us to the area where I was to remain for the next nine months. We had crossed the snow-covered eastern mountain range and descended to a country of steeply rolling hills, blanketed with beech forests. In this part the houses were grouped into small parishes and the rich soil was well cultivated. We halted on the evening of the second day at a village called Oruglica, where we had been advised to make our headquarters. A courier had been sent ahead to warn the Četniks of our arrival and we found an escort waiting for us, which conducted us to a building where lodging had already been arranged.

Oruglica appeared on the map as a tiny pinpoint amongst a mass of close contours hidden in the extreme south-eastern corner of the new Serbia which, under the new frontier demarcation drawn up by the Axis on the capitulation of Yugoslavia, had forfeited large slices of its southern territory to Bulgaria and Albania. The frontier between Bulgaria and Serbia met the Serbian-Albanian border two miles to the south and Oruglica, in Serbia, consequently lay less than two miles from both Albanian and Bulgarian territory. To the east lay the main railway and road from Niš to Skoplje, passing through Lescovac, a manufacturing town some twelve hours' march to our north-east and Vranje, a town now in Bulgaria, eight hours to the south-east. Between these two towns the railway circled the farther side of a high, rugged mountain, Mount Kukavica, while to the north-west, stretched the Lescovac plains rising to Mount Radan beneath which nestled Lebane, a small garrison town now held by a battalion of Bulgars. To the south-west, Albania was hostile country.

My primary target was to be the main road and the railway line. This was one of the most important lines of communication in Yugoslavia as the enemy used it to supply their army in Greece. My orders were to render passage along this railway as difficult as possible.

Apart from the troops in Lebane, garrisons were stationed in Leskovac and Vranje. In addition, the Bulgarian frontier, which skirted the southern slopes of Mount Kukavica, was heavily patrolled by Bulgar and Nedić police troops who lived in block houses, spaced at thousand yard intervals along the line. Friendly troops in these mountains were three Četnik guerilla formations, all allied to Mihailović. Manić, an ex-air force officer, controlled a formation based on Mount Kukavica, Andrejević, an engineer operated to the north in the hills bordering the Lescovac plain.

Oruglica was the base of a brigade under the command of a Captain Stefanović, who came to meet us at the outskirts of the village. He had been a regular officer of the Royal Horse Guards and his appearance was striking. He was of medium height but wiry and wore a fierce black moustache. He was carefully dressed in a short black fur coat, well cut breeches and shining field boots. His revolver hung from a leather cross belt and he carried a machine carbine of German pattern.

'Zdravo, dobro dosli' (Bravo, well met.)

Shaking hands I evaded his embrace and when we had completed the exchange of formal greetings I sent Harvey and Leban off to find a suitable place to set up the wireless, and settled down myself to talk business. Stefanović had heard of our recent losses and we discussed the attack, in the course of which the Germans had also passed through Oruglica but had failed to make contact with his unit which escaped without casualties.

After a reasonable interval, discussing the general situation for formality's sake, I started to outline the purpose of my Mission. I had by now been in the country three weeks and could talk slowly in Serbo-Croat.

'As you know, I've come here to act as British Liaison Officer with your formation and those of Manić and Andrejević. I have a wireless set which is in communication with our base in Egypt and I can arrange for supplies of arms and clothing to be dropped for your area. I have money which can be used to obtain arms and food. In return I ask that you send your men to me to be trained in the use of explosives and other material we have and to make troops available as I require them for attacks on the railway line.'

Stefanović rushed off into a long monologue. Yes, they needed arms, clothing and money very badly. They were true to the Allied cause and they wished to help in every way possible to hasten victory over the barbarians. They loved the Allies dearly and would sell their lives for the cause. It was well known that the Serbs were born soldiers, that they had thrown out the Turks, fought harder and suffered greater casualties than any other Allied nation in the last war and, though their country was over-run by the Germans, were fighting in the mountains, severed from all their friends, without support or help.

As he paused for breath I broke in:

'Yes, I agree, the Serbs are a very gallant people. But now you will get the support you require, if you will only agree to put troops at my disposal. I am not suggesting immediate action. We must get our supplies first, train the men and choose the targets. Only then will we be ready.'

Stefanović assured me of his agreement. He would do all in his power to help. Of course he must have the supplies, the arms and ammunition, the explosives and then it would be easy. When the invasion came they would be prepared and the great Serb nation would sweep the Germans out of Yugoslavia. In the meantime he would do all the sabotage I asked for, attack as often as the number of his men allowed . . . 'But' . . . and here was the proviso – I was to come to hate this sentence more than any other . . . 'but I must first have orders from Mihailović.'

'But surely,' I protested, 'you don't mean to say that you must first have permission for each separate attack?'

'At present, yes,' replied Stefanović. 'Later he may delegate discretion to us to order small operations. But now, our orders are to arm and equip as much as we can and prepare for the *Ustanak*.'

The *Ustanak* or uprising was to be the day when the whole country would turn against the enemy.

He continued:

'Now we may attack armaments depots or stores to equip ourselves, but we must kill the minimum number of Germans. Do not forget that for every German we kill one hundred Serbs are shot. If we were to kill twenty thousand Germans we would not win the war. We might thus help the cause a little, but oh so little, and the consequent reprisals would wipe out every man in Serbia. Then the enemy could withdraw every division in the country, as there would be no further need to police it, and those divisions could be transferred to reinforce another front. Can you not see that a policy of attack means racial suicide?'

'And are you permitted to do industrial sabotage?' I asked.

'Ah, that is another question,' answered Jovo. 'We will do all that you ask. If you will give us the explosives, we can carry out the work. Men will go slow, sand will be put in the machines, wheels will not be greased. Yes, that I will arrange' . . . He let his hands fall in a pathetic gesture . . . 'Please understand, I want to fight. I am a soldier, an officer of the King's Guard, and war is my profession. I took an active part in the coup d'état which put Yugoslavia into the war. But now I must obey my orders, which are to save the lives of the people. If I thought that I were strong enough to capture Vranje and hold it, I should do so. I could capture it, perhaps, but I could never hold it and the enemy would return and burn the town to the ground. I myself would not suffer because I would be safe here in the mountains but the people would be made to pay and perhaps, in desperation, they might turn to the Germans against us. No, *Gospodine Kapetan*, I long to fight but, until Mihailović, my General, gives the order, I must desist.'

There was sound reason in his impassioned speech, but it was logic to be ignored. Like Stefanović, I too had my orders – to carry out sabotage against the enemy. If I achieved nothing, however sound the reason, my continued presence in the country would be unjustified. I would try appealing first but if that failed I resolved to use other means of persuasion. For the present, however, it was clearly useless arguing further and my meagre knowledge of the language reduced any chance of persuading Stefanović to change his mind. I therefore decided to compromise:

'In that case I will agree to order a quantity of supplies if you will request permission from General Mihailović to start operations against the railway. In the meantime, while you are waiting for an answer, I want to carry out a reconnaissance of the railway line between Vranje and Lescovac. I presume that you can provide guides to accompany me. By the way, how will you communicate with Mihailović?'

His answer came at once:

'Oh, that's easy. We are in constant communication with him. I send a girl by train to Belgrade where she meets another, who knows where Mihailović is hiding. The other, acting as a post exchange, sends my message on. It takes two days to Belgrade and a messenger goes to Mihailović and returns twice every week. We will have the answer in well under twenty days.'

'Can't you send a courier direct? That would seem more reliable.'

Stefanović shrugged his shoulders. 'I do not know where Draža is. Perhaps he is forty days' march away, perhaps he is here. Some even think he is in England. Very few know.'

I took a great liking to Stefanović from the start; though suave, at least he seemed to be honest. When we went on to discuss our plans for the reconnaissance he was delighted at the chance of some occupation if not action and he immediately suggested that he personally should accompany me.

While we sat talking, the villagers were by no means idle and the harsh smell of burning hair drifted across the yard. A pig had been killed in honour of our arrival and was roasting on a spit over the glowing embers of a huge open fire. Three Četniks of bloodthirsty appearance squatted on their haunches and sang dolefully as they turned the carcase round and round.

Stefanović asked for *rakija* and, having learnt that Serbs love nothing more than talking about themselves, I asked him to describe his life as a cavalry officer in Belgrade before the war. He responded willingly and was soon relating his life history. He was a peasant's son and, passing out well from school, had gone into the military academy and later obtained a commission as a subaltern in the Royal Horse Guards. He described the good life he had enjoyed before the war in Belgrade, dwelling on parties at the Palace and the Embassies. Then came the war and as a member of the secret group of officers who, preferring to fight and lose honourably rather than not fight at all, had overthrown the Government and thrown Hitler's ultimatum back in his face, he had taken part in the coup d'état. After the capitulation he was taken prisoner but he escaped and returned home; a few weeks later he was summoned by Mihailović to join the Četniks and was given command of a brigade. He told me of the hardships the Četniks had undergone in the first early days, with every man's hand turned against them. Of how every rifle and round of ammunition was paid for, when the currency was blood.

Jovo's reminiscences were interrupted as the pig, now cooked to a turn, steaming and crackling, was brought forward to be carved. As the guest of honour I was asked to take my seat at the head of a table which had been set up in the yard and, greatly to my consternation, no sooner was I seated than the head of the pig was placed on the table in front of me. Observing my unpractised handling of this delicate morsel, Stefanović offered to prepare it for me, an invitation I accepted gladly, as without skilled assistance I envisaged sleeping on a stomach, empty save of *rakija*.

He inserted a penknife deftly just behind the crown, gave one quick turn and the head lay bisected, presenting two full sides each like a plate of prepared hors d'oeuvres. There is more flavour and variety in the head of a roasted pig than in any dish I know. The brains that melt in the mouth, the tongue like tender ham, the firm flesh of the cheeks . . . I was made to eat the nostrils. The eyes . . . I slipped my plate quietly aside, but Stefanović noticed and protested.

'You must eat the eyes, they are the best part. I will take one, you the other.'

Fearing to appear over-sensitive, I acquiesced reluctantly, though it was with a feeling of nausea that I bit into the rubbery globe. I never again refused the offer of an eye. The springy resilience of an oyster, a not totally dissimilar flavour, though stronger and subtler. The eye of the pig is considered a prize morsel in Serbia.

As we were about to leave the table a commotion outside heralded the arrival of a party of horsemen and a vaguely familiar voice enquired whether the English had yet arrived. A large figure, wrapped in a sheepskin coat, waddled portentously into the room. It was Cikabuda. When I enquired what brought him to Oruglica his large eyes twinkled.

'And should I ask you, O foreign Captain in the Army of Great Britain, every time I wish to visit my nephew, your host?' He went on, relentlessly, 'I came also to tell you that I do not like your name. I, Buda, do not like to talk about the Capitan Liss. What is your before-name?'

'My parents called me Michael.'

'Mikarel . . . hm.' A gleam came into his eye: 'Yes, Meekee Mowse, we will call you Meekee.'

Having settled this all important point to his complete satisfaction,

Čikabuda settled down to eat all that was left of the pig. It was my misfortune that the name stuck.

*

It was over a week later, and then only with the greatest of difficulty, that Leban managed to re-establish communication with base. Cairo at once confirmed my plans and promised a sortie of three aircraft due in twelve days' time. As Jovo Stefanović had in the meantime obtained the guides to take us across the mountain to the railway line near Vranje, I decided to carry out the reconnaissance right away, returning in time to supervise reception of the sortie. While waiting to get in touch with base, I had visited Manić and Andrejević, the commanders of the two neighbouring brigades.

Mile Andrejević commanded a small brigade whose headquarters were at a village called Barje in the foothills which overlooked the Lescovac plain. He was a pleasant person and seemed straightforward and honest. He had previously been a subaltern in the Engineers of the Guards Division and was a great personal friend of Stefanović. His brigade of only one hundred and twenty men was badly in need of arms and clothing and I promised to do all I could to help.

Manić was a very different character. He was young, an ex-air force pilot, and he possessed a dynamic personality. He was large for a Serb, being over six feet tall, and had the figure of an athlete with striking good looks, although his finely cut features, well drilled physique and thin cruel mouth gave him a Prussian appearance. I realised at once that Manić would be the key to the success or failure of my mission. Underneath his charming manner, I could see him sizing me up as an opponent and I realised that he was a man who would do nothing unless he personally benefited from it. He was of the strong unscrupulous type which, in any country, goes to the top or to gaol. Determined to impress me, Manić had arranged a full parade of his brigade on the occasion of my visit and I was indeed astonished by the appearance of his men. Unlike the Četniks I had seen till then, they were smart and well-disciplined in their attitude and, best of all, their arms were cleaned and oiled. This formation, the Letića (mobile) Brigade, was well armed, over two hundred and fifty strong and the biggest in my area.

I worried about Manić; it was plain that he could not be bluffed or browbeaten. Untrustworthy as a friend, he would be the very devil if made antagonistic.

I decided to take Harvey on the reconnaissance, relying on his expert knowledge of engineering to assist me in drawing up plans of the bridges and estimating the quantities of explosives necessary for demolition purposes. Dressed as peasants, in order to facilitate freedom of movement in Bulgaria, we were due to leave that evening at dusk and, observing ourselves in a mirror, we laughed happily as we wondered what would have been the reaction of the Cairo staff could they have seen us. Jovo had great difficulty in obtaining for me a sufficiently large suit of peasant dress and, after several vain efforts to squeeze into outfits belonging to men of his formation, we had dispatched scouts to find the tallest peasant in the vicinity. When he had been located he was ordered immediately to Oruglica and asked to strip. It was only when I had adorned myself in his roughly woven, patched trousers that I realised I would have to lend him my only pair of uniform trousers, complete with gadgets, until my return. He had only been gone some ten minutes when, scratching wildly, I was forced to accept the conclusion that when I recovered my trousers they too would certainly be verminous.

Apart from my not unnatural dislike of sharing my trousers with numerous vermin, I was satisfied with my clothes. I was at least completely disguised with a short fur coat, a black woolly Bulgarian cap and gaily knitted stockings. My feet were wrapped in cuts from the skin of a calf killed two days previously; they fitted snugly and prevented thorns entering the soles but, in all other respects, as one felt every stone and bump on the ground, one was little better off than barefoot.

The party consisted of Harvey, Jovo and three guides, all similarly dressed. Each carried a sten gun, stripped of the butt. The magazine and the short body and barrel section being placed separately in the big inside pockets of our peasant jackets. To a casual observer, we would appear to be a harmless group of peasants, perhaps returning from a party but, if questioned by police or a Bulgar patrol at close range, we carried enough fire power to give ourselves a fair chance of escape.

Our objective for that evening was a small village near Vranje, where we planned to sleep at the home of our first guide. The following day we were to work north through the hills bordering the Morava valley, the course of the main road and railway. I had picked out on the map various bridges and points where the railway ran close to the forest on the western side and I wanted to visit each of the places and determine which were most suitable for attack.

The path to Vranje from Oruglica led down into the valley of the Veternica and thence over a steep escarpment whose summit marked the Bulgarian frontier. Our guide, who knew the route intimately, explained that we should cross the line under cover of first darkness, so as to allow us the greater part of the night to reach our destination. Jovo and the guide led the way together, swinging along at a good pace as we wound our way down over the river and into a thick wood on the far side. As the light failed and I found it increasingly difficult to pick out an easy path, my feet, unaccustomed to marching without stout boots, began to feel the repeated jars of the rocky ground and I was thinking that we should steady our pace if we were to cover the fifty odd kilometres to our destination that evening.

We were climbing steeply up the wooded escarpment when Jovo and the guide suddenly stopped and beckoned to us. We came alongside quietly and they pointed to where a white building showed through the trees a quarter of a mile distant. Jovo whispered:

'That is a *Carinara* (frontier post). There are fifty Bulgars there; go quietly.'

Turning he started to creep forward, a picture of pantomime stealth. We followed silently and I was surprised when one after the other our Serb companions plucked at my sleeves as if with an urgent message and, pointing to the ridge in front, whispered, 'Ssh, ssh! the frontier.' They never tired of this drama until we reached the top of the hill and flattened ourselves out under cover by the edge of a ride cut through the trees. A single strand of field telephone wire marked the line. I waited for the signal to move on but Jovo made no sign and we lay in silence until the damp started to seep through my clothing.

Wondering at this delay, I leant over to Jovo:

'Why do we wait?' I whispered.

'To see if there is a patrol.'

In the moonlight the ridge showed clear into the distance. I looked to right and left, it was empty.

'But I can see nobody.'

He signed to me to be quiet. 'Ssh, we must look.'

I relapsed into silence, curbing my desire to tell him, 'There is no patrol but, if we stay here much longer, there probably will be', when suddenly Jovo leaped to his feet and with a fierce shout of '*Napred*' (forward) tore across the path and down the slope on the other side. Like men possessed, the guides ran after him and, taken completely by surprise, Harvey and I stumbled along well in the rear.

A hundred yards the other side, the fleeting figures stopped and, when we came up to them, they were sitting resting on a rock and Jovo was lighting a cigarette. If a patrol fired on us now, in full view and easy range of the ride, what would it matter? They had enjoyed their little drama and we had crossed the frontier.

We marched all night, travelling fast across country, often forging rivers waist deep. My feet were sorely bruised and ached abominably and I longed to be back in Egypt snug in bed, instead of trapesing about enemy country with a pack of melodramatic Balkan idiots! As we slithered and scraped along a mountain path, dislodging stones which fell with a clatter to the valley below, Harvey would burst into a whispered flood of invective followed by a roar of 'Ssh' from the Serbs. The whole performance was so ridiculous, however, that after a time my sense of humour reawoke and I found myself shaking with laughter at this absurd situation.

At last we saw the village in front of us. While our guide went ahead to ensure that his family were alone in the house, we sat by the roadside smoking, with burning cigarettes hidden surreptitiously inside our hands. I felt my legs stiffening up in the cold of the air before dawn and thanked God that we had finally arrived and would soon be lying alongside a fire with food and *rakija* warming our stomachs.

The guide reappeared, creeping back cautiously along the path.

'Quick, into cover,' he whispered, 'there are troops in the village.'

We rested in the woods that morning.

That reconnaissance was a nightmare. Each night we marched forty or fifty kilometres, following the railway northwards and skirting the villages, which were full of troops and police; by day we lay up in whatever cover was available, slipping out at dawn to reconnoitre targets, relying for food on scraps of bread and sour cheese fetched by the guide who had an identity card. On the third morning at dawn we found ourselves on the eastern slopes of Mount Kukavica resting in a gorse thicket. We were about eight miles from the last place to be seen, we had marched all night, my feet felt like a mass of bruised pulp and my head ached abominably. I felt hot and shivery and I groaned as Jovo tugged at my arm.

'We must go on soon, you and I,' he advised. 'We can leave the others here and return later. Unless we get back here by dusk we will be unable to reach the frontier tonight.'

'I feel ghastly,' I protested. 'I can't walk another step.'

'But you must,' insisted Jovo. 'We can't remain here tomorrow. We are expected over the frontier tonight.'

'I don't care. Let's just rest here today and leave the job. We have enough information for now and we can come back again later.'

We argued for some time. I pleaded that I was ill and tested my pulse. It was fast and I knew that I had a fever but Jovo was adamant, insisting on completing the task we had set ourselves. Eventually, shamed into acquiescence, I agreed and we started off on our own.

That day was hell. I lurched along demanding frequent halts, while the seemingly tireless Jovo nursed me along until three hours later we looked down into the Morava valley. Crawling through a field of maize we approached until we could look out onto the road ten feet in front of us. On the far side of the road the river ran muddy and stony and two or three hundred yards to the left was a large single span steel bridge which carried the railway across while the stone-built road bridge lay just downstream. Concrete pill-boxes had been constructed at each end of the viaduct and I could see a sentry in Bulgarian uniform standing by the door of one of them.

We waited for about ten minutes until some peasants appeared struggling along the road towards Vranje. Letting them pass we stepped out of the maize and followed them down the road. Two of them turned round to look at us but made no comment and as we reached the bridge Jovo stopped and bent down as if to tie up the laces of his peasant footwear. In the time thus gained I leant on the parapet, seemingly to look for fish in the river, making a brief sketch of the railway bridge and memorising the features of its construction. The sentry stared oafishly at us but appeared to notice nothing strange and Jovo soon straightened up and whispered to me to move on.

Two miles from the Morava valley on the way back to the rendezvous we had to pass through a tiny village which had been clear on our way down. We climbed painfully up the hill through the cultivated fields to the edge of the village.

As far as I can remember we both saw them in the same instant. The street was full of soldiers in brown uniform jackets and shorts. A group of ten lolled about smoking cigarettes, farther up another group were cooking over an open fire; two men walked past the house in front of us carrying pails of water on a stick between them and a light machine gunner sat examining his gun. I made to dive behind a haystack but Jovo, taking in the situation at a glance, hissed:

'Go straight on.'

With a lack of concern which shamed my trembling, Jovo linked arms with me and we sauntered up the street. I could see no signs of villagers, just soldiers, Bulgars. With their heavy featured mastiff-like faces they stared idly at us; bowing politely we walked through their camp. Three minutes, five . . . it seemed an age waiting for that one word '*Stoy*' which would seal our fate. In a daze, tired and desperate, I strolled along automatically, wondering vaguely whether we should have a chance to shoot our way out.

Then Jovo laughed. 'That was a near thing.'

I looked round; we were through. We had reached the end of the street and turned off. The village was a hundred yards behind.

Rejoining the others we set off again at once. To me the march to the frontier became a crazy blur of nausea and pain. My fever was worse but I had reached that stage when one goes on unquestioningly because one is past conscious thought. It never occurred to me to ask for a halt; when the others marched, I marched . . . when they halted, I halted. Nothing seemed to matter. At the frontier we were met by a new guide . . . This time we crossed, up an open hillside to the escarpment, a frantic scrambling rush, then past the 'phone wire and into the sweet secure cover of the thick green forest. Yugoslavia again. At dawn I staggered into Oruglica and collapsed seriously ill with malaria.

CHAPTER SIX

Četnik Internecine Strife
Second Lesson in Balkan Politics

For three days my fever raged. I lay on a pile of straw, alternately conscious and delirious, cursing all around me. No drugs being available, Stefanović procured the local 'wise woman', a bewhiskered nauseating old hunchback. With great ceremony she prepared a brew, a mixture of herbs and roots from the forest, entrails of some animals, pinches of spices. The pot, topped up with strongest *rakija*, was placed on the fire and the old witch leaning over to stir it, crossed herself and muttered unintelligible incantations. When it boiled she took a wineglass of the liquid, went out of the door and reappeared at the window. I was ordered to get up and receive the glass over the sill. This I did and drank to the accompaniment of a further string of mystical murmurings.

I was too ill to be amused at their antics but I noticed that even Stefanović, an educated man, took the ceremony seriously. The liquid, dark green in colour with a bitter taste, was very hot and strong and I felt the fumes, rising from my stomach, fill my lungs, throat and head. A few minutes later I fell into a deep drunken sleep. The following morning when I awoke I felt weak and ached all over but my head was clear. The fever had gone.

So-called witchcraft is practised in many wild parts of the Serbian mountains. The efficacy of such potions is undisputed but the women who practise these rites are no witches. They are merely possessors of a knowledge of natural medicine, gained through the centuries. Their materials are roots and herbs, used in civilised countries under the more credible name of 'nature cures'. *Rakija* is used as the basis of many potions, for it is strongly alcoholic and induces sound sleep. The ceremony no doubt has a great psychological effect on the simple peasant patient. Albeit, I felt better in body and clear in mind.

Harvey had done wonders during my illness. Lists of necessary stores and explosives had been prepared and despatched, the dropping ground chosen and signals arranged. The sortie was due that night but when he assured me that all was under control, I decided to stay in bed all day so as to be fit to cope with the situation when the stores arrived.

The day was fine and clear and at midday we received a signal ordering us to expect three aircraft at around and midnight. At five I got up, ate some food and went out with Harvey to see the dropping ground. The fires were to be lit in a flat open space about half a mile from the village, where a wood to the south would screen the glare from observation at the frontier. The turf was ready cut in ten places forming a letter H and stacks of wood lay piled along the side.

This sortie was intended for Stefanović's brigade. At eight the men paraded on the ground, guards were stationed at all commanding points and a machine gun was trained covering the path leading to the frontier against any possible interference from that direction. A small fire had already been kindled and I sat beside it wrapped in blankets while Leban fussed around preparing *slivovički čaj* (slivovich tea), by burning sugar into boiling *rakija*, a warming, satisfying drink.

We had been waiting about an hour when one of our scouts rushed wildly up to me; bursting into a garbled story, he stated that a peasant had just arrived with a report that a Bulgar force, a company strong, had crossed the frontier an hour and a half distant and were moving in our direction. I sent for Jovo, instructing him to send a strong patrol out to make contact and explained that, until we received further reports, or heard firing, we would continue with reception. Meanwhile I waited anxiously, listening for sounds of contact to the south.

My watch showed a quarter to midnight. The first plane was due soon afterwards. The men were standing ready by the fires, while Leban held a torch. All was ready and I had dismissed the report as an unjustified scare when suddenly there came a burst of fire from the north. This was followed by the repeated crackling of rifles and the steady drumming of a machne gun. Simultaneously a heavily armed Četnik, dripping with sweat, ran towards us, saluted and handed me a letter.

As I opened the letter I heard the murmur of an aircraft in the distance. I ordered Leban to signal to it but not to light the fires.

I tore open the envelope. The faint throb was now a steady roar as the plane flew straight in our direction. Leban's torch winked out dot dot dash . . . dot dot dash. The machine gun rattled in the distance. The letter was short and to the point:

> Dear Captain, At six this evening my scouts reported a battalion

of Germans moving towards us from Lescovac. I am deploying my brigade along the northern slopes of Kukavica to give you warning of their approach.

It was signed 'B. Manić'.

The aircraft had spotted our torch and was circling low directly overhead. A lamp from the rear gunner's cockpit tapped out its letter slowly at first, then petulantly as we failed to light the fires. The sound of battle came clearly nearer now. An enemy battalion to the north, a company of Bulgars from the frontier. Both must be less than an hour away. Manić cannot possibly hold and we have only one machine gun to protect our southern side. The stores would take at least six hours to collect and hide, but the enemy were reported one hour away – the aircraft circled impatiently.

I hated to lose those stores; my inadequate wireless equipment needed replacement; we had no clothing or medical kit; we were short of ammunition and arms; supplies would give me necessary power and prestige. God alone knew when we would get another sortie. Already I could hear in the distance the faint murmur of the second plane. The light from the air flashed furiously, revealing our position to the frontier.

'Leban, order the men to hide all signs of preparations. Pack your wireless set and stand by to move off to the woods. Give me that torch.'

Slowly letter by letter, I flashed my signal: 'SORRY . . . ENEMY . . . CLOSE . . . BY. GO . . . AWAY.'

We moved into the woods with Stefanović and his staff; the brigade was deployed and scouts sent out in all directions. I listened to the roar of the second and third planes, circling, circling, searching for our signals. The ground was damp and, weak from my bout of fever, I felt tired and cold; I wondered dispiritedly what would happen this time. The last attack had cost us dear enough. I cursed at the aircraft circling overhead revealing our position and prayed that, short of petrol, they would soon turn for home.

At dawn the section sent to the frontier returned. They had patrolled all the paths leading from the line. They reported that all was quiet and that no troops had passed during the night. From the north, scouts returned and insisted that no troops had left Lescovac the previous day.

I asked Stefanović: 'What the devil does it mean?'

'Think it out for yourself. Your stores would make me strong. There is a lot for you still to learn about Yugoslavia.'

My thoughts were very bitter. So that was the answer – Manić had shown his teeth.

*

Back in Oruglica, Harvey and I sat breakfasting. Thoroughly depressed, we were discussing the affairs of the night before.

'Well, what do you think should be done about it?' I asked him.

'Punish the bastard. Don't give him a thing and arm Stefanović and Andrejević till they are twice as strong as he is,' replied Harvey.

'Yes, that is the obvious answer, but it doesn't help much. Firstly, it would require many sorties, which I don't know if I can obtain, to arm up the other two. They can all get as many men as they've got arms for but they won't be trained. Manić's men are. Lastly, if Manić can play that sort of trick on me I don't put it past him to play one on someone else.'

'What do you mean by that?'

'Meaning Milhailović,' I replied. 'Jovo is a simple straightforward soldier and won't break orders. Manić is out for himself and, if I could convince him that the terms are worthwhile, I've got a feeling he might be persuaded to break loose from his fetters and act without permission from the old man; he's that type. As I see it, we're here to do sabotage or rather to make the Serbs do it. The place is a mass of political intrigue, personal and national. They're up to dirty tricks – we must be unscrupulous too. There's only one thing I can do, if I don't want to make a clear break with Manić. If he will allow me to do so, I'll play the honest English idiot. I shall try to make him assess me as a man with a one track mind. If he produces satisfactory results then I will help him: no results, no stores.'

'And Stefanović?' asked Harvey.

'He's the difficulty. I can't put that argument to him or he'll go writing to Mihailović and the cat will be out of the bag . . . I'll have to play a double game and bluff him off temporarily. If Manić can be made to start the ball rolling, who knows, Jovo may join in and, not to be outdone by his rival, carry out attacks too. I'll have to play one off against the other.'

'Well, it all sounds damn silly. Why can't they work together? They're both on the same side.'

I laughed bitterly. 'That question can be applied similarly to the troubles between Tito and Mihailović. Jealousy, ambition, selfishness, they all play a part but in that sort of trouble the biggest rogue usually wins. That's why I'm not breaking with Manić yet.'

Before leaving for Manić's HQ the next day I had a difficult interview with Jovo. I told him that I was fully aware of what I was doing, that I sympathized with him but that, as a British officer, I refused to be called upon to explain my actions. As a token of good faith I left Harvey, Leban and the wireless set at the headquarters in Oruglica, giving them orders to send all incoming messages on to me by courier.

On arrival at Kukavica I was greeted with a tremendous show of hospitality. Manić gave me a dramatic account of his action the previous night against the mythical enemy attack; the German battalion which had, in fact, never left barracks, had, according to him, been repulsed with heavy losses at the northern approach to the mountains. As he talked I could feel him probing to see if I credited the tale and I tried hard to give no sign to the contrary. With truly incredible effrontery he finished:

'So you see that we are prepared to fight hard for you but we must have supplies. Last night we used much of our precious ammunition and until we get some more we cannot fight again; we must run. Stefanović does not fight. Leave him and come over here to us.'

I recalled the village street full of Bulgars, Jovo's whispered: 'straight ahead,' his casual attitude as he sauntered along, calmly picking his way between the enemy soldiers. I wondered if Manić would have played that part.

He interrupted my thoughts:

'Establish your headquarters with us. Arrange a large sortie for my brigade alone. Then, when we have the ammunition, we will do whatever you ask.'

It was significant that Manić never mentioned the veto Mihailović had placed on aggressive action.

'No, I can't do that,' I answered, 'I'm here to support all the Četniks in my area, not one particular group. I shall order a sortie and it will be divided equally between yourself, Andrejević and Stefanović. All of you should have enough ammunition and explosives to start sabotage and then' . . . I looked him straight in the face . . . 'we shall see who uses Allied assistance most effectively.'

It was August and the weather was glorious. The rain which till then had fallen almost daily gave place to blue skies and warm, still nights. Five weeks had passed since my conversation with Manić and our sortie had not yet come. Base had put forward various excuses: shortage of aircraft, unsuitable Met, night fighter activity, urgent priorities elsewhere.

Urgent priorities . . . listening with Stefanović to the BBC broadcasts in Serbo-Croat, I had noticed the change in the political trend of the news. Three months previously the exploits of General Mihailović, Minister of War, had filled the bulletins. Now the name Mihailović, unadorned by rank or title, was only occasionally mentioned briefly. We had been hearing each day more and more of the doings of Marshal Tito and his National Army of Liberation, previously denominated 'Yugoslav communists or partisans'. Now no mention was ever made of Peter, the Boy King. This worried the Serbs and it worried us too. Obviously the Partisans were the 'Urgent Priorities elsewhere'. Now this change of policy only threatened our supplies, later it might mean that the Civil War would spread to us in Serbia.

It was during this period that Tomlinson had rejoined us, fully recovered. He had left Sehmer three days march away and carried a letter from him. John wrote that he was having great difficulties with Djurić, who was becoming more demanding every day and expected unlimited supplies of stores, although refusing to satisfy any of John's demands for the commencement of offensive operations. Experiencing similar troubles myself I was not surprised and wrote a sympathetic note in reply which I gave to Harvey who, to my regret, had to return at once to rejoin Sehmer.

Communication with base became a nightmare. We had only the one battery, by then battered and leaking, and the hand generator to charge it. Jovo had detailed a squad of men to do the turning for us but, even working the full twenty-four hours, they stored only enough current for half an hour's working time every day. In addition to this we had other troubles; the generator regularly broke down and valuable time was lost in repairing it and owing to Leban's indifference as an operator we had to confine ourselves to the absolute minimum of traffic. I prayed for the sorties to come before communication would peter out entirely.

We spent the time too idly. Till the stores came the Yugoslavs would not consider action. We could do nothing without explosives, even on our own. I passed the days travelling around getting to know the country and the people. In the evenings we bathed in the stream below Oruglica and slept each night in the woods. An occasional scare broke the boredom of inactivity and once a strong patrol passed through.

From the neighbouring forest we watched the Bulgars enter the village and ransack the houses. Any food they found they ate on the spot, took away or burned. To cook a meal they made a huge fire, burning furniture as fuel. Wanton destruction. Because this was Serbia — they were Bulgars. Satellites, they had entered the war on the side of Germany. Their troops, uncommitted to any fighting front, lived on the fat of the land, plundering and pillaging occupied territory. In the last war too Bulgaria fought on the side of Germany; defeated, she was treated well by the Allies, not with contempt, but with consideration. Once more a jackal, at war with us at peace with Russia, I wondered if Bulgaria would again escape her just fate. War is made at the peace conference table.

Lying at the edge of the forest, a light machine gun in front of me, I felt small and unimportant in the grip of controversy. There, in front of my eyes, in the sights of my gun, my enemies were lustfully destroying the belongings, the very livelihood, of those people who had been my hosts. I had only to squeeze the trigger to stop them. That hulking great soldier now passing through the peepsight, perhaps he was the man who drew Smith's revolver and shot him in cold blood .. Just a gentle pressure and those boys would be revenged. But my finger was tied. If I killed those men, the peasants of Oruglica would be the first to curse me, for they would then pay the price not in possessions but in blood. A country will fight, paying an eye for an eye, a tooth for a tooth, but courage alone cannot withstand reprisals which demand a hundred human heads for one dead dog.

At last the signal came: 'Stand by for a sortie tonight'. I had chosen a new dropping ground in the valley between Oruglica and Mount Kukavica. It was not a good ground, because an almost perpendicular slope rose up from the small river on the western side, but in deference to Manić the site had to be in territory common to all three brigades.

Andrejević and Stefanović were there already when I arrived with Tomlinson. They stood chatting amicably whilst their men collected wood for the fires. The night was warm and clear and hopefully I discussed with Tommy details for unpacking and distribution of the stores we were expecting.

Then Manić arrived; lithely marching at the head of the column, he towered head and shoulders above his men. The brigade halted, turned about and grounded arms. He swaggered up.

'*Zdravo, Gospodine Kapetan*. My men are at your disposal.'

Pure showmanship perhaps, but a very impressive show.

Having deployed his troops in defensive positions, Manić turned to greet Andrejević, completely disregarding Jovo. I felt that his little drama was intended more for Jovo's digestion than my own; the enmity between these two promised more serious trouble to come.

Two aircraft were expected that night, the first at 11 p.m. It was essential that they should come. That first episode at Oruglica and my subsequent friendliness with Manić had upset Jovo badly and he had many times taunted at my inability to obtain material support from base. All three were concerned at the pro-communist propaganda of the BBC. Yugoslav broadcasts and rightly guessed that the Partisans were obtaining the bulk of the support. They called this a breach of faith on the part of the Allies with Mihailović.

Hoping that further explanation would not be necessary, I vainly searched my mind for possible excuses in case of default. Time passed only too rapidly and my watch soon showed eleven. We waited in silence, listening for sounds of aircraft but nothing came.

Eleven thirty. The stars blinked in the clear dark sky. There was not a murmur of wind; it was a perfect night but still nothing came. Manić turned to me and with a grin on his face murmured:

'The communists control even the weather!'

But before he had completed the sentence the roar of engines throbbed loud and clear. Screened by the steep slopes of Mount Kukavica we had not heard the aircraft till it passed directly overhead. The fires flickered and then roared up to illuminate the valley. Not satisfied with their efforts the Serbs piled on more and more wood till the glow was reflected in the sky. The murmur of the aircraft passed away into the distance and reawoke as the pilot circled searching the hills, studying the lie of the land in order to come in low for the drop. Again the engines died away, then with a thunderous roar a great black ugly shape came swaying down the tiny light on the wingtip flashing past less than fifty feet from the steep mountain well above the river. With a fierce flutter, like the drumming of a settling pigeon's wings, the engines throttled back. Then, directly over our heads above the noise of the engines came a crackling rustle and, like shrapnel bursts, six round shapes opened in the air and floated down towards the fires.

The noise of the engines died away down the valley. Swinging crazily at the end of their harness the heavy metal containers crashed to the ground. The troops rushed to unhook the containers, and without hesitation a group of men plunged in after one which had fallen into the river.

As the plane circled, dropping again and again, I felt a strong link with my countrymen three hundred feet above. The pilot and his crew talked in English as they went about their work. In five hours' time they would be drinking cups of strong tea, smoking English cigarettes, reporting to their commanding officer that their load had reached its destination. That strong black shape boring its way intrepidly through the hard glitter of the Balkan night was a little bit of England. That Halifax, born of British brains and muscle had also known the gentle mists and felt the soft green turf under its wheels.

A light flashed in the sky to the south, then another. Quickly I seized the torch and flashed out the signal. The second plane had arrived. As the first had done, it circled high, searching, the engines sounding loud and clear then dying away behind the mountain screen. For a moment there was complete silence, then a roar from the south as the first aircraft swung in on its last run but, as it approached, a rival note sounded from downstream. The second had chosen to enter from the north.

Transfixed, impotent, I watched appalled as the two friendly monsters rushed straight at one another, both visible to the ground but invisible to each other. For one agonising moment it seemed that they must crash together head on in that narrow space; then at the last moment they saw each other and swinging slightly to the side passed by, their wing tips slicing one above the other.

Leaving Tommy to supervise the collection and unpacking of the containers I went with Leban to a miller's cottage nearby to code a signal for transmission to base. We were just finishing our work when Tommy followed by Andrejević rushed into the room. The latter burst into a flood of speech, gesticulating wildly and speaking so fast that I could not understand.

'What's the trouble?' I asked Tommy.

'Come down to the river quickly. That bastard Manić looks as though he's going to start a civil war.'

'But why?' I demanded.

'I couldn't understand exactly but we can't find two of the containers. It seems that Manić is accusing Jovo of telling the peasants to hide them so that he can collect them later and get more than his share.'

I seized my Sten and ran down to the ground. An extraordinary sight met my eyes. Stefanović stood unarmed, his back to the river, his face white but calm. His men, powerless to help, were grouped to one side covered by the ready mounted machine guns of the Letiča brigade. A foot in front of Jovo's body Manić, whose handsome face was contorted with fury, held a cocked sub-machine gun his finger quivering on the trigger. Beyond all self-control he screamed and growled like a wild beast.

There was no time to be lost; I ran up and thrusting my Sten into Tommy's hands touched Manić on the shoulder and spoke quietly to him:

'Put that gun down.'

His eyes blazed and he quivered all over with jealous rage. He was unaware of anything except Jovo's calm face in front of him. Disregarding my order, he burst into a fresh flood of invective. For a second Jovo glanced at me, his troubled eyes showing me that underneath he was frightened. Manić was dangerous.

'Manić, this is Kapetan Miki, put that gun down.'

His only answer was to raise the muzzle till it pointed at Jovo's heart. His finger tightened on the trigger.

There was no choice. With my left hand I pushed his gun aside and using all my strength I hit him under the ear with a blow that could have killed a small man. For one terrible second Manić swayed on his feet, his Schmeiser swinging in my direction. Then he collapsed slowly to the ground, his gun falling to one side . . . Tommy, with great presence of mind, retrieved it. Stefanović never moved but I heard him whisper:

'Look to the left.'

Without turning my head I glanced round. Three officers of the Letića brigade stood with revolvers levelled at us. Manić got to his feet. Quiet now, his eyes still blazed at me. I took the initiative:

'Order your brigade back to their posts.'

For a long moment he glared at me, then his eyes changed to a cunning look and he spoke quietly and sanely:

'Certainly, if you wish your stores to be at the mercy of a thief.'

Under Tommy's watchful eyes the equipment was unpacked, sorted and divided into three equal portions: three stacks of rifles, three of explosives, three of clothing. Manić and Stefanović watched like hawks to see that not a round of ammunition, not a sock, not a stick of gelignite was wrongly placed. In a small package we found a locked bag and an envelope addressed to me. It contained the key and the loading list prepared by the officer who, back in the desert, had supervised the packing of the stores. Twenty-four containers and thirty packages were listed. Quickly we counted up; yes, we were short of two packages. Tommy went to tick off the numbers so that we might ascertain which were missing while I took the key and unlocked the stout canvas bag. Inside was a packet of mail, the first we had received in two long months, and another bag, full of money – sovereigns, napoleons, and a wad of notes, dollars. Covertly I slipped the bag into my haversack, hoping that it had not been seen by the Serbs. When Tommy came back, he made a long face:

'What's missing?'

'Numbers eleven and twelve,' he answered.

'Well, you've got the list, what are they?'

For answer, he handed me back the page. Anxiously I checked it. 'No 11. rhomboid . . . one wireless set . . . clothing. No 12. ditto, motor generator, one can petrol.'

'Hell's bells, that's torn it,' I exclaimed.

Tommy looked at me oddly.

'Well, what is it?' I asked.

'It's no business of mine, Mike, you're running this show, but you may be interested to know that numbers 10, 13, 14 and 15 were brought in together. They fell just round the corner in the woods . . . and –'

'And what?'

He paused for a moment, then unable to restrain himself burst out, 'And they were brought in by Manić's men. I wouldn't trust that dirty rat, sir.'

For a moment I did not follow Tommy's train of thought, then I realised what he was driving at.

Understanding, I hated to believe it. Deep and cunning, the plot was diabolical in conception. Surely it could not be true – it must be a coincidence; but the memory of the first abortive sortie belied that hope. The facts were against me. They pointed to only one answer.

Before I arrived Manić had been in a strong position. His brigade outnumbered the others. He could sit back, secure in the knowledge that when the day of the uprising came he would get command of the army mobilised in the mountains. But my arrival had provided a problem. If I supplied stores to all three brigades, their strength would in time become nearly equal, and Stefanović, a senior officer, might be nominated commander by Mikhailović in preference to him. The obvious solution was to carry out my wishes and operate against the railway line, thereby obtaining extra supplies, but he realised that if he followed this course without permission, so would Stefanović and Andrejevic and then they too could co-operate and receive equal supplies.

The other course was subtle – simple, if dishonourable . . . He would stop the sorties by cutting off my communication with the outer world. He knew my wireless difficulties. It was easy to order a few trustworthy men to look inside the containers and hide those which contained signal equipment. I wondered if he had German blood in him: his appearance, his contempt for the Allied war effort, his true Teutonic attention to detail. In enacting that little scene by the river, he had tried to throw suspicion on to Stefanović for the loss of the containers. Whilst acting his part, his enmity for Jovo had run away with him and if Tommy had not been observant I should never have guessed. Guessing, there was little I could do, I only hoped that my punch had hurt him. Small consolation indeed.

For the second time I had been caught out by the tricks of that devious personality. For the second time I had to take it lying down. If I accused Manić he would just laugh apologetically and say that he was sorry that his troops had been beaten to the spot by Jovo's peasants. I could not write a report to Milhailović as I had no proof of my suspicions. Helplessly I asked myself why he had done this but I had already answered that question fully. I turned to Tommy.

'It looks as if Harvey was right in the first case. I've been too ambitious, hoping I could use Manić. So far he's made circles round us.'

'Well, we can still break with him now,' suggested Tommy.

'No, we can't. I may be acting the coward but I'm prepared to bet a quid to a rotten lemon that if I went down to the river now and asked Manić to hand over his share of the stores he would refuse. What's more, I think he'd take the whole lot by force, which would be easy.'

'But if he's prepared to do that why does he go to the trouble of stealing our wireless replacements only. We've still got the old set so why doesn't he pinch the lot or shoot us all?'

'That's easy to answer. If he took aggressive action against us, he'd be in the cart at once. But he knows only too well that our hand generator is practically useless. He knows too that if I go down and take away the stores without justifiable reasons he can refuse my orders, saying that I'm crazy; and everybody else would agree with him. Nobody would credit my suspicions.'

'Well, what are you going to do about it?' asked Tommy.

'Just nothing,' I replied. 'We'll beg base to send us more kit as quickly as possible and in the meantime either Leban or yourself must remain with the wireless set all the time. Lastly, don't move about the place alone; accidents might always happen.'

With our limited time on the wireless, it was impossible to explain the situation fully to base. I wrote out a short signal:

> Motor charger lost on dropping stop Please supply replacement soonest stop Unable charge batteries with present equipment stop Will stand by for sortie every night.

That should explain my plight to base. Then even if they failed to hear from us they would still send the sortie. I prayed that the 'urgent priorities elsewhere' would permit of one angel of mercy for me. That same night Leban came in to say that the coil of the hand generator had burnt out and that it was beyond repair.

'Will the battery be up enough to work tomorrow?' I asked.

'I don't know, I can try.'

I stood by him as he opened communication. Scowling, he listened to the faint call sign from base a thousand miles away. Then, whipping off his earphones, he turned to me.

'There's an urgent message to come in.'

'Refuse it and send our signal first; then take theirs.'

'Right, sir.'

He tapped out our signal, and received the sign that it was through. Then he spoke: 'I'll try to get it, but they're very weak.'

Checking and rechecking, he received the message. As he finished, the battery went flat. We sat down together to decode it. It was short and to the point, telling us to do all we could at once to reduce enemy movement on the railway line and to be available throughout the coming month.

CHAPTER SEVEN

Sabotage Operations Commence

'Tommy, let's open our mail.'

We had eight days in which to do the impossible. Far better to waste half an hour reading about home, forgetting the tangled webs of Balkan politics, than to set out bemusedly to tackle the problem at once. Tommy tore open the bag. There were three packages, one for each of us.

'Leban, you've got the smallest packet, run out and get a bottle of *rakija*. You might order some food too. I'll be going out in an hour or so.'

I turned to my parcel and cut the string. Two hundred cigarettes, pipe tobacco, a tin of anti-louse powder. I threw that at Tommy's head. Toothpaste, a razor, and a bar of Lifebuoy soap. Tommy had received much the same, but no soap.

'Why should you have all the soap?' he protested. 'We'll share it. Here, I'll cut it in half.'

'Oh no you don't; we're not with the Partisans! Look it's addressed to me. Doubtless one of my girl friends in the office slipped it in. Look at that smudge on it, that's where she held it in her darling fingers, pressing it to her lips....Tell you what, I'll be very generous and give you the bar I'm using now.'

He was furious. 'I don't want that filthy ersatz Italian sandpaper.'

'Well, if you want to look a gift horse in the mouth... but remember, cleanliness...'

'Bugger you,' said Tommy.

I turned to my letters and tried to read, if only to take my mind off my current pressing problems.

They were mostly from my mother, chatty, gossipy letters, from which accounts of the air raids and discomforts at home had been thoughtfully omitted. She asked if I were better and why I had been in hospital. It seemed that she had just received a telegram to that effect. To prevent anxiety on the part of one's relations, the organisation undertook to send weekly telegrams to any stated address. It seemed that they had sent the wrong number. But that was but a minor worry compared with those which confronted me now.

We had only eight days' grace. In two long months I had achieved nothing. Now I had a week in which to mobilise a force, train them in the use of explosives and move them across the frontier to strike. No mean task, even if they were willing to accept my orders, but in face of the Mihailović veto, it seemed a hopeless position.

The obvious target was the larger of the two railway bridges which I had seen on my reconnaissance. A massive steel viaduct across the Morava which, if destroyed, would take many weeks to repair. But that bridge was well guarded, for I had seen the blockhouses built alongside with machine guns mounted in the slits which served for windows. Two sentries watched at each end of the span. That would mean a guard of at least thirty soldiers. To destroy the bridge we should have to overcome the guard and hold it against outside interference while the engineers carried out their work. Once the enemy came to know of our activity, troops could be rushed by truck from Vranje, less than ten miles distant by road. I consulted Tommy.

'You're the engineer, and you've seen Harvey's report. How many men will you need to fix the charges and how long will you take?'

He scratched his head before answering: 'Twenty men and ten extra to help carry the stuff. I'll need twenty minutes if all goes well but I demand three quarters of an hour to be on the safe side.'

Three quarters of an hour. It would take a hundred men a quarter of an hour at least to deal with the guard in the blockhouse. That would give the enemy an hour to prepare a counter attack. He could do it in that time. Therefore a strong force, equipped with at least ten light machine guns would be necessary to be sure of completing the job... Manić was the only commander with the men and arms available. If he refused to go, Stefanović and Andrejević together might be strong enough but their men were untrained.

Of course this order could mean only one thing... The Allies now fighting in Sicily were to invade Italy shortly and we were required to prevent the German army in Greece moving north in support. The British officer with Mihailović must have received a similar order and perhaps he had persuaded the old man to lift the veto, but that couldn't help me out. A message from Četnik HQ would take at least six days to arrive. That would be too late.

'Tommy, there's only one thing to do. I've got to persuade somebody to break Mihailović's orders. I'm sure Jovo won't and, even if he will, Andreović won't. I've got to try Manić.'

It was the test of my policy. Now I would see if I had been right in my judgement of the man.

'I'll go at once. You hang on here till I send for you.'

'And the wireless set?' he asked. 'It's useless.'

I paused and then an idea came to me.

'Leban.'

'Yes, sir?'

'This generator, have you told anybody else that it's burnt out?'

'No, I don't think so; the chaps know it broke down, but that's happened often before.'

'Excellent,' I went on. 'Now listen carefully. This evening take it to pieces, and pretend to fix it. Then set the men to turning the handle as if nothing was wrong. Tomorrow, and until I come back, hook up the set and make a show of using it. Don't let anyone think that we've lost contact with the base.'

Leban looked puzzled. 'Yes, sir.'

'Just that, nothing more. Maybe I'll tell you why tomorrow.'

All night I argued with Manić. No, he could not disobey orders. He couldn't take responsibility for the reprisals that would follow. If he had orders from Mihailović he would be the first to volunteer.

'Don't you see, Mihailović must agree under these circumstances but he cannot get the orders out to you in time. The war can't wait for him.'

Manić interrupted me. 'Yes, yes but if he hasn't given permission and I go ahead with your attack, where do I stand then?'

'You stand then with me behind you. If you carry out my requests I will do all in my power to give you whatever you ask for. And don't forget the radio broadcasts: we haven't been getting supplies because the Partisans have had all available sorties. Why?... because they are doing more for the war effort.'

He seized the red herring. 'That is just where your government is wrong. The Communists are fighting us, not the Germans, but the blood-thirsty English are happy so long as they fight somebody, no matter who. Tito has hoodwinked the English to think that he is fighting the enemy but as he always keeps his liaison officers under guard they only see and hear what he wants them to.'

I silenced him. 'Perhaps that may be the case but you've got to prove yourself. My offer still stands.'

'But how can you help me? You cannot get in touch with your base. Your wireless set is....'

Quickly he stopped himself. Realising that he had slipped up, he reddened slightly.

Looking straight at him I spoke slowly and clearly. 'No thank you, my wireless equipment is in perfect order.'

Manić was on the run. At four in the morning, after our third bottle of *rakija*, he agreed to put his men at our disposal to attack the bridge.

Before lying down to sleep I wrote out a short message to Tommy. 'Come to Kukavica at once. Leave Leban where he is and tell him for Christ's sake to keep pretending to work the wireless.'

Finally committed, Manić was efficient and helpful. At once we set about detailing the many tasks. Thirty men, armed with pistols only, were handed over to Tommy for the demolition – a company one hundred strong was selected to carry out the attacks on the blockhouse and the capture of the bridge – six machine gun teams for covering the approaches to the valley – men in civilian clothes to cut the telephone wires before our arrival. Scouts were sent out to requisition horses necessary to carry the heavy machine guns over the mountains. Manić was a brilliant organiser and thought of everything. One problem had been worrying me all the morning.

'Manić, how can we get this large force across without observation from the frontier posts?'

'Bravo, Miki, the perfect soldier. For a soldier that is a difficult problem, for a diplomat it is easy. Tonight we will have a guest to dinner.'

'Who?' I asked.

'You will see,' answered Manić.

We were eating cheese and drinking *rakija* while supper was being prepared, when I heard a clatter of heavy boots outside and the door swung open. Manić entered followed by five soldiers. The first, a slight young man, had the gold-braided epaulettes and cream collar indicating him to be an officer. All wore the dark green uniform of the Nedić police. With a broad grin Manić introduced the leader.

'Kapetan Miki, Poručnik (Lieutenant) Popović. Commandant of the frontier police in the Lescovac area.'

Popović saluted smartly and held out his hand. 'I am very pleased to meet you. I have heard much about you. The German commander in Lescovac is very concerned because we have not apprehended you yet.'

'I am sorry if I have embarrassed him – or you.'

He smiled. 'You have embarrassed me considerably. In fact he has already threatened that if you are not caught by the end of August, I shall be replaced.'

We laughed and Manić gave him a glass. He raised it:

'To the victory of the Allies.'

Manić explained that he had been in touch with Popović for some time. The latter had wanted to join the Četniks bringing his entire company of police with him but they had decided that he would be of greater use carrying on in enemy employment and warning the Četniks of impending anti-guerilla operations. I drew Manić aside.

'How can he help us? Do you really trust him?'

'Good God, yes. He has a platoon post on the frontier near the top of Mount Kukavica. I told him that we wanted to cross the line in that region. He has offered to lay on a big party and invite the Bulgarian guards opposite to come and join in. The Bulgars love drinking but they are paid so badly they cannot afford to buy *rakija* and in the mountains there is no place near where they can loot it. They are sure to accept and will get very drunk. We must wait half an hour's march away from the line. When the way is clear Popović will come and guide us across.'

That sounded an excellent plan. It was essential that we should cross the frontier without raising an alarm. Returning it was immaterial whether we were discovered or not. We could fight our way back. It seemed that, in spite of the many difficulties, we were at last ready for our first attack.

The morning of the day scheduled for the operation dawned clear and warm. We were ready to leave at midday, crossing the frontier that evening to attack the bridge on the following night. Tommy and I, stripped naked, were washing in the stream, beside Manić's house. I threw a stone, splashing my companion.

'Well, today's the day. Have you got your charges made up?'

'Yes, and the men trained. They're a grand team. Very keen and quick to learn.' He broke off, exclaiming:

'Listen, what's that noise?'

Down the path leading to Oruglica came the sound of voices raised in a marching song. The song was 'Lily Marlene', but the words seemed strangely familiar.

> We're in the bloody desert lying in the sand,
> Miles and miles from anywhere, O Christ it would be grand,
> Next year to spend our leave with you...

We stood naked and aghast as, round the bend of the path, strode two figures. One tall and strongly built with fierce red hair, the other short and dark. Both unmistakably English. They wore stripes on their arms.

I called to them, 'Who are you?'

They checked, came across and saluted.

'Are you Captain Lees? We're reporting for duty, sir.'

It was the red-head who had spoken.

'My name is Faithful, sir. Sergeant Johnson is to be your wireless operator. We dropped six days ago to Major Sehmer because your communications were out of order.'

Turning to Johnson, I asked quietly, 'And did you bring a new generator with you?'

'No, sir.'

'Are you good at telepathy?'

'Pardon?'

'Oh, it doesn't matter. Why didn't you bring any equipment?'

'Well, sir, at base they said that you were using an untrained operator. I'm an instrument mechanic and they thought I should be able to put your set in order.'

As if that wasn't enough for one day, Faithful spoke up:

'Major Sehmer gave me a message for you sir. He said it was very important.'

'Well, have you got it?'

'He wouldn't write it down. Base told him to let you know that you should postpone operations against the railway line till further notice.'

I walked slowly to the house to find Manić. He sat listening intently to a portable radio. As I broke the news to him, he turned the knob so that I might hear the broadcast. 'The Partisans report that they have amassed a fund of reliable evidence of Četnik collaboration with the enemy.' Manić smiled grimly. 'The Allies are consistent, if only in changing their minds.'

*

Each night we waited for planes that did not come. The fine weather held and soon it became impossible to find excuses for my failure to provide supplies. With the attack postponed, there was no further reason to conceal the fact that my communication with Cairo had ceased. By courier I sent a message to Sehmer, explaining my plight and asking him to intercede with base on my behalf.

Manić made no secret of his attitude:

'I do not understand your policy. We Četniks are ready to fight. I agreed to help you blow up that bridge. It was you, not I, who gave the order to wait.'

'That was not because I want to do nothing,' I protested. 'We had orders to wait. Possibly the Allies had to postpone their plans. If we had blown the bridge the Germans would have repaired it by now and you know only too well that we could not do it twice. Our work must fit in with the general plan of the higher command.'

'I quite agree but I have given you proof of my good faith and still the Partisans receive stores whilst we do not. The war is easier for you British; you have been bombed, yes; you have fought alone, yes; but we have had the Germans in our country butchering our people and now, under the guise of a resistance movement, the Communists, helped by Russia, prepare to seize power. We cannot think only of defeating the Germans; we must remain strong to protect ourselves against this other enemy inside our walls. If you give us the arms then we can do both but if you arm our enemies and not us then we must save ourselves for the civil war which you British have fostered. Believe me, the Partisans think first of killing Četniks.'

Fiercely, Manić went on: 'The Serbs are nationalistic; we love our king. Can you see our peasants in a communist state? Here each man has his *svojina*, his patch of land, his stock, his *rakija*. He is master in his own house. Once I have shown my willingness to help you. Until you can show that supplies will come, I cannot agree to give you troops.'

Back at Oruglica, the Mission, now five strong, had moved into a house about half a mile from the Četnik headquarters. I was still on good terms with Stefanović and, kindly, he did not taunt me with the lack of Allied support. The old enmity was still fierce between him and Manić and he was therefore glad that I had returned, and willingly provided me with men to wait at night on the dropping ground and to act as guides and messengers. He had written once again to Mihailović, requesting his permission to start operations, but he had not yet received an answer. I considered taking my mission and starting some small sabotage on our own but, on reflection, I realised that I must wait till my sortie arrived.

Then, on the first of September, came a courier from Sehmer. I tore open the letter: 'Dear Mike, Base are very worried because they can't get in touch with you' – the fools I thought, 'send me a generator' – 'They want you to do your utmost to cut the line from Skoplje. Djurić refuses to move.'

I knew it was hopeless to ask Manić again but I tried. Once more we argued through the night. Once more I made promises which I now knew for certain I could not fulfil. But this time Manić knew too. He was adamant; he would do nothing. I called on Stefanović; worried and upset he wanted to help but could not. All the old arguments passed but he had only one answer to them – he had not yet received an order from Mihailović and therefore dared not act.

Then, from a completely unexpected quarter, help came. In desperation I visited Andrejević and surprisingly he agreed – on one condition. He demanded that the whole of the next sortie, whenever it came, should go to his brigade. I promised readily. Our luck had indeed changed.

That same night it was Tommy's turn to watch at the dropping ground. Just after midnight I was awakened to find him beside my bed.

'Listen, Mike.'

Faintly in the distance I heard the sound of an aircraft. I leapt up and started putting on my boots.

'Well, why did you come down here?' I asked. 'Haven't you lit the flares?'

'Yes, of course I have but planes have been passing all night; they come from the south-west and pass over to the east.'

Together we went out. In the valley the fires glowed, forming a letter H. A torch flashed intermittently.

'How many times have you heard planes?' I asked.

'At least four times. The first about half an hour ago.'

That was queer; never before had we heard aircraft at night except those dropping stores. The German transports, which we often saw in the daytime, never flew over the mountains at night. As I listened to the engine note now directly overhead, it seemed smoother, quieter than a Halifax.

'I think they must be bombers. I wonder where they are bound for?'

Tommy agreed. 'Yes, what shall we do about the fires?' he asked.

'We'll have to keep them burning low,' I answered. 'If they're sending bombers over we might get a supply plane.' The surmise was right. At two a.m. a deeper roar broke the murmur of the bombers flying high on their return journey and our signal was answered from the sky. The black shape of a Halifax flashed past low over the dropping zone and the parachutes fluttered down.

That was a happy morning. While Johnson was unpacking his new generator and Tommy sorted the stores ready for collection by

Andrejević's brigade, Jovo came into the room. He was beaming all over his face. He rushed up and shook me warmly by the hand.

'Wonderful, wonderful. I've just listened to the news, Sofia has been bombed.'

I walked back with him and tuned in to the British service.

'...a force of Wellington bombers attacked Sofia last night. Observers report that large fires were started in marshalling yards.'

*

Some three to four weeks after Faithful arrived with that cryptic message preventing our first attempt to do something active to justify our existence, I set out with Tommy and thirty men, heading for the railway line. Without the help of Manić we could not hope to capture and destroy the bridge, so we had decided to blow a length of the line itself. The plan was to march straight across the top of Mount Kukavica till we arrived within two miles of the Morava, then to turn north and keep parallel to the valley till we reached the spot where the railway ran out into the Lescovac plain.

At that point the Bulgar guardhouses, placed at intervals along the line, were situated about three thousand yards apart. Covering parties of two Spandau machine guns and six men would establish themselves on the railway within five hundred yards of each house, barring a mile of line from enemy access. A group armed with knives and tommy guns were detailed to clean up any sentries on this stretch, silently if possible, and to clear the way for the demolition party under Tommy who hoped to complete his work in less than fifteen minutes.

The route chosen for withdrawal was due west across the Lescovac plain parallel to the northern wall of Kukavica and back into the mountains at Barje. This route avoided the frontier and provided a flat stretch of easy country for withdrawal.

We set out at midday travelling slowly as the men were heavily laden with explosives. By evening we had crossed the highest point of Kukavica and were wending our way down the long eastern slope towards the Morava valley. Far from any human habitation, we camped for the night in the middle of the forest by a spring of mountain water. A goat which had been led that far by the Četnik cook was slaughtered, we dined well and slept.

The following morning the explosives which till then had been carried in bulk were sorted and prepared. The charges, one pound of plastic high explosive each, were to be placed at each joint about twenty yards apart on the line; they were fitted with a primer and two feet of detonating fuse. Five men carrying fifteen charges each would in theory be sufficient for up to a 1500 yard stretch or 750 yards blowing both rails. Another five men with thousand yard reels of fuse were to connect up the charge. The signal for withdrawal was a series of blasts on my whistle. To reach our objective we had a further five hours to march; so we planned the attack for ten o'clock, allowing ourselves eight hours to reach the safety of the mountain before dawn.

We could see the valley below, five miles distant, wending its way through the hills. A line of tiny black spots, a convoy, moved along the road towards the north. Faintly I heard the whistle of a train in Grdelica station and puffs of white smoke appeared above the red roofs as it pulled out of the junction. If all went well Grdelica would be idle for some time to come!

Pesić, the commander of our thirty Četniks, had previously been a sergeant in the Engineers. Young and active, he did not worry about reprisals and politics and was glad of a chance to fight the enemy. Before the war he had lived in Grdelica, working in the railway yard. I was asking him about the capacity of the railway.

'Before the war they used to pass about ten trains a day. Now I'm told it's often as many as thirty or forty.'

'But it's only a single track.'

'Yes, but they've got a brilliantly organised system of running the trains into the sidings so as to allow two way traffic.'

It sounded important enough. If we could hold up this line for only one day much enemy reinforcement would be held up but the Germans are very quick to repair damage. How long would it take them to repair a mile of line?

'Pesić, you don't happen to know where the nearest railway repair depots are from here?'

'There's one at Lescovac. They've got rails, sleepers and a crane there; but to the south there's nothing for miles.'

That was good news, if they could only work from one end, lifting the rails and sleepers, dumping them clear and replacing with new ones, it would take some days to mend the line however quickly they worked. Night fell, still and dark. The moon was not due to rise until after midnight. Wind or rain to cover any noise of our approach would have been welcome. We marched silently in single file, following a narrow track down towards the plains. Then as the ground levelled out Pesić raised his arm. We halted. He touched my shoulder and whispered, pointing: 'There's the railway.'

I looked ahead, my eyes straining into the darkness. Across a pasture field showed a long back shape like a low wall. It was the line of the embankment. I signalled to Tommy to close up.

'Keep the party here, make sure everything is ready and wait until I come back.'

Taking two men with us Pesić and I moved forward. Keeping to the hedge we crawled along till we were within twenty yards of the embankment, stopped and lay still watching... listening. For two minutes there was silence. Then, from the north came the sound of voices and the footsteps of men walking unevenly along the wooden sleepers. I strained my ears to catch their words; they were talking Yugoslav. At that moment I heard the whistle of a locomotive and the throb as the rails vibrated. The throb turned to a rumble and the engine came into sight, its headlights blazing down the track outlining the sentries standing in pairs. They were in civilian clothes, unarmed. We had seen what we wanted and covered by the roar of the train rushing past we slipped back quietly to join the group.

Tommy sat with the commanders of the covering parties. I whispered to them:

'All set?'

He nodded.

'Right, we'll start right away. We must be finished before the next train passes. Come with me now and when we reach the line move off at once... you five hundred yards north... you five hundred yards south. Send the sentries you capture back to me under guard. If any escape don't shoot at them unless the alarm has already been raised. Tommy, bring your men down exactly three minutes after we've started. All clear?'

We moved off quietly and, reaching the embankment, the covering parties disappeared into the night. Pesić and I stood waiting on the metals. To the left I heard a voice raised, then a soft thud, then silence... As the third minute passed the demolition party clattered on to the line. They had been well drilled in the mountains and within seconds the fuse was tied to a sleeper and the reels were being run out in both directions. Following close behind, saboteurs placed and taped charges to the rails. Two minutes, four, five; the work was going well, when I heard a whirring ringing sound... Someone had spotted us and was tapping the rail. Ten seconds later from the north a single shot rang out followed by another. Tommy came running up: 'They've done about 700 yards.'

'Excellent. How much longer do they need?'
'About five minutes'.
'Good, well come with me. There seems to be trouble on the line.'

As I spoke heavy firing sounded and I could pick out the deep tearing note of our Spandau machine guns. Running up the line towards the firing, I saw the demolition party ahead of us frantically fixing their last charges.

'Tommy, give me a shout when everything is ready.'

I ran on to the covering party. They were deployed with their guns in action on both sides of the embankment. Three hundred yards away I could just pick out the wall of a building. From around the white patch came short red flashes. I threw myself down beside the Spandau.

'What's up?'

A Četnik answered. 'One of the sentries escaped and gave the warning. That's the Bulgar guard house they're firing from.'

'Can you hold till we finish?' I asked.

'Yes, but hurry, because I heard a party of men moving round to the right; they'll come in behind us soon.'

'All right.'

I started back; as I ran, I heard a yell.

'Mike, we're ready.'

'All right, fix the fuse.'

As I came up to him Tommy was bending over to strike a match. It flared up and he held it shaded.

'All set?' he asked.

I blew my whistle. The demolition party ran from the line and disappeared into the darkness on their way to the assembly point. A few seconds later the Spandau ceased fire. Tommy fumbled with the fuse and struck another match. Pesić stood alongside covering us with his sten gun. Tommy swore under his breath.

'I can't get this blasted thing alight.'

'You'd better hurry, we haven't any time to waste,' I answered.

Two minutes later Tommy asked for a knife to recut the fuse. He tried once again.

'It's going!'

A fizzling sound came from the end of the black snake which he held in his hand. I checked the time.

'Good... let's...'

As I spoke a hoarse challenge sounded a few yards along the embankment. We threw ourselves flat as bullets cracked over our heads. Answering the fire with our stens and bending low under cover of the embankment we ran from the line. The assembly point was where we had first halted. I counted the men and found that all were present.

'Tommy, how long's that fuse?'

'It will take three minutes.'

I looked at my watch, two minutes, fifteen seconds had passed. I gave the order to lie flat. The scuffle of heavy boots on the embankment showed that the Bulgars were closing in towards the fuse. Two minutes fifty, fifty-five, three minutes... Nothing – the enemy must be up to the fuse by now... Three minutes fifteen seconds. I whispered to Tommy...

'Get out your second fuse, we'll have to...'

At that moment the charge went up, the blast slapping our faces as a line of flame lit up the scene; a sharp crack was followed by the screech of flying metal – screams... The explosion, perfectly timed, had caught the enemy patrol as it arrived to investigate. Some wooden sleepers ignited by the heat blazed merrily.

We moved away across country. Behind us whistles shrilled, desultory firing continued and the searchlights of an armoured train wove patterns around the scene of destruction. When the moon rose, the railway, now useless to the enemy, lay ten miles behind.

We travelled all night. After the rugged mountain paths to which we had become accustomed, it was sheer joy to march again on flat soft grassland. We skirted several prosperous-looking villages and helped ourselves to bunches of small sweet grapes from the vineyards that we passed. Elated at the success of our operation, I swung along happy and tireless. As the sky turned from black to grey, we turned south towards Kukavica and halted in a small village nestling in the foothills. Pesić announced:

'This is Dobri-do. I have good friends here because often I come down to buy food for Andrejević in their village. The men are tired. Can we halt for a few hours before climbing into the mountains?'

'Well, what about the enemy? They'll be combing the plains for us today.'

'They can't get here for some time. There is no road.' As an afterthought he added:

'Besides, we will get food here, milk and cheese, eggs and wine.'

After some months of subsisting on beans with an occasional bite of meat, the promise of a real breakfast was too tempting to refuse.

'All right, I think that's an excellent idea.'

Pesić posted a machine gun on watch and knocked at the first door we came to. The village was charming. The little red-roofed, two-storeyed houses were whitewashed and their walls were covered with wistaria. With its neat farmyards and duck pond, it was very similar to an English hamlet.

Once we had aroused the inhabitants, they could not do enough to make us comfortable. The women fetching mats and blankets so that we might lie down to rest ran off to kill chickens and collect eggs for our meal. The men, who were superior to such menial tasks, repaired to the 'podrooms'... returning with large supplies of the excellent but fierce grape *rakija* which is the speciality in the plains. As custom dictated that we should sample each blend we were soon in merry mood.

The meal was superb; great bowls of rich creamy sheep's milk; eggs, boiled and cooked in fat, young tender chicken, *Gibanica*, a form of lardy cake, all washed down by great beakers of rough red wine. When I had eaten till I was all but bursting I told Pesić that I should have to go on ahead. The president of the village overheard our conversation and immediately offered to lend me his horse. I thought for a moment. If I rode quickly, I should be in time to prepare a message for the midday contact.

'Yes, if there is one ready now.'

The head man called out to one of the peasants, who disappeared into a stable, reappearing three minutes later riding one horse and leading another. Having bade my farewells, I warned Tommy not to stay long and cantered off towards the mountains. My companion led at a good pace and two hours later we reached Barje, Andrejević's headquarters in the mountains. Leban had come down from Oruglica to meet us, bringing his wireless set with him and we sat down at once to encode my report. We were just finishing when Andrejević came rushing in.

'Mike, come outside, quick!'

I followed him through the door.

'Listen!'

Faintly, from the direction of Dobri-Do, came the sound of intermittent firing. Andrejević hurried off to gather a patrol together and telling Leban to get the signal despatched I picked up my sten and followed him. Andrejević quickly summoned all his available men and about thirty were already forming up. Without waiting for the remainder, we started off.

We had just reached the plains when we met the sabotage party returning. They moved deployed, a Spandau section in the rear of the column. As Tommy approached I saw that his face was contorted with rage. Behind him a Četnik staggered along, supported by two comrades.

'Well, what happened?' I asked.

'We were ambushed just this side of Dobri-Do,' answered Tommy.

'Good God, they must have followed our tracks quickly to be there so soon from Leskovac. Were they Germans?'

Tommy answered bitterly, 'They weren't Germans or Bulgars either; we were ambushed by the Partisans.'

CHAPTER EIGHT

Deal with Partisans Fails
Third Lesson in Balkan Politics

It seemed that the civil war was with us sooner than I had feared. It constituted yet one more factor to impede our work against the enemy. Two days after the ambush had taken place, definite reports came in. It appeared that a force of two hundred Partisans had established a base on Mount Radan just across the Lescovac plain and that strong patrols had been seen canvassing daily in the large villages around Lescovac. These patrols eked out a precarious existence lying hidden in vineyards or plantations by day and slipping into the villages at night to requisition food and hold meetings to spread their communist ideals.

According to witnesses the propaganda was having little effect on the peasantry who, living in terror of the occupying forces, wished only to be left in peace. Again, the peasants, the key to whose hearts lay in their pockets, resented the Partisan assumption that it was their duty to produce food without remuneration. The Četniks had always paid and were popular amongst the peasants but the Partisans were reported to have enlisted considerable sympathy amongst the workers in the German-controlled factories of Lescovac, particularly so as at this time they demanded not sabotage but support in wiping out the nationalist Četnik organisation in the mountains. Amongst the Partisans were a number of Albanians and Macedonians from the south-west of Skoplje. This raised great resentment amongst the Serbs, who considered that internal politics were their own affair, not that of wandering Mahomeddan brigands.

This Partisan invasion increased my difficulties considerably. The Četniks at once united in one primary purpose to destroy this political menace in their midst and were even less than previously inclined to use their men against the common enemy, lest expending ammunition they should weaken themselves whilst the Partisan movement gained strength. Even the enmity between Stefanović and Manić died in face of this common peril but that availed me little under the circumstances. Entirely apart from this difficulty, there was the added complication of possible Partisan ambushes in the plains, the shortest and most satisfactory route to our objective the railway line.

I realised that it would be hopeless to try to conduct successful sabotage operations in face of these two problems in addition to the purely tactical question of outwitting the defence of the occupying forces and I soon came to the conclusion that we could only organise continuous sabotage operations if we could arrange some local rapprochement between the two political parties. I hoped that this seemingly impossible task might be facilitated by the numerical superiority of the Četniks over the more belligerent Partisans.

I called a council of war of all the Četnik leaders and put forward a plan. I suggested that through the peasants in the plains we should effect a meeting with the Partisan leader, a Gypsy known locally as 'Black Marco', and fix up a truce on the understanding that they operated only on Mount Radan and interfered in no way with the area held by the Četniks who, in their turn, undertook not to attack them. I did not tell my hosts that, having established contact with the Partisans, I intended to offer them supplies of explosives if they could be induced to use their influence with the armaments workers to conduct industrial sabotage in Lescovac.

Manić was adamant; he for one would not consider a pact with the Communists unless they agreed to stop all propaganda and place themselves under Četnik command. Knowing this demand to be hopeless, I appealed to Jovo but this time his sympathy, though unexpressed, tended to lie with Manić and the others thought likewise. After much argument I got them to agree to climb down in their demands in one respect. They would not insist on the Partisans coming under command, but all leftist propaganda must stop.

We left it that Andrejević would establish contact from his headquarters in the foothills at Barje, where I had remained since our return from cutting the railway. The report on that action had just come in. From the progress made by the enemy in repairing the line, it seemed that it would be out of order only for one week more. I sent off a courier to Lescovac with orders to return at once when trains started running again and sat down to work out plans for another attempt. Communication to base, never good, was very faulty again. In the last sortie, in addition to the motor charger, we had received an odd form of generator, designed to be worked by a man sitting on a stationary bicycle, driving it with the pedals. Our motor charger had run a bearing and we were obliged to make use of this machine. Charging more efficiently than the hand type, it was very liable to mechanical failure, the chain constantly slipping and breaking, so that, with the batteries seldom charged, we could only make very cursory contacts and send out the minimum information.

The Serbs were still uncompromising in their attitude. They demanded many more sorties before they would consider granting my requests for large scale sabotage. They had, they said, received from me, only three sorties in four months, a supply sufficient only to maintain their forces against normal wastage and allowing nothing to permit them to indulge in constant effort. In vain, I pointed out that apart from ammunition and explosives expended we had incurred no losses in my one attack but they countered that we had been lucky and that the enemy would now be more alert.

In face of this opposition I had to be ready to operate again within a week, and in desperation I decided to plan for a derailment which, if the Serbs were still adamant in refusing to provide troops, could be carried out by myself and members of the British mission alone. This had recently been strengthened by an escaped prisoner of war, an Australian sergeant, so that we were now six strong. I estimated that such an action would hold up the railway traffic for a further three days at least.

Lesar, the ex-prisoner of war, had an extraordinary story to tell. He had been captured in Greece and, after a period in camp there, had been sent by rail with other prisoners bound for Germany. Crowded into a cattle truck he and three others had decided to make their escape. They had climbed through the narrow skylight window and dropped from the moving train. One of his comrades was injured and they had been forced to leave him to be recaptured while they made good their escape. Arriving at a village they discovered that they were in Yugoslavia.

Lesar related how he had lived for months travelling around avoiding the enemy. Although he had neither money nor documents, the peasants had taken him in, fed, clothed and protected him. He had tried to escape to Greece and thence via Turkey to the Middle East but having no funds to pay guides he had been forced to turn back. Finally he had joined Mihailović in the mountains and watched the growth of the Četnik movement and he remembered when, shoulder to shoulder with the Partisans, they had fought together against the common enemy. Born in Melbourne, Lesar was the Australian version of the British cockney. A quick-witted little man, he longed for one thing only... to get out of Yugoslavia. He had been there just two and a half years too long.

On the evening of the conference, after I had returned to the house occupied by our mission, Andrejević came bursting in. His face was a mask of fury but he spoke politely.

'Did you listen to the news tonight?' he demanded. I shook my head as he went on, 'On the Yugoslav broadcast, the sabotage carried out by my Četniks under your command was reported.'

Gratified, I replied: 'Excellent, what did they have to say?'

'They spoke well of it and the facts were quite correct except in one respect.'

'Well?'

'It was reported to have been carried out by the Partisans!!'

Pathetically, he added, 'We have difficulties and I admit we don't do much but you might give us, not our enemies, credit for our small successes.'

*

After nine days, the courier came back to report that the line was again in order. He told us that the traffic passing was heavier than any yet known. I had to act at once and, to save time, I decided to go to a point between Grdelica and Lescovac, some distance north of the scene of our last demolition. We would take the shortest route across the plains, thereby avoiding the frontier crossing.

I called Andrejević in to tell him that I wanted to leave that same afternoon. Surprisingly he answered, 'I'm sorry, you can't go.'

'Good God, why not?' I protested. 'I've already detailed the men I need.'

I was to take Pesić and nine of his men who knew the area intimately. He was adamant.

'I'm afraid I can't allow my men to go.'

'All right, give me a guide then, and I'll use the British.'

'I'm sorry,' he said again. 'But I can't allow that either. You see the Partisans are in force at Miroševce.' This was a large village on the direct route.

'Oh, how many Partisans?' I asked.

'I don't know exactly, but they're strong.'

'Well, that doesn't matter to me. I'm British and they are our Allies. If they arrest me I shall merely have the conference I planned a little sooner.'

My speech had no effect on Andrejević.

'No, I'm sorry I can't allow it. You must remain here until they've moved on.'

He was not concerned about my personal safety, but he knew well

(Right) Lees with the hindquarters of Goebbels and Goering

(Below left) Lees on Hitler

(Below right) Winter quarters 1943/4 with packhorses

(Left) Sgt Red Faithful and Peter Solly Flood on home-made skis *(Right)* Major Peter Solly Flood, my 'accomplice' in sabotage after the official break with the Četniks

Winter quarters

that a British officer was a very strong bargaining factor in the mountains and if the Partisans captured me they would not allow me to return. He was also afraid that I might be influenced by their propaganda and that, if the Partisans persuaded me theirs was the right cause, my presence would influence many of the local peasants onto their side. I tried persuasion.

'I'm not trying to meet the Partisans today. I shall avoid Miroševce, but I must cut the line again tonight.'

Andrejević was firm. 'No, I can't take the risk.'

We were talking in the Mission headquarters. Apart from Andrejević there were only British present. In English I told Tommy to stand by the door. As he moved round behind Andrejević I talked to him as soothingly as I could:

'Now, listen, we've been good friends and we've both kept our word to each other but it is apparent that you don't trust me now. I'm a British officer, you're a Serb. I don't give you orders, I shall certainly not accept any. I am going to the railway tonight. If you put any difficulty in my way I shall go to the Partisans who may be more helpful in fighting the enemy. Please be good enough to sit down and write out a note to Pesić with an order to accompany me now. If you don't, I am ready to start and I will go straight to the Partisans whilst my men keep you company here.'

Andrejević looked around and saw he was beaten. 'All right, I'll give you the men.'

Amicably we discussed the plan. It was decided by Andrejević that I should take a large enough force to ensure that I would not be captured en route by the Partisans. Apart from Lesar and myself, there were thirty men under Pesić and a further thirty under an ex regular sergeant major, Vlada by name. The latter was a great ally of mine. More than anyone else he had convinced Andrejević of the necessity of co-operating with the British and to disregard the veto placed by Mihailović on offensive action. He was a great fighter and had many actions to his credit in the early days of the movement. Unfortunately he was completely undiscriminating and fought both Germans and Partisans at every opportunity.

At two in the afternoon we set out down the mountain side to the plains. The double column moved fast, keeping away from paths and villages, in a direct line towards our objective. We passed Dobri-Do where the chimneys smoked peacefully in the pretty hollow, and marched on across fertile country past Miroševce, another village often visited by Partisan patrols, till at dusk we came in sight of another large village frequented by Partisans. Halting till dark, we made a detour to avoid any widely placed sentries and passed by without challenge. Eight hours travelling brought us to the objective and we halted in a plantation of firs overlooking the railway, which showed up in the moonlight three hundred yards distant.

Sending for Pesić and Vlada, I gave them their orders. Vlada would take command of the full force which was to be deployed in two groups, one to the right and one to the left. Each group would move forward till it found a commanding position from where they could cover the line. I intended to place my charge at a point where the line curved slightly away from us. Lesar and Pesić would accompany me, the former carrying a second charge to guard against the possibility of the first failing to detonate and the latter coming to give local protection while we fixed the charges.

When the main party had been organised and despatched, we crawled forward along a ditch which led towards a bend in the line. The moon was high and the embankment showed up clear in front.

Halting I whispered to Pesić, 'How far do you think it is?'

'Fifty yards.'

I agreed. 'Yes, we'll wait here. Let one train pass and attack the second.' The headlights of the first train would show up the line clearly.

Ten minutes later a distant whistle followed by a faint rumble proclaimed the approach of the train. Its headlight illuminated two sentries standing on the path alongside the railway line. They appeared to be civilians... fifty yards nearer... we could see another civilian... then... two soldiers carrying arms.

As the lights picked out the curve, I saw something I had not bargained for. Just on the other side of the line a building, looking like a large galvanised iron hut, was hidden amongst the trees. Outside stood two soldiers on guard. That must be a recently constructed emergency guard house! There was no alternative however; to be sure of a successful derailment we would have to place the charge on a curve but we would have to do it under the noses of the guard. I whispered to the others:

'Wait till the next train is well in sight before moving.'

The station master was kind to us that night. Exactly twelve minutes after the first, the whistle of another train sounded and the metals reverberated with a singing hum. In the distance came the puff puff of the locomotive as it drew out of Lescovac station. Then far away up the line the headlights blinked into view. Lesar started to get up but I pressed him down. It was still a mile away and moving slowly. In an agony of anticipation I waited until we could see the great black shape of the engine with its cowcatcher fixed on front, belching sparks about seven hundred yards away. I leapt up.

'Now!'

Sprinting forward we raced towards the line, scrambling up the embankment into the glare of the headlights less than two hundred yards off. 'No time to look at the sentries, that's Pesić's business. Fix the charge' – a ten second job – 'clamp on the fog signal and fix the fuse... wedge the five pounds of explosive under the line... a stone to keep it in position... Pesić hasn't fired yet'... a glance up the line, the great red and black monster thundered down on us only sixty yards distant by then... a last quick glance at the charge... 'all set.' We dived back down the embankment and started to run clear and, as the ground levelled out, I glanced again at the train. We had been spotted by the driver; I could hear him scream as, too late, he slammed on the brakes, and a second later jumped clear of his cab. The sentries, too intent on watching the train, had seen nothing.

We were running now, all three abreast and over my shoulder I watched the leading wheels of the locomotive rushing on to the detonator only fifteen yards behind us.

'Down!'

As we threw ourselves flat lumps of metal and stone from the permanent way sung past our heads. The engine mortally stricken tore on slewing sideways off the rails. With a scream of rending metal it lurched drunkenly and toppled over the embankment, the leading wagons zig-zagging as they telescoped into one another.

We were on our feet and running again when Vlada opened up. Passing over our heads the bullets from his Spandaus crackled into the wreckage. A burst of tracer from a Bren pierced the boiler of the wrecked locomotive and, with a fierce explosion, it blew up, the wreckage catching fire instantly. By the time the Bulgars, stupefied by the carnage on their doorstep, had gathered their senses and started to return the fire we were back with Vlada.

'All right, that's enough, let's get out of it.'

Our guns stopped firing and still deployed we moved away. Half a mile back, heads were counted and the column started home. Swinging along, happy, I laughed and thought of that Bulgar post commander reporting to his chief in the morning. Without incident we marched the twenty-seven miles back into the hills arriving just seventeen hours after our departure the previous day.

Back at Barje it was a red letter day. During my absence we had unexpectedly received a drop from one Halifax. I arrived to find Tommy and the others busy sorting the stores. They had already guessed our success, having seen the flash in the sky from the explosives. Tired though I was after my long march I decided to postpone my rest until everything was distributed and out of the way, in case there might be any trouble.

Manić and Stefanović had arrived with men to carry away their share. It had been a good load and I was able to hand out a machine gun and a number of rifles and stens to each brigade.

At about ten o'clock, as the work was finishing, we were just going in to a much needed meal when we heard shooting in the Veternica valley, about half a mile away, where the river ran out into the plains. The rattle of rifles and light machine guns was broken by periodical heavier explosions. Manić spoke up:

'That's my *bacač* (mortar) in action. It must be men of my brigade.'

'Did you send them down there for practice or anything?'

'No, not for practice, Miki, they're on patrol. We've been covering these approaches pretty thoroughly since the Partisans came in to the plains.'

The firing continued, heavier now. It was too consistent to be just casual firing by a patrol.

'Well, what do you think they're shooting at?' I asked.

'I don't know,' replied Manić. 'It might be the Germans coming up to attack us after your provocation last night. I'm going to see.' He turned to Andrejević.

'Mile, will you get your brigade standing by in case we need reinforcements?'

As Manić set off Andrejević called his officers in for orders and Jovo sent his men to carry their stores back and stand by in Oruglica in case anything developed. I was left alone with Tommy.

'Well, personally I'm going to have some food and rest; I've done enough in the last twenty-four hours. Tell Johnson to get the wireless kit packed up. If the Germans are going to beat up the area, we shall probably be chased all over the place.'

A few minutes later Andrejević returned with the news that Manić's men were in contact not with Germans but with a large force of Partisans. The fighting sounded closer now and another company was despatched to help. Two wounded were brought into the Mission headquarters to be treated as best we could.

I wondered how to stop this useless conflict. Here we were in the middle of an enemy-occupied country supposed to be fighting that enemy, yet both Četniks and Partisans were far more concerned with eliminating each other than attacking the occupying forces. Those Partisans attacking us were in all probability using British rifles and ammunition against the men using similar weapons supplied by me. Senseless, yes, but how could I, alone, avoid it? The decision must come from the top. If there were no rapprochement between Tito and Mihailović there never could be any permanent accord between their sub-commanders. If I succeeded in my plan of calling a conference and arranging a local truce it would only be broken again by orders of one or the other of the big men.

It was a curious state of affairs – but one thing was clear – the British Government had first followed the policy of supporting Mihailović, then, when he had not come up to their expectations, they had turned round and were supporting Tito primarily and Mihailović to a small extent, although at the same time they denounced him openly. That policy had to stop; it could only serve to foster the already intense civil war. But why not stop supplies to both sides, stating that sorties would start again on an agreement being reached to fight the Axis only and stop the civil war? Why not? I didn't know. Meanwhile I could only carry on with my task and do as much sabotage as possible under the circumstances.

The firing had died away gradually and half an hour later Manić returned. He looked tired and despondent.

'Well, what's happened?' I asked.

'The Partisans attacked across the Veternica; there were about two hundred of them. We took one prisoner and he admitted that they were trying to capture Barje to take the stores dropped last night. Fortunately my patrols happened to bump into them as they were crossing the river and attacked right away. When I arrived they were already withdrawing to Miroševce, I think. They had a few automatic weapons and seemed short of ammunition.'

Manić slumped into a chair, loosened his boots and looked at me. 'Miki, you have seen with your own eyes now that these Communists are nothing but brigands. They ambushed your party returning from an operation against the Germans. They tried today to raid your British stores dropped last night. Why does your Government go on supporting them?'

I didn't answer him. How could I? Manić hit the table with his fist and burst out:

'You British made a pledge with us, with Mihailović in 1942. You told us to come into the mountains to support him but now you are deserting us in support of a self-seeking communist, a Russian agent. If Tito comes into power after the war, we will be under Russian influence, not British. But we Serbs like the British and we want to be friends with them. We know the Russians and we don't like them. We're afraid of them. They want to include us in their Soviet. We want independence.'

Manić was right. Everywhere I had been in Serbia the people had always told me that. They prayed for an Anglo-American invasion through the Balkans so that on liberation they would be free to have a nationalistic democratic government. They knew the red terror and they did not want the Russian influence in their country.

Manić went on, 'The British have broken faith with Mihailović but we still get token support, one sortie against perhaps fifty to Tito, and we still have our British Liaison Officers.' He looked straight at me. 'We will always have you with us even if your government decides to break with us completely; for propaganda reasons I don't think we could afford to let you go.'

Manić meant what he said. If there was to be a break with Mihailović, the Liaison Officers would surely be held by him as hostages. At the time it seemed unimportant. Later it worried me a lot.

News came in about our derailment; it had been a great success. The train, careering sideways along the embankment, had torn up a hundred and fifty yards of line, which would have to be levelled and relaid. The coaches lay on their sides, burnt out and useless and each in turn would have to be lifted and dumped aside. The work would take the enemy at least three days to complete. That night on the wireless we heard the news we had been waiting for. Allied forces had some days previously landed in Italy. The Italian Government had surrendered unconditionally and fighting was going on around the bridgehead established at Salerno in Southern Italy. I was glad that we had been able to help our countrymen in their adventure.

Since the start of sabotage operations, we had been living at Barje, where Andrejević had his headquarters. It was a small hamlet of some thirty houses set on the edge of the mountain overlooking the exit of the Veternica into the plains. We had taken over a house at the edge of the village for the accommodation of the British Mission. Our host was a young man called Dragan, a hardworking peasant, uninterested in war and politics, who only wished to be left in peace to cultivate his land. He liked having us in his house, because we paid him well for the food he gave us and he took pride in obtaining anything for which we asked.

Married to a woman five years his senior, he had one great sorrow in life. He was childless – for a peasant this constituted a real tragedy. If he is without a son he has no one to care for him in his old age. There are no systems of social security or institutions for the aged in Yugoslavia. Families are completely self-supporting and, as a man becomes too old to work, he hands over control of the household to his son and spends a happy old age sitting around, talking politics, giving orders and drinking *rakija*. If he has no son, he works till he can work no more; then he must die of slow starvation.

Dragan's wife was an attractive woman but very concerned with her inability to produce the necessary children. Failing in the consummation of her marriage with her husband, she turned her attentions to other men and slept promiscuously with anyone who was willing. I am convinced that Dragan was well aware of the fact that she was regularly unfaithful but it did not seem to perturb him unduly. If he could not obtain a child from his wife it seemed to him the lesser of two evils if the very essential offspring were provided by someone else.

Promiscuity in Serbia takes a curious form. When a girl marries she must be a virgin. Marriages among the peasants are generally arranged by the parents, to the mutual benefit of both families, and it is decreed by custom that the bride brings a dowry, representing a certain percentage of her father's livestock and money; she must also provide the marital bed. The day before the marriage, ox carts arrive to carry away these goods. On the day of the marriage the bride's mother goes to the bridegroom's home to prepare the connubial quarters and makes up the bed with a specially embroidered clean white undersheet – a most unusual luxury in the Serbian mountains.

The reception ceremony is conducted at the girl's home amidst much feasting and drinking of *rakija*. After toasts have been drunk the man carries his bride away on a horse. That night the marriage must be consummated. If the bridegroom finds that the girl is not a virgin he at once sends for her mother who inspects the sheet which she herself prepared. If the evidence is against her the man may turn out his wife and keep her dowry. She cannot return to her parents, because she would stand no chance of finding another husband with her dowry gone and her promiscuity proven. She cannot work because she is illiterate; no one will employ her and she has no choice but to go to the town and on to the streets. The enforcement of this harsh rule is considerably facilitated by the custom of postponing the church service until three days after the girl has been carried away so that where the husband has justification he can expel his bride because he is not already legally married to her. Public feeling would prevent him doing so unless he were truly justified.

In view of the strict observance of this custom all young girls are very carefully watched. They are never left alone with men or allowed away from their homes. When I slept with a peasant family all together in one room I was sometimes forced to take my place on the floor next to a young girl, but the mother would always tie the girl's legs firmly together, even though I had given no sign of any interest in her.

Conversely, after marriage the peasant women are very free with their attentions. Many of them flirt quite openly with other men. They are safe because they know that if their husbands object they cannot expel them because every man needs a wife to work and provide him with children and, having married legally, the husband cannot marry again. Sometimes advances were made to me by these women but it was essential not to reciprocate in any way. Apart from principles, if I had made a move everyone would have known because, like news of enemy forces, scandal always travelled fast and wide, increasing in savour at every telling. Though the Serbs would probably have been amused, my prestige would have suffered enormously.

Andrejević had made no headway in his efforts to arrange the conference with the Partisans. Whenever I asked him about it he would confuse the issue by going off into an unending tirade against the 'Communist brigands' as he called them, until, in desperation, I would have to change the subject.

I think that the Četnik commanders had conspired together to avoid the conference at all costs. To me they would always appear willing but it was obvious that Mihailović had ordered them to have no dealing with Tito's men. Finally, in desperation, I decided to arrange a meeting with the Partisans myself and to go and see them alone, after first obtaining a guarantee of safe passage.

I sent a peasant, Dragan's brother, down to Miroševce with a letter to Black Marco. I explained briefly who I was and asked him to meet me in Miroševce, guaranteeing me free return. I told him that I would come without an escort and that I wished to discuss the possibility of co-operating together to fight the enemy. I received an answer the same night written in English. It consisted of one sentence only:

'Come to Miroševce at six tomorrow night.'

I told Andrejević nothing of this, but made my preparations alone. The following day, during the morning, I sent for Dragan and his brother and told them that I wanted them to help me. I swore them to secrecy and promised each a sum of money, which was to them a fortune, if they would do exactly as a I said; they agreed readily. I told Tommy of my plans and gave him full instructions about what he was to do if I did not return by midnight. Base were to be informed, so that they could use their influence with Tito. If the Partisans kidnapped me it was certain that they would try to take me away to their headquarters on Mount Radan so Tommy was to get Andrejević and Manić to seal the route there. We fixed certain pinpoints where he guaranteed to have a covering party if I had to make an escape. Miroševce was over two hours' march away and with my two companions I set out at two in the afternoon, slipping quietly out of Barje towards Kukavica, so that if I were seen by any of the Četniks they would think I had gone to see Manić.

We descended into the Veternica valley and then turned left down the course of the river. An hour's march brought us to the river exit from the mountains. We set off unobserved across country, avoiding the paths, and by half past four we could see Miroševce about half a mile in front of us. To the north of the village there was a small mound on which was a cemetery which rose fifty feet above the surrounding countryside. Making full use of the cover of the hedges, I led the way till, ten minutes later, we rested hidden in the graveyard. The village and its approaches could be clearly seen from our commanding station. I turned to Dragan and asked him:

'Do you often go to Miroševce?'

'I sometimes go to buy things for the house,' he answered. 'There's a shop that sells buttons, cooking pots and other things we can't get in the mountains.'

I gave him some money. 'I want you to go down there now. Go to the shop and buy something. Then if you meet any friends hang around and have a drink with them. Wait there till the Partisans arrive and then come back and tell me how many there are and anything you can learn from them.'

Dragan set off. I waited with his brother until the sun sank low in the west, throwing the great black shadows of the mountains across the peaceful countryside. I looked at my watch – it was five fifteen. I got out my field glasses and started to search the countryside. I was examining the village with my glasses when Dragan's brother plucked at my arm.

'Look over there.'

He pointed past Miroševce in the direction of Strojkoyce. In the lenses I picked up a long column of men moving towards us. They were hugging the hedges.

The column closed up to the outskirts of the village and halted. I saw a large man with a rifle slung over his shoulder collect a group around him and start to give out orders. A few minutes later the force split up and about thirty men with the leader disappeared amongst the houses. The remainder in small groups moved off in all directions. Quickly a cordon formed around the village, each group taking a sector, and the men moving into concealed positions. Only one route was left open, the route from Barje.

I had informed Marco that I would come without an escort and had asked him to do likewise. This cordon could mean only one thing. They intended to prevent my return. It was still not half past five. If I had arrived at the correct time, instead of two hours before, I should not have seen these preparations and would have walked straight into a trap. We waited hidden. At six Dragan had not returned. His brother spoke up.

'I expect they are holding the civilians in the village in case someone comes out to warn us of the cordon.'

'Yes,' I answered, 'I think we'd better go back. They may send out patrols.'

Using a circuitous route we set off back to Barje. Dragan did not return until the following morning and when he got back he was furious.

'They kept me locked up all night because I was from the mountains. I said I'd only come down to buy something in the shop. I'd got some very nice silk for my wife with the money you gave me. I showed it to them as proof and they took it all away from me – bloody bandits.'

I laughed: 'Don't worry about the silk, you shall get some more, but what happened?'

'Black Marco was furious because you never came. He was asking all the peasants about you and the British Mission and about the sorties we get. He had intended to get you inside the village and then if you didn't agree to leave the Četniks and join him voluntarily, he was going to take you prisoner!'

It seemed that my efforts at rapprochement had failed.

CHAPTER NINE

We Carry War to the Enemy

With all hope of an agreement with the Partisans for safe passage across the plains abandoned planning for sabotage on the Lescovac side of the mountains become increasingly more difficult. It seemed a hopeless task if, every time we set out to cut the railway, we should have to use a huge covering force to prevent ourselves from attacks en route.

It might also mean that I, personally, would get involved in actions against the Partisans, which I particularly wanted to avoid, as it was against British policy and would provide good propaganda against us if the Germans came to hear of it. The only alternative open was to divert operations to the Bulgarian side of the frontier. This would mean enlisting the aid of Manić or Stefanović, as Andrejević operated only around Lescovac. I decided to try Jovo first, as I knew that I had little hope of getting help from Manić since he had told me categorically that he would do nothing to assist me.

I bullied Jovo for three days. I pointed out that Andrejević had twice provided me with men and had not yet been reprimanded by Mihailović for doing so. Nevertheless he talked of reprisals that had taken place and insisted that, even if others broke orders from their commander, he personally could not do so. I argued that the war against the Germans was the only thing that mattered and that in any case the best policy for the Četniks was wholehearted co-operation with us to redeem themselves in the eyes of the Allies. He gave in finally, and agreed to co-operate, but only with the firm condition that I should give him extra supplies. Although I was fully aware that I should probably be unable to keep it, I made him a promise and moved my headquarters and the dropping zone back to Oruglica.

Once he had decided on a course of action, Jovo became very keen. We agreed that I should lead the first operation, taking five of Jovo's officers to demonstrate how the task should be carried out, so that they could later lead parties of their own men, and Jovo insisted on accompanying me himself. It was early in October. Snow had already fallen on the higher mountain slopes and fierce purple clouds massing to the north gave promise of more to come. We set about making up white hooded overalls for camouflaging ourselves against the snow.

We had established ourselves in the same house at Oruglica as we had occupied previously. Our host, Bogdan, was glad to have us back again and showed his contentment with much bad language and good *slivović*. I set Faithful and Lesar to work making preparations for the winter, as I had decided to keep a base permanently in Oruglica if we were permitted to do so by the enemy.

Bogdan, who, in comparison with the other peasants, was a rich man, owned two houses built alongside one another. He used one for himself, and the other had only one room and had been designed as a place in which he could entertain his guests. We requisitioned this one; it was a nice room with a wooden floor, which was a most unusual luxury in Serbia, and had a cellar underneath which made an excellent store room for our explosives and other equipment.

Like all British soldiers, the Mission party were very skilful at making themselves comfortable and, now that I had given them the warning that we might be there a long time, they set to work with a will. Ox carts were requisitioned to bring planks and, within a couple of days, three makeshift beds had been knocked together. In deference to my position, I was allowed one to myself; the others slept two to a bed. There were only five of us as, being no longer in need of his services as wireless operator or interpreter, I had sent Leban back to Sehmer. When the beds had been completed, tables and stools were scrounged and the walls plastered with pin-ups. A large Union Jack provided the patriotic touch and the house soon took on a friendly air. Finally, caches were prepared so that we could hide our stores in case of any sudden emergency.

One unfortunate episode took place during the settling-in operations. Johnson, the wireless operator, had requested Lesar the Australian, to obtain a long pole from which to suspend the wireless aerial. Lesar, a townsman, had departed with an axe and cut down the longest tree in the vicinity. He cut off the branches, borrowed a bullock and came back proudly dragging his prize. Shortly afterwards a very incensed Bogdan rushed in, swearing and gesticulating. It transpired that Lesar had cut down his largest and most productive plum tree, from the fruit of which, Bogdan stated, was distilled a fantastic number of kilos of *rakija* each season. However when I had bought the tree for I suspect the current price of his whole orchard he regained his sense of humour and we drank to the bargain in a bottle of our wireless mast's *slivović*.

Another disaster overtook us two days after our arrival at Oruglica. The pedal charger, always erratic, broke irreparably. I cursed the nitwits who had neglected to answer our requests for another charger. Altogether we had three wireless sets complete with batteries, but nothing with which to charge them. There were no mains or private electric lighting sets in the Serbian mountains and there was therefore no possible alternative way in which we could charge our batteries. As a result our communication with the outside world was again cut off.

I sent off a courier with a message to Sehmer, asking him to inform base of our troubles and to insist that they send us a motor generator at once. Again I gave orders for a party to stand by with fires ready every night until a sortie came.

The following day I set off with Jovo and his party. Apart from Jovo and myself, there were his five sub-commanders and a guide. The latter was a great character. Vuk was about thirty-five, of medium height, with a young, sensitive face. Slightly built, he was very strong and was possessed of terrific endurance. Before the war, he had been a professional smuggler of cigarettes, tobacco and currency from Yugoslavia into Bulgaria. He did it all on foot, slipping across at night between the frontier patrols. His career since the war had been an extraordinary one. His profession, particularly where currency was concerned, had become remarkably lucrative. So for two years he had continued dealing in contraband and made a tidy fortune. Then he heard of the Četniks and joined them. Delighted at recruiting such a useful man Jovo had used him as a courier to carry any dispatches or stores which had to be taken across the frontier. He had twice been captured by the Bulgars and escaped both times. On the second occasion, as he was being led out to be shot, Vuk kicked the man who was leading him, and, bending down, snatched his guard's grenade which was fastened by the pin to his belt. The pin came away igniting the grenade and, dropping it, Vuk ran while the guards threw themselves flat. In the four seconds that the grenade took to detonate he covered a considerable distance, and miraculously escaped any injury from the explosion. Ducking and dodging, he avoided the fire of the guards who had not been killed or injured by the grenade and eventually he got right away.

His home was about two kilometres from the frontier at the highest point of Mount Kukavica, an area which he knew intimately.

Carrying the white overalls with us to use when we reached the snow line, we left Oruglica at about ten in the morning and headed for Vuk's cottage, where dinner was to be ready at five. We had planned to leave there at seven and cross the frontier during the night.

It was a dull, cold day and towards the summit we came into mist and low cloud. The ground was rugged and broken with great ravines which swelled into deep valleys intersecting the mountainside; large rugged rocks hung drunkenly where they had halted, displaced by some avalanche years ago. Trees, luxurious on the lower slopes, but higher up sparse and stunted, their limbs now bare of leaves, grew thicker as we approached the summit of the mountain, whose table top was covered by a dense beech forest stretching for miles, unbroken by paths or signs of human habitation.

Vuk had gone on ahead to see that all was prepared. We last saw him moving lithely over a ridge in front. We were climbing slowly to save our energies for the long march in front of us.

Suddenly a single shot rang out ahead of us. We stopped to listen but hearing nothing further we moved on thinking it to be nothing worse than a frontier guard shooting at a hare or a fox.

Vuk's home was situated on the top of the mountain at the edge of the forest. Two other houses were built alongside and below, on the far side, the ground descended to a small hollow, where the smoke rose from the chimney of another small building.

As we came into view a woman who had been standing at the door of his house rushed up to us and started talking rapidly to Jovo, who explained that she was Vuk's wife.

'The Bulgars have just been here. Vuk fired a shot to warn you. He is following them to see where they are going. They ate all the food that I had prepared for you.'

'How many Bulgars?' Jovo asked.

'Three. They are from the frontier post. They come to loot. They took all my neighbours' chickens and now they have gone down to steal a pig.'

She went off into a long tirade against the Bulgars and in passing she mentioned the names of two of the men. Jovo turned to me.

'Those two men are devils. They're stationed up at the frontier post and they come over regularly to loot. One of them raped a girl just the other day. Come on, we'll go after them.'

That was all very well but three dead Bulgars wouldn't help the war much, and I didn't want to incur reprisals in this area. It might make the Serbs shy of doing sabotage.

'What about reprisals?'

'That's all right. There won't be any. These men aren't on duty. They're acting against orders.'

We gathered from the woman that they were inside the building in the hollow. As there was no time to be lost, Jovo gave his orders at once. Two men were sent round to the right and two up into the forest on the left to stop them escaping across the frontier. We waited for the others to get into position.

I took off the magazine of my sten and pressed the top round to be sure that the spring was free. Fixing it on again I cocked the bolt and slipped it into the safety notch. I pressed forward the catch to the 'Automatic' mark.

'All right. We'll move off now.'

The three of us slipped silently from rock to rock down towards the cottage below. Fifty yards away Jovo knelt behind a rock and beckoned to me.

'There they are.'

I saw three men in brown uniform with rifles slung over their backs standing by the door of the building. One of them was shouting at a peasant who stood holding a pig by a length of rope.

Jovo whispered, 'Wait a minute till they get clear.'

Unaware of our presence the three looters moved off up the path which led through a ravine towards the frontier. They were followed by the peasant with his pig, who moved directly between us and the enemy. We waited, holding our fire. Then, as they turned a bend in the path, we got a clear sight.

'Now!'

Simultaneously our automatics stuttered out. The Bulgars stood for a second, astonished, petrified. We got their range and one fell as the others started running for cover; another was limping heavily.

As I pressed the trigger for another burst, it came to me that this was the first time in five months that I had had an opportunity to avenge the members of the Mission, murdered by these men's compatriots. This was slaughter too, but at least it wasn't murder. I enjoyed it and rejoiced as my bullets smacked home.

The men who had been sent to the flanks opened up and in ten seconds it was all over. One Bulgar surrendered, slightly wounded. The other two were shot to pieces.

Quite unperturbed by the hail of bullets smattering around him, the old peasant came rushing back to his cottage, whooping and yelling with joy as he shepherded his precious pig. What did it matter if he had nearly been killed? What did anything matter? He still had his pig, which he would butcher soon and make into bacon and biltong to keep himself through the winter. A few minutes later he came tearing up the hill towards us. He was mud-bespattered and ragged and blue bruises showed where the Bulgars had hit him with their rifles but his wrinkled old face was wreathed in smiles. He carried a full bottle.

'Oh, thank you, thank you! God preserve you!' He held the bottle towards us. 'This is my best *rakija*.'

The prisoner was brought in. He was a big heavy man with thick lips and a mastiff-like face and he quivered with fear.

Jovo questioned him. He appeared to be very simple; he was from the frontier post; he had just come there and could give us no information of which we were not already in possession.

'What shall we do with him?' Jovo asked me.

Before I could answer the men chorused, 'Kill him!' I thought for a moment: it would serve no purpose to kill that quivering terrified jelly. Better let the Bulgars do their own dirty work.

'Take his arms and equipment. Send him back with a letter explaining that they were looting and that if there are any reprisals I shall order a bombing of Sofia. They'll probably believe it – the subhumans that they are!'

We sent him off; just as we were going shots sounded from the frontier and a bullet whistled harmlessly over our heads. Jovo led us away from the skyline.

'That will be the counter-attack coming in. We'd better be on our way.'

As we entered the forest I noticed that the Bulgar was following us like a sheep. I turned round to shoo him away.

'Go back to your post.'

He made a remark in Bulgarian. One of the men translated: 'He says that if he goes back without his rifle he will be shot.'

Waving the man away, I replied in English, 'And that is exactly what I'm hoping will happen.'

*

We carried out the derailment the following night. Our journey across the frontier to the Morava passed uneventfully enough and during the day we laid up in a hut overlooking the valley. All day we watched the trains roaring past, belching black smoke and sparks

(Above left) Captain Boon (escaped Australian POW) with Peter Solly Flood

(Above right) 'Tired' Peter and horses resting on way back from the railway

(Left) 'Bringing home the bacon' — the author and Peter Solly Flood carrying a sucking pig

(Left) Captain Robert Purvis, another active saboteur before the break with the Četniks, on railway line between Vranje and Skoplje. His mission chalked up a number of successes

(Below) British group including Lt-Col Bill Cope, Maj Rupert Raw, Maj John Sehmer, Sgt Harry Lesar, prior to evacuation

British group including Lt-Col Bill Cope and Captain John Stott on way out to evacuation

from their squat funnels. Two northbound convoys passed along the road and one halted opposite us; through glasses I could see the men stretching their legs and smoking cigarettes whilst an officer strutted up and down the line of halted lorries.

Moving off at dark we reached the line at ten and placed the charges at the point where the road and railway ran close alongside one another on the bend which Jovo and I had reconnoitred three months previously. The sentries were not vigilant and were quickly rounded up. Vuk made an excellent job on a Bulgarian soldier passing along the road on solitary patrol. Creeping silently up behind his unsuspecting victim, our smuggling guide slipped one wiry hand over the Bulgar's mouth while, with the other, he drove a knife deep into his ribs. The man died without uttering a sound. Watching from the shadows alongside the track, it was easy to see that Vuk's was the hand of the practised killer.

When our explosives were ready in position we started back but before we had reached the end of the path leading up the steep slope from the road we heard the train which was to be our victim whistling as it turned down the line. As its leading wheels crushed the detonators, the charges exploded and the locomotive leaped high off the rails. The train crashed across the road into the steep valley wall. Jubilantly we left the scene of carnage and, marching fast all night, we reached the frontier, which we crossed with the usual pantomine but without incident as dawn was breaking.

Our guide's knowledge of the frontier zone was amply illustrated that night. The ground was covered in snow, hiding any paths which might have existed, and the night was moonless and cloudy when Vuk led us back through the thick forest. How he found the way was beyond my comprehension. We travelled straight and never once did he falter. When I asked him his secret, he smiled.

'I know the mountain,' he answered.

But under those conditions a man could have lost himself in his own garden. This forest stretched for miles on every side. Jovo's explanation was that Vuk recognised the trees. But the trees all seemed identical to me – tall, bare, beeches. I think that it was just another instinct which the animals have and which a man can develop if he travels often, at night and alone.

*

October and November passed and the forests on Kukavica were bare of leaves. The snow stood deep rendering the mountain impassable at times. At Oruglica we had falls of snow, and frosts but then the weather would change and rain would wash the ground clear again. Apart from sending one strong patrol from Lebane up to Barje, the enemy did not venture into the mountains and my headquarters at Oruglica remained secure and snug. Our wireless was still useless, as we had received no more supplies, though fires were prepared and men stood by waiting every night.

We continued sabotage as best we could. Disappointed by my failure to keep up supplies for them and worried by the prospect of another winter in the mountains without help from outside, the Serbs were loath to indulge in offensive activity. They argued that if we were too active we would incite the enemy to carry out an intensive anti-guerilla drive through the mountains. With the forests bare of cover and snow on the ground to show our tracks, we would be very vulnerable and would find escape difficult. Lacking sorties, our ammunition was running short and we had not enough for a pitched battle.

Although they refused to carry out a comprehensive sabotage plan, I managed to persuade the commanders to give me men from time to time to cover small demolitions which I could carry out alone. In this way, with sections from Stefanović and Andrejevic I was successful in derailing three more supply trains and, goading him into action by eulogistic descriptions of the co-operation of his rivals, I finally persuaded Manić to lend me a number of his troops. Once committed, he decided to do the job properly, and detailed his best company comprising about eighty men to accompany me. I later heard that he had given the commander instructions that at all costs they must march me off my feet.

We set out from Oruglica at dawn one morning and, marching all day across Mount Kukavica, reached Grdelica by dark. Without resting we attacked at once, capturing a Bulgar guard-house and demolishing one thousand yards of railway line. With our mission completed, we marched back across the plains, arriving at Barje at dawn the following morning. When I later measured it on the map I found that notwithstanding the weight of the explosives we were carrying we had covered sixty-three miles of bad country in twenty-four hours. The company commander certainly obeyed his orders!

Apart from these operations which I conducted personally a party of Jovo's men, led by Vuk, carried out a successful ambush of a convoy in the Morava valley, destroying four lorries and damaging others, and Pesić from Andrejević's brigade, together with one companion, visited Grdelica station disguised in civilian clothing and left some delay action bombs behind them attached to the boilers of the locomotives in the repair sheds.

Reviewing the last six months I tried to analyse whether my Mission had justified its existence and upkeep. Without question we had failed in our primary task, which was to mobilise the full striking force of the Četniks to operate all out against the enemy's lines of communication. We had certainly carried out quite a considerable amount of sabotage but, with fifty determined men, I could have achieved as much or even more as I had succeeded in doing with the thousand Četniks in my area. But we had failed through no fault of our own; the veto which Mihailović had placed on offensive action had immobilised the Četnik commanders before we ever arrived and even coercion by the British Government had failed to shake the old man's determination to lie low and avoid reprisals. Similarly, in six months, I had received only four aeroplane stores sorties, a number quite inadequate to give me any real bargaining power.

I consoled myself with the thought that at least we had succeeded in cutting the railway when it was most needed by the enemy and that we had been a source of constant anxiety to them since that time. Those attacks would never have been carried out by the Četniks on their own without our persuasion; we had at least achieved something. Reports from other Četnik areas indicated that few or no operations had taken place in most of them. And the Partisans . . . I wondered just how much they really were doing. Those on Mount Radan had certainly done little except hinder my operations. If they had carried out any sabotage I should certainly have heard of it. So far I had received only one such report, when they burned the wooden bridge on the Lescovac–Lebane road; a singularly useless operation, as this was only a by-road going no further than Lebane.

I wondered how it would all end, and when. Would we carry on indefinitely, short of supplies, living with this forgotten army until the day of liberation. That day, which in the summer had seemed imminent, receded now into the back of our thoughts as we prepared to weather out the winter.

My greatest problem was the lack of communication to base. It was over two months since we had been able to receive or transmit any messages. I had sent further couriers to Sehmer, but he replied that he too was receiving no sorties and had no spare generator to give me.

Johnson had become ill with a skin disease not unlike scabies, which had developed into running sores all over his body, and a few days later I too started to itch all over. Our stocks of ointment and antiseptic were exhausted, so we called the 'wise-woman' in again. She told us that ours was a complaint common in the mountains and one particularly active in the winter. Locally it was called 'Sugar'. She advised us to go to Sirinske Banja, one day's march away, where there was a natural hot water spa where we could take a course of sulphur baths.

We started the next morning. I had recently acquired two horses for the Mission and, as Johnson was unfit to march, we rode. Leaving Oruglica at nine, we travelled west along the trail by which I had come into the area six months previously and by three in the afternoon we reached our destination. Sirinske Banja was a delightful surprise. At the top of a very deep valley a large modern village had been erected to house the would-be bathers; a tarred motor road led towards Medvedja, a neighbouring village which was occupied by the enemy from time to time. There was a smart three-storey hotel, numerous cafes, and a row of shops. We were fascinated by all this splendour. After months of frugal living in the tiny mountain cottages, devoid of any comforts, it was inspiring to come just around the corner to find this.

The hotel was empty. Earlier in the war the Germans had used it as an officers' rest camp and, since they had vacated it, it had not been reopened. We searched around and found ourselves lodgings at one of the cafes.

The baths were excellent. At one, boiling water bubbled out of the mountainside, was caught and cooled into an iodine bath. Another was hot lime water, a third sulphur. Obeying our medical advisor, we chose the latter.

It was sheer heaven to feel hot water around one's limbs again. This was my first bath since I had left Cairo. Johnson and I washed, splashed, and wallowed happily for half an hour, until the attendant came to warn us that it was unsafe to stay in too long, and advised us to get out.

We dressed and wandered back towards our lodgings. It was just getting dark, and lights twinkled through the unshuttered windows of the houses down the street; a pony cart drawn by a high-trotting grey clattered past; a group of men wandered along in front, their pipes glowing, heading for the cafe.

As we turned in at the gate, I noticed a fine black horse with an army saddle on its back, tied to a post by the door of the cafe. The saddle was festooned with leather bags, rolled blankets and other fittings, a phenomenon which made us wonder who could be the owner of this fine outfit.

The cafe was brightly lit and full of people drinking and arguing vociferously. In the far corner sat a group of Četniks in British battle dress. Hanging my sten gun and equipment on a peg behind the door, I turned to find a chair as one of the men detached himself from the group and came across. I realised at once from his appearance that the stranger was British. Tall, heavily built, with a handsome face under thinning black hair, he wore crowns on the shoulders of his battledress.

We shook hands.

'How do you do! I suppose you must be Mike Lees? I'm Peter Solly-Flood.'

'How do you do, but if you don't mind my asking, what the devil are you doing here?'

'Well, let's get a table to ourselves and I'll tell you all about it.'

Peter told me his story. He had dropped two months previously to Mihailović as Intelligence Officer to the British brigadier who was Liaison Officer there. After a month at headquarters the brigadier had sent him on a mission to visit all the Četnik commands and to bring back a report on their potential value as a striking force if Mihailović could be persuaded to give orders for an all-out offensive against the occupying armies. Carrying out this task he had covered hundreds of miles on horseback and on foot through the mountains. Sometimes he had been forced to cross the plains which were strongly held by the enemy, travelling at night or in disguise. He had met all the well-known Četnik leaders and visited their British Liaison Officers.

Since our wireless had failed we had been without any news of the other British Missions in Yugoslavia and I was delighted to get this opportunity of hearing how the others had fared. It seemed that all had experienced the same difficulties, lack of support from base in supplying adequate sorties, poor co-operation from the Četnik commanders and, of course, the civil war with the Partisans.

Peter finished his account:

'I left Sehmer two days ago and I was on my way up now to visit you. They told me that you were at a place called Oruglica, and I was planning to spend the night here and go on to you tomorrow.'

I explained the reason for our visit and suggested that he should return with us to Oruglica the next day. While I arranged food, he went off to the stable to feed his horse.

It was such a novelty after the months of solitude to meet another British officer that natural reserve soon broke down and Peter and I became firm friends. He was about thirty years old, an Irishman and not yet married. After leaving Eton, he had joined the Foreign Office and taken up an appointment in San Francisco. When the war started he had been refused permission to return home to join up on the grounds that his was an essential service. Nothing daunted, he had continued pestering the authorities until, in desperation, they allowed him to go. Since joining the army he had seen service with the Eighth Army in the desert and had later been given command of an intelligence training school near Cairo. After a month or two in the fleshpots, he had again become impatient for active service and he had volunteered to come to Yugoslavia.

Peter was able to give me an unbiased view on the question of the civil war:

'The whole crux of the matter is that the Četniks won't fight. You say you've managed to do something in your area, but that's an isolated instance and in any case only a small contribution. Mihailović has a very large force of men under his command; it's impossible to estimate the exact figures. He maintains they number a hundred thousand but that is certainly an exaggeration. I should be inclined to believe that there are fifty thousand mobilised Četniks and the greater proportion of those are making no contribution to the war effort at all.'

'But they are tying up German troops and they will fight when the Allies invade Europe,' I protested. 'They are holding back now to keep themselves intact.'

'Agreed. But people outside Yugoslavia don't understand that. For propaganda purposes they must be active if they want support.'

'Do you really believe that the Partisans are so much more active?'

'I don't know. They're boosted up to be. On the other hand I've seen or heard very little evidence of it. But the Russians like the Partisans and we have to keep sweet with the Russians.'

'Meanwhile storing up a lot of trouble for ourselves after the war?'

I asked Peter if he had found sympathy for the Partisans amongst the population of any of the areas he had passed through.

'So far hardly any at all but I've only met Serbs. Occasionally one meets someone from the towns who doesn't mind much who comes out on top. But the Serbian peasants are all united behind Mihailović.'

Peter went on to confirm that even at Headquarters they were receiving very few sorties indeed while, as early as August, when he had been in Cairo, he had heard that the allocation of airlift to the Partisans was considerable.

Next day, leaving Johnson whose sores were still open, to complete his cure, I rode back to Oruglica with Peter. He proposed to spend three days with us and then to cross the plains to visit a Četnik group on Mount Suva, ten miles north-east of Lescovac.

The time was spent busily poring over maps, detailing targets and trying to assess our strength and armaments accurately. I called a conference of the Četnik commanders and introduced them to Peter. Afterwards he asked me about Manić.

'He's a brilliant man – and he has the best trained, best disciplined brigade in the area – but he's very unco-operative and entirely out for himself.'

'I'm interested to hear you say that because when I was leaving Headquarters Mihailović particularly asked me to see Manić and bring back a report on his progress. Apparently he was at Headquarters before he came here.'

Because of the danger of Partisan ambush in the plains and the necessity of crossing the railway line, Peter needed a large escort for his journey to Mount Suva. As he would have to return to Oruglica afterwards, I decided to accompany him myself and to carry out an operation which I had been planning for some weeks.

Niš, a large manufacturing town, lay about thirty miles north of Lescovac. About five miles from Niš, at the foot of the mountain, there was an aerodrome on which the Germans had based a squadron of Messerschmitt fighters, which they used against the American heavy bombers which passed over en route to raid the Rumanian oilfields at Ploesti. For some time I had been playing with the idea of carrying out a night attack to blow up or set fire to the aircraft on the airfield. It was impracticable to mount such an attack from Oruglica, the distance to the airfield being far too great, but the aerodrome lay only about five hours march from Mount Suva and was therefore well within the radius for a night attack.

The plan was our most ambitious yet. Using Pesić and about fifty men from Andrejević's brigade we would cross the plains north of Lescovac on the night of 10th December, if possible derailing a train en route, and cross the Morava at the foot of Mount Suva. Peter needed three days to conduct his business with the Četnik commander, whilst I would borrow guides and, with a party of twenty men, attack the airfield on the second night. We planned to return by the route south of Lescovac and cut the line for a second time on our journey back.

On the 9th we moved to Barje to collect and organise our force. Andrejević raised no difficulties and Pesić was delighted with the plan. He was soon busying himself sorting his explosives, preparing the special charges that we would need for the aircraft, and instructing his men in their use. The plains were reported to be clear of Partisans, so we planned our departure for noon the following day.

We spent the night with Dragan. Two Russian officers, recently escaped from prisoner of war camps, had joined the Četniks at Barje. We asked them to dine with us and also invited Andrejević with some of his officers. The party lasted late into the night and after the *rakija* had been circulating for some time the Russians started to sing. They were both Ukrainians with excellent voices and we sat enchanted by their lilting songs. Then Andrejević tuned in and we listened to Serbian and Russian melodies in turn, until sometime in the small hours we rolled ourselves in blankets and lay down to sleep by the fire.

Our departure was timed for noon and I ordered Pesić to give his men a meal before starting. They had finished eating and were outside making a final check of their weapons when we arrived. I took Pesić aside to discuss final details of our route of approach to the railway lines and method of attack, and we were talking to one of the guides, when Peter, who was standing nearby, suddenly burst out:

'Who the devil's that, with my horse?'

Down the path from Oruglica, a horse was galloping towards us. As he drew up I saw that it was Mile, my orderly from headquarters. He was riding Peter's black horse, which was lathering freely. Before I could question him, he handed me a letter.

'Lieutenant Tommy told me to bring you this letter. He said that it was very urgent and that if you had started I had to follow and catch you up.'

I tore open the envelope. Inside was a short note from Tommy and another envelope which had already been unsealed. Tommy's note read:

> Dear Mike. This message from base, for all Missions, arrived from Sehmer this morning by fastest courier. I'm sending Mile on the Major's horse so as to catch you before you start.

There was a coded signal form inside the other envelope. Tommy had decoded it and written the message underneath:

It has been decided to discontinue all support of Mihailović and his forces. Cease all operations. British Liaison Officers should plan to evacuate if possible, or make their way to Partisans. Mihailović has not yet been informed. We will instruct you of date to move.

I handed it on to Peter.

'So much for your survey, old cock!'

CHAPTER TEN

Ally Dumped

For months we should have understood that this would be the inevitable outcome of the civil war but, optimistically, we had never allowed ourselves to believe it and these orders, preceded by no warning, came as a stunning blow. For some minutes our minds were immobilised by this dramatic upheaval, which would completely overthrow all our conceptions and plans, and Peter and I just stood and stared at each other as the full import of that signal sank in. I pulled myself together. It was essential to say nothing in front of the Četniks.

'Pešić. Orders have come for the British major to return to Mihailović. We shall not go to Mount Suva today. You may dismiss the men.'

We walked away from the group and sat down to think things over. The real question to be decided was how we should evacuate! By air? But I knew of no place in the vicinity of our area suitable as a landing ground, even for light aircraft, let alone the large planes which would have a range long enough to reach us and return to Allied territory. Peter confirmed that there was none in any of the neighbouring mission areas. But how else could we evacuate? On foot? We could march south towards Greece, but that route had already been attempted, without success, by escaped prisoners of war. To the coast through Albania? With a civil war there, and many fascist sympathisers and groups of straightforward bandits, there would be little chance of survival a day over the border. If we marched due west, making for the coast, we could avoid the Germans by sticking to the mountain routes but we should have to pass through other Četnik and later Partisan held areas. The Četniks would surely not allow us to escape, leaving them to eventual destruction at the hands of the Axis or the Partisans. All those alternatives seemed hopeless.

There was only one other possibility: to escape direct to the Partisans on Mount Radan. But would we be better off then? My experience of them already made me wonder what sort of a reception we would get and, when we arrived there, we could not stay with them and supply them with arms with which to fight our erstwhile allies the Četniks. They certainly had channels of communication to the larger groups of Partisans to the west but I suspected that those channels were only practicable for disguised couriers and not for the exodus of a body of Englishmen. Apart from these objections, I doubted whether we would ever succeed in reaching Mount Radan. Alone it would be easy but with a party of six and Johnson dead lame it would be impossible to travel fast enough to avoid interception by the Četniks.

From every angle the problem was a grim one. Without further details it was impossible to decide on a course of action. Peter suggested:

'There's no point in going back to Mihailović now. In fact I doubt if I could get there but I'll go as far as Sehmer's HQ where there is a wireless set working. If anything further comes in I'll ride back and let you know. What do you say?'

I agreed readily. We returned to Oruglica and Peter started the same evening. At the last moment I decided to send the Australian Lesar with him.

During the next three days we buried all our kit, leaving ourselves just a small haversack each to carry essentials and stood by for further news. It came soon in a short note from Peter:

Dear Mike. Come to Sirinska Banja at once. Peter.

This note arrived one evening. We started at midnight slipping out of the area without giving the Četniks any warning of our departure. It would have been impossible to devise a satisfactory excuse for the sudden departure of the whole Mission and they might easily have guessed the trend of events and detained us forcibly. We reached Sirinska Banja by midday, but Peter was not there, and I decided to push on at once towards where Sehmer's headquarters had last been reported.

After about two hours' march we stopped at the top of a steep hill by some farm buildings for a rest. Faithful went off to find some *rakija* with which to revive Johnson, who was very lame from the sores on his legs, and Tommy and I sat on a log looking out over the snow covered countryside. Suddenly we heard the jingle of harness from the path to the west and two horses trotted into sight. Their riders were Peter and Lesar. They drew up alongside us; Peter pulled a solemn face.

'Turn round and go back at once, Mike. The cat's out of the bag.

Sehmer and all his party were shot by Djurić this morning. We escaped because we were staying at another house and were warned in advance.'

I stared at him dumbfoundedly. I was capable of believing anything that day. I thought for a moment:

'There's no choice. We'll have to cross into Albania and take our chance there.'

For answer Peter smiled broadly. Lesar slumped off his horse and collapsed on a log, weak with laughter. I was furious.

'You dirty bastards. What's the true story?'

The true story was as surprisingly fortunate as the other had been grim. Mihailović had been informed of the situation and had agreed to the evacuation of British Missions with only one proviso: that they travelled through his channels and did not go via the Partisans, to whom he feared they might divulge secrets of his formations. The brigadier had given orders that for the present we should remain dispersed until, with the help of Mihailović, we could prepare an airfield at Headquarters on which we should concentrate to be evacuated later.

I shall always remember the manner in which Mihailović's decision was made. Publicly denounced and deserted by the Allies, he held no rancour against us as individuals. He could not have acted with greater dignity or forbearance. It was a gesture of a true gentleman and soldier. Under similar circumstances, would Tito have done the same?

The evacuation was delayed for six months and for half that time we lived in the mountains around Oruglica. The British contingent was swollen by outlying Missions until we were twenty strong. The other Missions brought wireless equipment, so that we managed to contact base for the first time in three months. Each day we listened, waiting for the order to move; each day there was news of further delays. This became nerve-racking after a time because by virtue of its size our group was unwieldy and we had to be always on the alert against enemy moves to effect our capture. Knowing that we were serving no purpose in the war effort, and with little to do to amuse ourselves, time passed slowly and tempers became frayed.

Although they knew of our plans for departure the Serbs were still disposed to friendliness. By common consent we did not discuss the rights or wrongs of the decision which had been made for us. I often went with Peter to visit the commanders and to eat a meal with them. One day we were riding back from Kukavica, after lunch with Manić, when Peter reined back his horse so that I came up alongside him.

'I don't know about you, Mike, but I'm fed up to the teeth with doing nothing.'

'So am I, but what can we do about it?' I answered.

Peter paused, thinking, then went on speaking deliberately, as he analysed the situation:

'Well, as I see it, we're serving no purpose sitting on top of a mountain eating and sleeping. They can't evacuate us, yet, agreed, but I for one hate wasting my time. We're supposed to be fighting the Germans in this war. Well here we are right amongst them. Let's get on with it.'

'I quite agree, but we've been told to cease operations with the Četniks – not that they would do anything for us now.'

'Yes, but why the devil shouldn't we do something on our own? You know the area and the possibilities. What could we do?'

There was sense in what he said. We talked over the possibilities, coming to the conclusion that the best plan would be to try to derail a train. Any other scheme would be impossible without troops to carry charges and cover us while we worked.

We told the others nothing of our plans. They might have raised objections. There was always a point of view that the reprisals which were bound to follow action would, under present circumstances, anger the Serbs against us and, possibly, cause them to place us under arrest. We were prepared to take that risk; months of inactivity had made us desperate from frustration. At least this would be something to relieve the prisoner mentality into which we we were slipping rapidly. More importantly it would help the Allied war effort.

In daylight we rode as far as Veliki Milanovac in the plains, which was about three kilometres from Lebane, and stabled our horses to wait until dusk fell. The village was a small but rich one, surrounded by fertile pasture. We were taken in by the head man, a charming old peasant with a young wife and a most attractive baby daughter who sat on my knee and called me 'Uncle'. She was fascinated by the scant and dirty beard, which I had been forced to grow, since my stock of razor blades had become exhausted. Our host plied us with large dishes of sumptuous food, washed down with *klekovačka* and a pink wine. We fed so well that, as dusk fell, it was an effort to tear ourselves away from this hospitable place.

As we had no guide, I had chosen a point on the railway just north of Lescovac as our objective. It lay about four hours' march from the starting point and I hoped to navigate by marching across country towards the lights of the town and turning off to the north as we reached the outskirts. As at this point the railway line was straight and the trains would be running slowly I had made up a more powerful charge than usual: fifteen pound blocks of gun cotton nailed onto a board three blocks deep, connected by a short length of fast-burning fuse to the igniter, a fog signal device which was formed so that it could be fixed quickly onto the metals. I cut the fuse to burn so that the charge on the outside of the rail would detonate directly against the leading bogey wheel of the locomotive as it passed and I calculated that the force of the explosion would be sufficient to punch the front of the locomotive off the rails and hoped that the momentum of the heavy train would do the rest. We were both armed with sten guns and revolvers; I carried the charge packed into a sandbag ready for use.

An hour's march brought us to the Lescovac-Lebane road, which was little better than a rough gravel track built up above the wet countryside. The moon had not yet risen, a fine sleet was falling and the night was very dark. We stumbled up from a heavy ploughed field onto the road; as I slipped across, I heard a muttered curse and a rattle behind me. Peter whispered close to my ear:

'There's a trip wire, I've dropped my gun. Get across and I'll follow.'

As I ran into the fields on the far side, I heard shouts and the sound of heavy boots pelting along the road. I whistled softly but no answer came. The boots sounded closer and I whistled again, but still there was no answer.

Reluctantly I moved on to the cover of a hedge about forty yards further on and lay down to wait as the Bulgar patrol arrived to investigate.

A few minutes later, having found nothing suspicious, the Bulgars passed on out of hearing and I went back to the road but could find no signs of Peter. Whistling and calling softly, I searched unsuccessfully. It seemed that he had crossed the road and gone ahead expecting to find me. In the darkness it was easy to miss one another.

As it was hopeless to waste more time searching for him, I tried to visualize what Peter would do when he failed to contact me. He was carrying no explosive, so he could do nothing on his own; he could either go back to our starting point, or go on towards the line to search for me there. But he had never been there before and he did not know the exact spot I was making for – not that I did for that matter. I was marching to strike the line somewhere north of Lescovac. Knowing Peter, I felt sure he would not go back.

Having come that far, I decided to carry on and try to complete the task. If I happened to find Peter by some lucky chance, well and good. If not, I should have to work alone.

Keeping the twinkling lights of the town on my right, I hurried on over the wet countryside. Ploughland, wet from the melting snow, clogged my boots, which felt more leaden at every step.

Passing close to the outskirts of Lescovac I veered away due north; as I waded across a dyke a line of telegraph poles loomed out of the gloom ahead. Behind them lay the railway embankment like a long low wall.

In the darkness it was hard to estimate distances but I guessed that the telegraph poles would be placed within fifty yards of the permanent way. I moved up close to them and lay down beneath the humming wires.

I had intended to allow one or two trains to pass through unscathed, to give me an opportunity to spot the sentries and pick out a good spot on the line to place my charge but as I lay there the time lengthened to an hour; an hour and a half; two hours and still nothing came. The drizzle had stopped and in the east a moon began to rise.

Twelve o'clock . . . It was imperative that I be on my way back by one a.m. if I were to reach the security of the mountains before dawn. This was a factor I had not bargained with; in normal times the railway carried at least two trains per hour during the night.

At last, far in the distance to the north a whistle sounded. I dared not let this train pass by as there might not be another for some time. The job would have to be done without previous observation of the line.

To free my hands, I slung the gun over my back, slipped the charge out of the sandbag and took the heavy gun cotton block in my right and the fog signal in my left, the direction from which the train was coming.

As the headlights twinkled in the distance, I crouched waiting. The light came nearer. It must be six hundred yards . . . I started to run towards the embankment. In the dark I had misjudged the distance to the line. My lungs bursting, it seemed that I had been running for hours as I sprinted forward racing the train which mercifully had slowed down for the station ahead. Closer and closer it roared towards me as I strained to reach the embankment in time.

Forgetting all thoughts of sentries I forced myself faster and faster to beat that great iron monster, belching red hot fumes and rushing down upon me.

Across the path – scrambling up to the track – the locomotive was less than fifty yards away. Both hands together – an automatic movement – the charge against the rail – no time to wedge it – clip on the fog signal . . . Ten feet away the smoke stack of the engine towered above me; I jumped backwards, rolling over down the slope, my sten clattering onto the ground.

As I collapsed on the path at the bottom, the charge exploded. Shielded by the high embankment, the blast roared over my head. Flying stones spattered all around. The scream of tearing metal followed by a furious crash sounded from above. Without looking back, I picked myself up to run from the scene but I had not covered ten paces before flashes from an automatic shone just ahead and bullets cracked past. I threw myself flat, slipped my sten forward and levelling it I pressed the trigger. Nothing happened. I slid my hand along the weapon. The magazine had fallen off – it must have slipped when I jumped clear; I felt in my hip pocket where I carried three spare magazines. There were none there either.

Throwing my useless weapon away, I started to run towards Lescovac. The automatic was still firing but the bullets cracked away from me now. After a hundred yards parallel to the line I turned south towards the mountains, but first I looked back for a moment towards the railway. The locomotive was invisible, thrown clear to the other side. The leading carriages leant over drunkenly, telescoped into one another. There were other guns firing now from the railway, wildly, without target into the darkness. Half running, half walking, I commenced the long journey back.

At Veliki Milanovac Peter had not yet returned. While I debated the next move, I fed and watered the horses. It seemed foolhardy to wait in the village so close to the Bulgarian garrison at Lebane. After last night's performance it was more than likely that they would comb the plains. Peter might have lost his way and taken a different route back into the mountains rather than be in the plains at dawn. As an afterthought I saddled Peter's horse and left it tethered outside ready for him to leave at once.

Then I rode off slowly, alone.

I arrived back at Oruglica by noon. The afternoon was fraught with anxious waiting but at midnight I heard Peter clattering in and went outside to meet him.

'Goodness, I'm glad to see you, Peter.'
'Congratulations on an excellent derailment, Mike.'
'So you were there after all, you old devil.'
'Yes. After I tripped over the wire and lost you on the road I went on alone. I didn't know what you would be doing, so I made my own plans. I borrowed a rope at a house, intending to pull down some telephone lines, but I was delayed on the journey and, just as I arrived, you blew the train. So I emptied a couple of magazines into it and buzzed off. Not knowing the country, I got lost coming back.'
'So it was you. Do you realise you damned nearly shot me, you crazy devil? And if I hadn't lost my sten magazine, I'd have shot back.'

Peter roared with laughter. Sobered now, after the initial pleasure of seeing him safe and well, I remarked:

'Well, I hope the reprisals won't be too terrible.' Peter looked at me in a queer way and answered sombrely:

'I don't think there will be any reprisals, Mike.'
'Why?'
'Because, though the Germans will be angry at the smashed rolling stock and the lines all buggered up, they might otherwise be rather amused.'
'Why?' I asked again.
'It was a civilian passenger train; I heard that on the way back this morning.'

*

One month later we left Oruglica for good. During that period Peter and I carried out one other similar attack with fair success. Before our departure we wirelessed base a demand for the arms and equipment necessary if we were to undertake the hundred and fifty mile journey through the mountains to Mihailović's headquarters. Our boots were worn and we needed ammunition and portable rations. Base promised to send us a plane load.

Somehow the secret got out, and the Serbs discovered that we were to receive a sortie. We prepared the fires and waited through two nights when the weather was unsuitable. On the third night the plane came but, no longer needing to remain in favour, the Serbs had not been idle. Spies had observed our preparations and, when the first of the approaching aircraft was heard, exact replicas of our fire plan twinkled out amongst the hills in neighbouring Četnik areas. I later heard that competition to 'steal' the drop had been so intense that even a group of peasant women in one of the villages had laid out fires too. Fortunately we alone knew the correct code signal to be flashed by torch, so the load arrived at its proper destination. Some months later I met the pilot of that Halifax and he recalled the occasion at once as the 'time when Yugoslavia had looked like Piccadilly Circus on Guy Fawkes night'.

We started our journey in March, arriving at Headquarters six weeks later. The journey was remarkable only in that such a large group of British could travel in uniform without interception by the enemy's occupying forces and by the time we arrived our party had been increased to sixty heads by the addition of the crews of two crashed American Flying Fortresses.

I saw Mihailović once. He was a wiry, studious-looking little man, with a huge black beard and glasses. He looked a professor, rather than a great commander. Though a bad soldier, he was a brilliant guerilla. The Germans never caught him, although they offered thousands of pounds for his arrest. In those days it seemed impossible that Tito ever could capture him.

The airfield was short but the Dakotas came. On the first night the RAF piloted them and the first to leave hit the trees at the end of the runway. Advised by his leader to limit his load the second took only eight men and things looked bad. Next day it seemed that the RAF were having second thoughts about the pickup when suddenly the USAAF took over and sent in a large number of planes, combining the pickups with drops to Tito's Partisans and lifting only a few men in each plane. Wisely our Mission Command had packed the first two planes with American bomber pilots.

I was detailed for the fourth aircraft, and found myself sitting opposite Sehmer. The engine roared, the pilot released his brakes and we bumped forward along the rough runway. Slowly, ever so slowly, as we gained speed, the shaded hurricane lights marking the border flashed past. Watching through the open doorway I counted them – eleven, twelve, thirteen, fourteen – that was the last light, I remembered, waiting for us to pull up; then our wheels lifted, bumped again, and lifted – and I watched the ground dropping away below. Exhilaration at my release, regret at our failure . . . I knew not what to feel. Our small successes, our tragedies . . . The plane banked and the stars shone through the door. I turned my head to look at Sehmer and our eyes met. We each knew that the other was thinking back, a full year ago, remembering that other night in a cave when Smith and Blackmore died. If we could have called for

a plane then? . . .
Ninety minutes later we landed in Southern Italy.

COMMENT WITH HINDSIGHT WRITTEN IN 1986

Reading the preceding chapters I feel that I was less than fair to Bora Manić. Less amenable than Stefanović and Andrejević, he was both physically and intellectually a big man. My insistent demands for sabotage action without regard to reprisals, Partisan attacks or the Mihailović on/off veto – and my ruthless playing off of one leader against the other – must have tried his patience sorely. My official Mission report shows that drops to my Mission in seven months brought in only sufficient arms for 300 men, a miserable quantity divided between three brigades, when compared to the tens of thousands of tons thrust into the hands of their mortal enemies, the Tito Partisans.

It is indeed remarkable that the Četniks cooperated to the extent that they did and that they did not take us hostage when our masters abandoned them and denounced them as collaborators. American sources show that Manić continued subsequently to succour and pass on crashed Allied bomber crews in spite of Allied-supported Partisan attacks on his positions.

A fair-minded observer reading my story must recognise that the Četniks were indisputably patriots and that they constituted a genuine resistance movement. Yet, in the atmosphere of Titomania which has manipulated thinking on the subject, an incident, such as I related, where Manić did a deal with the local Nedić guards in order to get the Bulgar troops drunk so that we could pass by on a sabotage mission, would surely become recorded as another incidence of Četnik collaboration!

The SOE files are still kept under wraps at the Foreign Office. However copies of our Mission reports and an operational log are now available in the War Office files in the Public Records Office and make fascinating reading. Inter alia they prove incontestably that, contrary to the pundits' pronouncements, effective sabotage with help from the Četniks was carried out by myself and at least two other British Missions – one of them also on the key main line to Skoplje –

and that our attacks were actually being stepped up when the decision to abandon Mihailović was taken.

These files make nonsense of the fashionable wisdom that the Četniks in Serbia were straightforward Fascist collaborators from early on. Rather the Mihailović Mission HQ exchanges with M04 Cairo indicate that Mihailović had to contend with vacillating, provocative and even deceitful treatment apart from a lack of material and moral support.

The truly massive assistance given by the Allies to Tito from the autumn of 1943 – which equalled in some days what Mihailović had got in two years – ensured Tito's victory in the Yugoslav Civil War and spared the Red Army the bother of manipulating the position as they did in Poland. It is sad and unworthy that objectivity and balance have been lost in the frenzy to rationalise and justify what was a cynical exercise, whatever its expediency.

The Četniks lost everything – other than their honour – but they gave the Allies a lesson in good manners. History should have the grace to recognise that.

CHAPTER ELEVEN

Back to the Fleshpots

From the moment our Dakota touched down at Bari airport, events seemed to flash by as in an intoxicating dream.

The reception party at the airport; hand-shaking and year-old vintage jokes, resuscitated for our benefit; that nightmare first drive to our hotel, the street lights flashing past at a terrifying pace; the bottle of Scotch whisky, weak stuff after the *rakija* to which we were accustomed, which Peter and I knocked back together; the luxurious bedroom with a private bath and, best of all, the clean white sheets on the bed.

Before getting into bed, I piled my clothes carefully on a chair with my boots alongside. It was only as I was examining the bolt of my sten to leave it loaded and ready by my pillow that full realisation of my surroundings awoke. I stripped the gun, emptied the magazine, and with a wonderful feeling of complete exhaustion, slipped between the sheets. Thirty seconds later I was asleep.

We had been accommodated in the officers' club, a palatial hotel overlooking the harbour. Accustomed as we were to roughing it in mountain huts we wallowed in the comfort of the place. The most insignificant things were an unending source of pleasure; hot water in the taps; a shave and haircut in the barbers shop; scented soap; an easy chair . . . The civilised way of life, however, had a few disadvantages. For the first two days the traffic was terrifying and I often hesitated for minutes before crossing the road; then, sleeping with one ear listening for the murmur of engines heralding a supply sortie, I was awakened by every plane circling the nearby airfield; accustomed to a 'breakfast' of strong *rakija*, we all suffered severe physical discomfort waiting for the bar to open at noon.

Our old clothes were taken away to be burned. With regret, I handed in my sten and ammunition when we were given the run of the quartermaster's store. The unit accountant arrived with money; the messing officer with a crate of whisky; the doctor brought his stethoscope; a clerk telegraph forms. Everyone was charming, everyone helpful. In every way we were made to feel welcome on our release.

Until: the second morning after our arrival, Peter and I decided to go round to the office to find out what was happening in Yugoslavia. I considered asking about opportunities to go back again, perhaps to some other part, possibly Slovenia or Croatia, somewhere where there would be no Četniks and no civil war. It seemed a pity to waste my knowledge of the language and the experience I had gained.

We found our way easily enough. The warden at the desk, saluted.

'Good morning, sir. Whom do you wish to see?'

Peter answered, giving, in turn, the names of the various staff officers dealing with Yugoslav affairs. As he mentioned each one, the clerk shook his head.

'I'm sorry, sir, the major is out', and again, 'I'm sorry, sir . . .'

We went back again the following afternoon.

'I'm sorry, sir . . . in conference . . .'

They assured us that we were welcome. Perhaps our opinions were not.

*

After a week, the novelty of civilised living wore off and I started to think of the future. Then there came news of the Allied invasion of Europe: big advances in Normandy, hard fighting in Italy, the devastating Allied bombing of Germany itself . . .

Within ten days of my arrival in Italy, my mind was made up. The war would be over soon, if I marked time I should miss it all. I must go off on another job, somewhere, at once, and be 'in at the kill'.

Orders came to report to the officer in charge of personnel. At his office we queued for interview. When my name was called I went in, saluted, shook hands and sat down. My personal history dossier lay on the table.

'Well, Lees, what do you want to do?'

Presuming that I should be employed automatically on a similar mission again, I asked him, 'What are the alternatives, sir?'

'Well, you can go back to your regiment if you want to. Let me see, you were Parachute Regiment, weren't you?'

'Yes, but –'

'There's a brigade somewhere near here. Or I suppose we could give you some form of staff job.'

I interrupted him. 'No, sir, I want to go on another similar operation.'

He looked slightly surprised. 'Oh, do you? Well you must go on leave first. We'll send you to Cairo for a month or six weeks.'

'But I don't want to go on leave. As I know the language and the people is there any reason why I should not go back to Yugoslavia to some entirely different province?'

'I'm afraid you can't go there again. Nobody who has been with Mihailović is allowed back. You'd better go on leave and we'll think up a job for you.'

Again I felt as I had when Peter and I had been rebuffed in the office: they're afraid of our Yugoslav opinions.

For half an hour we argued about the leave. Apparently it was the regular rule that everyone should take a month's leave after returning from a Mission.

Eventually I lost patience. 'You can't order me on leave, sir. I'm not mental or odd in refusing it. I just happen to believe that the war will finish soon, and I don't want to hear the news over the radio in Shepheard's Bar.'

'All right, you can stay and prepare but we probably won't send you off for a month. Would you like to go to Hungary?'

Bitterly disappointed, I did not mind where I went as long as I got a job. I accepted with alacrity.

One by one the others dispersed, some on leave, some back to their regiments, a lucky few home to England, until I alone remained at Bari. Embittered by the course events had taken, the majority wanted a change. Peter had managed to arrange an air passage to Cairo and I went to see him off. In the car driving to the airport we discussed our plans for the future. Peter explained . . . .

'I'm going to Cairo because I can find out much more there. At GHQ they'll know about jobs in England and the Far East, as well as in this theatre. I want to find some form of soldiering similar to what we've been doing but without one's hands tied by politics all the time.'

'I couldn't agree more, but I think we've just been unlucky. Also the war will be over soon and I don't want to miss the kill searching around for the Utopian Mission.'

Peter was sceptical.

'Don't you worry about the war finishing. It's sure to last through another winter. Apart from that, I should not be too optimistic about going to Hungary if I were you. I had to wait three months before dropping last year and they were rushing chaps in then.'

If I had been as far-seeing as Peter, I should have joined him on that plane to Cairo.

The transport Dakota stood on a tarmac park beside the runway with its engine ticking over. We shook hands.

'So long, Peter. If you stumble into anything good let me know and I'll try to join you.'

'Of course. I'll send you a wire. Good luck.'

The days dragged by slowly and I fought against the apathy which threatened to encompass me. Waiting for evacuation from Yugoslavia we had endured months of frustration and inactivity but at least there had been occasional moments of excitement to break the boredom. This was different. Each day, tanks, freshly unloaded at the docks, rumbled past, heading north; officers on a few days leave from the front sat around in the hotel foyer swapping reminiscences of new battles; daily reminders of the war which was passing me by. I pestered the authorities to give me a promise or at least to fix a date when I might expect to be off. Always I got the same answer: nothing was fixed yet. Nothing this month, certainly; possibly during the next moon period. They wouldn't guarantee . . .

In desperation I wrote out an appreciation, detailing a suggested operation in which I would drop in alone to neutralize a certain important rail junction in the Balkans. My plan was turned down as too hazardous. This annoyed me, as I considered my experience qualified me as a better judge of the risks involved.

For a change of air and surroundings, I moved from Bari to an unfurnished villa some miles to the south. I shared the villa with another officer whose employment was similar to mine . . . waiting!

My companion, Andrew, born of Swedish parents in England, was British by nationality and held a commission on the General List. Good looking, and friendly, he had been educated in England spending only short holidays in Sweden. He had come to Italy about a week previously from North Africa. He too, hoped to go to Hungary.

We had been at the villa about three days when Andrew asked me to join a dinner party he was arranging at a little Italian black market restaurant in a town a few miles from Bari.

'We'll only be four. I've asked my sister and another girl.'

'I didn't know you owned a sister around these parts?'

'Well she's not really my sister; she's my sister-in-law. She's a nice little person. I think you'll like her. She's working as a staff officer in headquarters.'

As was the usual custom, permissible in those days, we took a service truck to collect the girls. They lived with half a dozen others in a bungalow overlooking the sea. We pulled up in the drive and knocked on the front door. Feet scuffled inside, and a voice called out:

'Who's there?'

Andrew shouted our names and we were ordered to walk round to the verandah and help ourselves to drinks whilst our companions finished their preparations.

A tray with glasses and soft drinks had been put out ready on a table. A bare arm appeared through the window curtain offering a bottle of whisky. Andrew poured out two strong ones and a few minutes later two girls came out, patting their hair and smoothing their frocks.

One was tall, dark, and vivacious. A mop of unruly hair set off her pleasant face with very striking large brown eyes. She wore a red frock with a white printed flower-pattern, and was introduced as Anne. Andrew's sister-in-law, Gwen, was a small, stocky, capable-looking person. Tidily curled hair, perfect features and a firm mouth gave her a look of hardness but that first impression was belied by her eyes, sometimes grey, sometimes green, large and kind under long black lashes. She was simply dressed in a plain blue frock, with white sandals, her legs bare. Andrew greeted her vociferously. It was the first time they had met since his arrival in Italy and they were soon engaged in animated conversation, discussing their respective adventures since leaving England.

Talking to Anne, I had a feeling I had seen her somewhere before. It transpired that she worked as a secretary in the office which controlled the 'Joes'.

'I'm having a battle with that colonel of yours,' I remarked.

'Oh, why? He's a poppet!'

'Doubtless, but he's a bit too much of a poppet to me. He seems unduly concerned about my health of mind and body and is determined to make me spend my time gallivanting around at parties in Italy instead of doing a job of work.'

She thought for a moment . . . .

'I remember now. You must be the chap who refused to go on leave?'

'That's quite correct.'

'They all think you're a bit mad,' announced Anne.

'That can only help to prove more conclusively that the staff officer mentality is out of sympathy with that of the combatant soldier. I'm quite harmless really.'

'Well, I'm afraid they hold the whiphand. If they don't want to use you, there's nothing you can do about it.'

'That's what I'm afraid of; only I wish your boss wouldn't prevaricate.'

The restaurant at Polignano was hidden away in the squalid back streets of the town. At the top of a rickety outside stairway we were greeted by a cheerful Italian maître d'hôtel, who conducted us to a table in a private room.

Gwen sat on my left. Completely unaffected, she talked intelligently in a clear quiet voice. Andrew and Anne giggled together, gossiping and laughing over the latest scandals.

Gwen talked interestingly about her job; she appeared to be completely absorbed in it – I was glad to find one person at least who had the interests of the 'Joes' at heart. She told me that she worked in the signals department, planning frequencies and other technical matters.

'You don't by any chance have anything to do with supplying wireless equipment to missions in the field?'

'Yes, that's all part of my job. We have to equip people before they go off and see that they have everything they want. If communications break down we have to find out what's wrong and if possible send any replacements necessary.'

I remembered the months I had been without a charger for my batteries. Surely this girl was not responsible.

'Oh, it looks as if you're the Aunt Sally I've been looking for. When did you start your job?'

'I came out from England about Christmas last year,' she answered.

'In that case you're saved. By Christmas I'd given up trying to contact base as a bad job. But before that I only wanted a tiny little generator, nothing else, for which I waited in vain for six months.'

Gwen looked at me queerly.

'What was your wireless name?'

When I told her, she burst out laughing.

'So you were that station. We wiped you off the slate as incorrigible.'

'Incorrigible be damned!'

*

With nothing else to occupy our time, Andrew and I often visited the bungalow during the following week. The girls worked in nearby offices and we used to hitchhike the thirty odd miles from our villa, arriving in time to lunch at their mess. Then, as they worked tropical hours, in the mornings and evenings only, we spent the afternoons below the bungalow, lazing on the rocks in the hot July sun and diving off at intervals into the clear blue sea.

We dined again at Polignano. Andrew had arranged a larger party and organised a small string band to play. Half way through dinner they struck up a foxtrot and couples moved onto the floor to dance. I sat on Gwen's left and we talked quietly through the first dance. When the band struck up again, this time with a slow waltz, Gwen asked me:

'Don't you dance?'

'To be honest, I'm so bad, I'm far happier sitting and talking.'

With a charming natural smile she stood up. 'I want to dance with you, come on.'

I unravelled my legs from under the table and stood up, towering a foot above her head. I warned her. 'I'll be heavy on your toes, keep them well away.'

I noticed how well she cared for her shapely, capable-looking hands.

After dinner the band played classical Italian music. Sitting on the balcony, looking out over the sleeping town I felt my nerves, pent up by frustration and delay, relaxing in the soothing atmosphere. For the first time in weeks I forgot my impatience in contentment and happiness.

About a mile from our villa there was an officers' mess where Sergeant Carter had set up his, by now, famous bar. I often wandered over there in the evenings to drink and play poker with the 'Joes'. Carter was the same as ever, a little plumper perhaps, but still the same hardworking, helpful philosopher. One evening I had been over there to play cards with Andrew and a few others but by midnight I had lost enough money for one evening, so I returned home to bed.

Some hours later I was awakened by Andrew barging into my room. I started to curse him, but he interrupted me.

'Wonderful news. I've got a job.'

I woke up immediately and pestered him to explain.

'After you left, a chap came in and I got talking to him. Eventually he told me that he was going to North Italy soon, to open up a new area. He apparently doesn't like the chap assigned to go with him and was looking for somebody else. Finally he asked if I'd like to take it on.'

'Excellent but what about going to Hungary?'

'Oh damn that! I don't think that's ever coming off. I'll get out of it somehow.'

I was inclined to agree with him. Our plans for Hungary were still nebulous in the extreme.

'Oh, by the way, who is this great benefactor? His name isn't Temple, by any chance?'

Andrew looked surprised. 'Yes, it is. Do you know him?'

I knew Temple well. Having been introduced in Cairo, before I went to Yugoslavia, I had met him again on a short course which we had both attended about a week previously. The son of a famous pianist, he was a charming rather cosmopolitan person and a great athlete. We had passed the time pleasantly enough, on the course, playing practical jokes on the good-humoured instructors and at the time he had mentioned to me that he wanted someone else but, stupidly, I had not pushed the matter further, thinking that my orders would materialise soon.

'You're an opportunist,' I remarked enviously, 'but I rather think you've made the right decision.'

For the next few days Andrew was busy with his preparations. His room became piled with odds and ends of equipment; wireless sets, tommy guns, rations and clothing. No orders had materialised yet regarding my future and I found myself visiting the bungalow more and more often till the journey became a daily affair.

Sometimes, when I had been lucky in obtaining a lift in a fast car or jeep and arrived early before the morning's work was finished, I would go to Gwen's office and potter about amongst the wireless stores or sit on the verandah reading a novel whilst she finished her work.

One day we decided to organize a picnic supper party on the coast near our villa. We made the most elaborate arrangements, conserving our rations carefully for some days ahead, to enable us to provide a palatable dinner. Andrew arranged to bring three members of the Polignano band and I scoured the countryside for some bottles of good wine.

When the day came, assured as we were during the Italian summer of a clear blue sky, we were lucky in that the sea was calm and the evening warm. For our party we had chosen a little cove which was hidden away and unfrequented by Italians or British troops. It was a beautiful spot, quiet and peaceful. Though less than fifty yards across, it was perfect for bathing, its sandy bottom showing silvery clear beneath twenty feet of water.

It was the perfect setting. As the sun sank behind the hills to the west phosphorescent twinkles shone in the sea which lapped soothingly against the rocks. We dived and swam, ate and bathed again, till, comfortably tired, our senses dulled by the rich red wine and the murmur of the sea, we lay back on the rocks to listen to the band. True Italians, they entered into the spirit of the party and accompanied softly by an accordion the violins played sweet, tender airs: La Traviata, O Sole Mio, Sante Lucia.

Overcome by the spell, I lay back wishing that this could last for ever. Unconsciously I moved my head till it lay resting against Gwen's outstretched legs and turned my face to feel the soft, firm flesh. A nebulous dream became reality and I realised for the first time that I loved this girl, outwardly cool, efficient and practical but underneath so feminine and real. The war was distant . . . it did not matter. Nothing mattered if only I could stay there by that little bay, always, with the music playing softly and the whole world in tune.

Morning brought reflections. I tried to over-ride my feelings and told myself that all I wanted of life was to be given the opportunity to taste the excitement and interest of the mountains again; that I must not let anything interfere with that object; that my feelings were the natural outcome of meeting any lovely woman in romantic surroundings after months spent in purely male company. But the more I tried to disillusion my mind, the more sure I felt in my heart.

Desperate, I determined to put an end to the situation. I went direct to the officer in charge of North Italian activities; I had never met him before but I barged into his office without ceremony, told him my name, and asked if he needed any officers. Surprised at my behaviour, he asked me if I had any previous experience. I told him about my work in Yugoslavia, adding that I was prepared to do anything in any capacity, provided that I was sent on operations at once. He looked at me carefully, searchingly.

'You seem unusually determined. As a matter of fact, we will be wanting people soon and you might do. If you can persuade your people to let you go I'll promise you something within a month.'

Exuberantly I talked over the various possibilities. I left with no definite task agreed upon but, with that promise to hearten me, I felt elated as I walked away from the office. But as my excitement wore off reaction set in. If only this could have happened a month sooner, if only I had not arranged that party last night, if only I didn't know. I felt uneasy. Was I running away from life? Was I afraid of being forced into a decision? 'But you're not being forced into a decision!' I told myself. 'It's only a passing infatuation. When you get back to work you'll soon forget it.'

I found myself at the crossroads; ahead a small lane wound away up the hill to the villa; to the right the wide arterial road stretched like a ribbon across the flat countryside towards Bari in the distance.

It was not yet noon. I had intended to return to the villa right away and to forgo my daily visits to the bungalow. Now I faltered; the heat haze glistening on the tarmac road winked at me. It seemed to say: 'What does it all matter? Enjoy yourself while you can. Go to the bungalow – for the last time if you like. Just to tell her your news. Why hurt her? You will if you shun her.'

It was a hot day and I was sweating hard. Behind, the sea glistened clear and cool, beckoning, inviting me to those rocks where we bathed together.

A jeep buzzed past: the driver looked questioningly at me but I waved my hand. I decided to compromise . . .

'I'll stop the first truck that comes, whichever way it's heading I'll go with it. Damn and blast you,' I added to the winking tarmac.

A staff car drew up and an officer leaned from the window.

'Do you want a lift?'

Without asking his destination, I opened the door and got in. The driver let in the clutch, put out his hand, and swung the wheel to the right.

*

During the week I managed to extract some details of the job I was to do. It was suggested that I should drop at the end of August to the Italian Partisans in the north western province of Liguria, somewhere in the area to which Temple was being sent. I was warned that I might be taking a war reporter with me, as it was considered advisable to publicise the resistance of the Northern Italians in an effort to obtain better co-operation from their southern brethren in the liberated territories. I wondered how the war reporter would despatch his copy from enemy-occupied territory but was informed that he would take his own W/T set and signaller for the purpose. I pitied the signaller who would have to handle pages of extravagant journalese, every word to be coded and tapped out in Morse.

CHAPTER TWELVE

Journey to Pino

We were staying at the officers' club near the operations aerodrome, which was some way south of Bari where we had been married. The last month had passed in a wave of ecstatic happiness. That deep contentment and perfect joy which can only come once in a lifetime had been mine. A miraculous change had come over Gwen. Gone was that hard look. Her eyes sparkled and her mouth twitched in constant laughter, making dimples in her cheeks. Only one discordant event had come to mar our gaiety together. Andrew, who had dropped some nights previously, had been reported wounded and missing.

Ironically enough, I had been detailed to take his place. We had taken off once but after three minutes in the air the plane had been forced by engine trouble to crash land back on the aerodrome. Now I was waiting for suitable weather to try again.

The evening came and we drove to the airfield together. It was dusk when we arrived. Aircraft stood dispersed around the drome; the great black shape of a Halifax loomed ghostly in the fading light. Around its belly men moved quietly, and unconsciously they pitched their voices low. The scene was quiet and still – this gateway to the other life.

A faint cool breeze stirred the air; feeling Gwen shiver and clutch my hand, I cursed my selfish thoughtlessness in bringing her there.

'I think you'd better go back now.'

She held on harder. 'No, I'd like to stay.'

I did not want her to because I knew how she would feel as we took off, standing alone and straining her eyes to catch a last glimpse of those lights on the wing tip, red and green, before they merged into the night.

The suspense was shattered by the splutter of engines starting up . . .

'Come on, you must push off now. I've got to get my 'chute on.'

I helped her into the truck. Morris, the driver, had been given strict instructions what to do.

'Please come back. Look after yourself for my sake.'

'Of course. Thank you for being *you*.'

Reluctantly I took her hands from my shoulders and placed them together in her lap. One last look, deep into her eyes, searching for all those wonderful things we had known together . . .

'Au revoir!'

'Bon voyage!'

As the truck turned the corner of the airfield, half my mind went dumb. I turned back mechanically towards the plane.

My companions were a war reporter, an artist, and one Italian. The reporter, Paul Morton, was a frail-looking man of around thirty years of age. He had waited some weeks for an opportunity to join the Partisans. A pleasant enough fellow, talkative and outspoken, I was rather worried about him. He complained of a strained ankle contracted during his training jumps and had tied every conceivable form of bandage and brace around it as a precaution against further injury. For good measure he wore rubber pads on every part of his body that might conceivably come into contact with the ground, so that his final appearance was somewhat like a foreshortened Laurel prepared to be Hardy on a motor cycle.

The artist, Geoffrey Long, was charming and very keen. Loath to be separated from his paper and chalks, he carried them in a bag suspended from his chest. He was about the same age as Morton and was small and very slightly built. He was thrilled at the opportunity of being the first war artist to drop to the Partisans.

I was deeply impressed by the last member of the party. He was a well educated Italian, whom we knew as Roberto. He was calm and determined, belying the concept that Italians are by nature hysterical.

My orders were brief. We were to be dropped to a ground on the edge of the plain south of Turin, about thirty miles north of Temple's hideout in the Maritime Alps. The reception would be organised by a group of Partisans commanded by a Major Mauri.

I was to make contact with Temple to be put in touch with the local situation. I took no wireless equipment with me, as Andrew's operator, who had not been captured, was still in that area and would be at my disposal. Morton and Long were to remain with me until I managed to contact Temple when they would come under his orders. Roberto would leave us immediately on arrival, to carry on with his separate task.

The aircraft throbbed on its way through the skies. Flying first due north up the Italian mainland, we turned west over Rome and headed

The wedding of Mike and Gwen Lees: Major Charles Maidwell (best man), Commander Hume Hendersen, FANY, the author, Gwen Lees, Maj-Gen Stawell, Anne St Paul Butler FANY

Wedding group. August 1944. Bari

Secchio village. Mission HQ with Mount Cusna in the background

(Left) Scalabrini, American Italian who commanded my dropping zone very successfully and very dangerously. *(Right)* Secchia valley, winter 1944/45

out to sea; then turned north again, crossing the coast at the Italian Riviera, to climb over the high mountains separating the sea from the Lombardy plains. It had been hot in Southern Italy and would be hot too in the plains to the north. I was dressed only in shorts with a battle dress tunic and a light parachute overall. High above the mountains the draught of cold air forcing its way through cracks in the hatch pierced my clothing and made me shiver; I moved forward to the warmth of the navigator's compartment.

As I sat down the pilot turned round and beckoned me forward to his cockpit perched high in the nose. He took off his mask and shouted, pointing below. I looked down at the fierce black tracery of peaks and gullies below. A good hideout, surely, if food were available. We were due to drop the stores here and then fly further north to the flatter country for our descent. Temple had signalled that his ground was too rocky, suitable for stores but not for bodies.

I remained with the pilot, seated alongside and finding a pair of earphones, I put them on and plugged in to the intercom. As we crossed the highest peaks we throttled back to lose height. Dead on time the bombardier called up:

'Light to Starboard'.

Looking down as the pilot banked I saw a tiny red speck flickering below. Then other fires glowed till there were twelve shaping a square. In the centre a torch flashed intermittently.

I went back to help despatch the stores; after two circuits the task was finished and the plane turned, climbed and headed north.

Ten minutes later, as I felt the plane bank and turn again, the despatcher signalled us to get ready. I fixed the static line from my parachute pack to the strop marked 'one' and hooked up Morton, Roberto and Long to the others.

A puzzled look crossed the despatcher's face as he listened in to his earphones. He leant down and spoke to me . . .

'Pilot says we're over the target but no fires have been lit.'

We circled around, moving further afield and searching the dark countryside, but we could see nothing below and, as the plane banked to turn back again, there was a sudden jolt and the fuselage rattled.

'Flak!' explained the despatcher, laconically. 'We're too close to Turin.'

Ten minutes later when the pilot called up again I took the earphones.

'Pilot speaking. I can't find the fires. We'll have to turn home soon, as we're short of petrol.'

Turn home . . . that contingency had never occurred to me. What would it mean. Days, perhaps weeks, waiting for another fine night and an available plane. I would be with Gwen again, but would we be happy with that constant shadow of separation hanging over us? She knew too much about our work living always in its atmosphere. She had said farewell bravely but I knew that underneath she was gravely shaken. Could she stand another parting? No, another return must be avoided at all cost. Apart from that, this was the last day of the moon period. That meant we should have to wait at least ten days when, weather permitting, we might try again. The American Army in southern France was pushing forward and had reached the frontier. This area might be over-run soon; if we were to be of any use we must drop tonight.

I looked at the others. Would they think the same? There was no time to ask them; I could find out later. If they wished to return with the plane they could do so. I was sure they'd all agree to drop. I spoke back into the intercom:

'If you can't find the flares, take us back to the mountains and we'll take our chance on Temple's ground.'

The pilot's voice crackled in my headphones . . .

'No, sir, I can't do that. I've had specific orders. That ground is dangerous.'

'Then drop the Italian and myself, blind, at the place you think the fires should be. We'll take our chance.'

'I'm sorry, sir . . .'

'I'll take the full responsibility.'

'No, sir.'

He was a sergeant pilot but in the plane he was in charge.

'All right. But give us every moment you dare.'

After a long pause while he checked his fuel tanks, his voice came back again.

'I'll take a risk and try for fifteen minutes more. But we will probably not get back to base. I'll have to land somewhere near Rome.'

I took up position again and waited, wondering what thoughts were passing through their minds as I watched the expressions of the others around the hole. Disappointment, relief, frustration, determination – all showed in their faces.

I had almost given up hope when the despatcher smiled and jerked his thumb. He shouted:

'Fires below. Pattern's right. No signal, but pilot will drop if you wish.'

For answer I slipped my legs into the hole and nodded tersely, gripping with my hands as the plane banked round to run in. The despatcher leaned down:

'Pilot says the drinks are on you.' He held out his hand. 'Good luck!'

The red light . . . I tensed my body. Paul sat opposite. I glanced at him and grinned encouragement . . . red . . . the engine fluttered . . . green . . .

It was a perfect night; under the moon the country shone clear as a map beneath me. I floated, swinging lazily in the warm night air. Three fires in a line blazed on an open patch which looked like a village green. A church spire which pointed itself at me was surrounded by a cluster of small houses. In three directions white roads stretched away and I cursed the bloody fools who had chosen their ground so badly; if one of us hit those houses, he would certainly be injured. My legs swung forward jerking apart and through the sight they formed I could see the steeple, three hundred feet below, levelled directly at my body. A ridiculous fear beset me: I should be impaled on the weather cock and there would be no ladders long enough to reach me. The Germans would come and find me there. How undignified a fate.

The earth rose up towards me as the steeple floated past to one side. I pulled on the lift webs, holding tight till suddenly the ground came into focus ten feet below. I released the straps, allowing the parachute to belly wider, thus checking my descent. The silk rustled and my feet hit the ground.

I slipped quickly out of my harness; the sleeping village lay fifty yards to my right; just in front of me the fires were untended, dying to embers.

There was no sound of movement in the darkness and the place appeared deserted. I had expected to find a large reception party and becoming suspicious of the silence I moved to the cover of some bushes, quickly assembling the sten gun which I carried in a bag across my chest.

While I lay there, I could hear the plane come roaring in for its second run. I fumbled for my torch, wondering whether to signal it away. Then three men rushed up and pounded my discarded parachute which lay open on the ground in front. One glance at these ragamuffins reassured me that this was no trap set by the enemy.

I whistled to them and rose from the bushes. They rushed up, looking astonished and gesticulating excitedly . . .

'*Americano? Inglesi? Tedesci?*'

In halting Italian, I explained that I wasn't German.

'*Bene, bene, Americano?*'

'No. *Inglesi.*'

My nationality decided, we were stuck. They rolled up my parachute and we walked to the fires where another group had materialised. I asked if any of them talked French.

An emaciated middle-aged man wearing a leather jacket introduced himself as Major Antonio and stated that he was in charge of the underground movement in that village. One glance at his men convinced me that they must be very subversive indeed. Antonio asked me:

'Where are the stores?'

'There are no stores. Just four parachutists.'

'But there must be stores as well?' he insisted.

'No. Just our personal kit,' I explained apologetically.

'Oh.' He looked crestfallen.

It was obvious that we had been dropped to the wrong reception party. I told him to send out men to bring in the other parachutists and find the three packages containing our personal kit which had been dropped with us.

When the villains had departed on their mission, I set about determining our exact location and found that we were about thirty kilometres north of the target in a province of low rolling hills. Antonio explained that the local Partisans were organised in small groups of ten to forty men and eked out a precarious existence, hiding in the woods by day and coming to the villages for food at night.

He informed me that the area was well served with roads and that in many of the villages there were fascist or German garrisons, the nearest of them being only four kilometres away. This made central command of the Partisans an extremely tricky task, so each group operated independently, conforming only to the general policy laid down by higher command. The divisional commander, Nani, had no fixed headquarters and no staff, spending his time visiting the various units in turn.

'Have you heard anything of a British major in these parts?'

He answered reservedly, 'I heard that one had arrived but I don't know where he is. We are not in contact with the British.'

'Well then, why do you put out fires?'

He looked away.

'We have orders from our commander. He tells us what patterns to use. We put them out whenever we hear aircraft.'

His manner as well as his words awoke my suspicions. I wondered how this wandering commander Nani obtained his information as to the correct fire plan. Clearly he could not know the correct torch signal, which was changed every day.

I asked Antonio if he knew where the groups of Partisans, commanded by Major Mauri were located. He looked uncomfortable and answered brusquely:

'They are Badogliani.'

The Badogliani were the right wing group named after Marshal Badoglio who surrendered to the Allies. For the main part this faction comprised old units of the Italian army who had escaped to the mountains when the Germans came to disarm them after the capitulation. Temple was working with the Badogliani formations.

'Are you not Badogliani then?'

'No, we are communists.'

As he answered I heard a shout from the road and a group of men approached. Paul was amongst them. He came up limping heavily.

'Hullo. What's happened to you?'

'B . . . it I've strained my ankle.'

"Oh, I'm sorry. That's a curse. I thought those bandages an straps would have supported the weakest leg.'

Paul sounded embarrassed. 'It's the other bloody ankle.'

Controlling my laughter I asked him if he had seen anything of Long or Roberto. He told me that the artist had landed safely and was on his way but he had no news of the Italian.

I sent the men off to search again and sat down to think out the situation. Remembering the political embarrassments in Yugoslavia, I wondered whether the communists and the right wing parties had a similar relationship towards each other here. It was clear what had happened. For some reason, possibly enemy activity, Mauri had not prepared our reception as ordered. Hearing the aircraft cruising around, these people had put out fires in the hope of stealing a load destined for their rivals. They must have been bitterly disappointed when four bodies only arrived on the scene.

I should have to weigh up their political opinions carefully before deciding on the next move. I wondered whether they would put difficulties in our way when I came to explain that I was leaving to join Temple with the Badogliani.

Men arrived carrying the packages containing our personal stores, and we opened them up to sort out our kit. Geoffrey Long joined us intact, having landed on the road about half a mile away. In as few words as possible I explained the situation, advising them, as we were in dangerous country, to get their kit properly sorted at once so that if we had to move quickly they could jettison any surplus.

At that moment a messenger came running up with news of Roberto. He had been injured on dropping and they were carrying him in on a ladder.

Leaving Paul, Geoffrey and I went at once to meet them, and found the party halted beside the road. Roberto lay propped up on a ladder, with his parachute under his shoulder. He smiled wryly.

'I'm afraid my thigh is broken. I landed in a tree and released myself. It was a long way down.'

'Are you all right on that ladder?'

'They are getting a cart. I think that will be better.'

As he was suffering considerable pain, I took a morphia ampoule out of my pack and gave him an injection.

The leader of the squad pointed to a village which showed up in the moonlight across a small valley.

'Fascisti – cento.'

The village could be no more than half an hour's march from us. If they came to know that we had landed things would be difficult with a sick man on our hands.

After a seemingly interminable delay, a rough farm cart arrived. It was drawn by a shaggy pony and had been filled with straw. We lifted Roberto carefully inside. He endured the movement bravely, groaning quietly only when we jogged his leg.

Back at the village I sent for Antonio. There was no time now to worry about our plans for joining Mauri. It was three o'clock in the morning and we should have to get Roberto securely hidden before dawn.

Antonio suggested a house in the village but I turned that down at once because he admitted that he could never hold out if the Fascists attacked in the morning. They would soon discover that there had been a sortie there during the night and would assuredly search the place.

Eventually he suggested a small farmhouse in the woods, about two miles away to the south which, he added, was the hideout of another Partisan group commanded by a Frenchman but, to the best of his knowledge, the enemy was unaware of the fact. That sounded better. Taking half a dozen of his men as escort we started off. The morphia which I had given Roberto had begun to take effect and he was lying more comfortably. I leant over to ask him:

'Have you any secret documents with you?'

He nodded.

'You'd better give them to me,' I suggested.

He thought for a moment. Then he reached into the inside pocket of his jacket and handed me a thick envelope.

'And my money?' he asked.

'No. Keep that. I'll let you have these back when we've got you into a safe place.'

The cart moved slowly. After an hour's journey we turned off the road onto a farm track up which we climbed to a ridge and entered a thick wood which stretched away to the valley on the farther side. A short way down we came to an isolated farm building.

One of our guides had gone on ahead to give notice of our arrival and some men were coming up the path to meet us. I noticed that three of them carried British-made sten guns; one of these introduced himself as the formation commander.

Jimmy, the Frenchman, was a wiry little man about thirty years old. He wore shorts, a flannel shirt and a pair of old gym shoes through which his toes protruded. His arms and face were burned almost black by the sun and he looked as hard as nails. He talked incomprehensible argot, gesticulating and blaspheming wildly. I liked him at once. After the rather insipid Major Antonio it was reassuring to find this little dynamo.

We carried Roberto upstairs and put him to bed. Rather than mess about trying to set his broken thigh Jimmy despatched a man for the nearest trustworthy doctor. Roberto was dressed in civilian clothes but we took away his parachute and all other equipment which carried British markings, leaving only his revolver placed ready to hand under the edge of the mattress. I gave him another morphia injection and he was soon asleep.

Dawn was breaking when I came downstiars. Paul and Geoffrey lay stretched out asleep in the yard with their heads resting on their pillowed packs.

I felt tired too but there were many things to be done before I dared rest. Using Antonio's men I collected together our parachutes and the empty packages which had been brought up on the cart. As an afterthought I added my pack keeping only ammunition, one blanket and a small haversack of the barest necessities. I had a feeling that we should have trouble very soon and I knew that Paul and Geoffrey would have difficulty in carrying their kit unaided. Apart from their ample personal equipment Paul had a typewriter which he declared he would never jettison as it was irreplaceable even in liberated territory and Geoffrey had a stock of heavy blocks of drawing paper packed into a bag with his paints and collapsible easel. Against my advice they were both armed with revolvers only but they would have had difficulty in carrying ammunition for a more effective weapon.

With my map spread out I questioned Jimmy about the locations of all neighbouring garrisons, marking them in with pencil, while on a loose sheet of paper I made notes about the Partisan formations. I asked him what he was doing in Italy and he replied that he had been with the Maquis in southern France but had been captured by the Germans. Escaping he had crossed the frontier into Italy before the Allied invasion in the south. He had met Nani who offered him command of this formation. By the way he talked I could tell that he was uninterested in local politics.

'Are there any Badogliani groups nearby?' I asked.

'Yes, there's one about three miles away.'

'Do you have anything to do with them?'

He answered frankly.

'We help each other when the enemy attack and we exchange intelligence reports but otherwise we avoid them, though I personally have nothing against them. This isn't my country and its politics don't interest me but sometimes the men quarrel when they meet.'

'There's never been any warfare between you?'

'No. There have been little incidents of course but now they keep to their territory and we to ours; we're both under orders of the Underground National Liberation Committee in Turin who direct the Partisans and keep the peace amongst them.'

Jimmy seemed reasonable. I thought he would probably help.

'How can I get to see Major Mauri?'

He spat pensively. 'Mauri. He's a long way from here. If you want to join him, you'd better get in touch with Nani, the divisional commander. He's got a motor car in which we could send you by night. It would be difficult to walk there because you've got to go through the plains which are heavily garrisoned by the Fascists.'

'And how do I find Nani?' I asked.

'I can send a courier if you wish.'

I wrote out a note to Nani, explaining that we had been dropped into his area by mistake. I pointed out that we had orders to join the British major with the Badogliani and asked him if he could provide transport or guides to take us as far as Mauri's formation. I wrote in

French in the hope that, if he did not speak it, he could find someone else who did. Jimmy did not know Nani's exact location at the time but he sent off a man in civilian clothes on a bicycle to find him and promised that my letter would be delivered by the following day at the latest.

Jimmy's men were an assorted crowd. Their clothing was ragged and their boots threadbare. I noticed that a number of them wore dirty bandages over fleshwounds and they told me that they had received a number of casualties in recent actions in nearly every case from mortar fire because the Fascists, affectionately known as the Brigata Nera, or Black Brigade, always preferred to fight at long range with mortars rather than close with the Partisans. Jimmy's formation was about fifty strong and fairly well armed; apart from the three British sten guns they had five Italian Breda light machine guns, a number of Beretta sub-machine guns, and rifles.

My fears of early action by the nearby garrison were realised when, about an hour after dawn, firing broke out from the direction of the village where we had landed. A few minutes later our patrols came in to report that the Fascists had occupied the village and that Antonio and his men were retreating in our direction. I asked Jimmy what he was going to do, and whether we could move Roberto to a safer place, but he assured me that as regards the injured man it would be better to keep him where he was. He explained that there was no really secure guerilla base in the province and the Partisans depended solely on their mobility to avoid being wiped out. He suggested that we try to hold the ridge above and, failing that, we should withdraw in another direction, attempting to divert the attack away from the farmhouse.

Reluctantly I agreed to leave Roberto alone, as I realised that he was not fit to be moved about the woods and that, if we tried to fight a last ditch battle around his hideout and were overcome, as assuredly we should be, he would stand no chance of passing himself off as a harmless civilian who had broken his leg on a bicycle, which was the cover story we had concocted for him. I hoped that the bogus identity papers, which he had prepared in Southern Italy, would allay any suspicions.

On the ridge above, Jimmy deployed his small force. I noticed the efficient, clear manner in which he gave out his orders and the excellent siting of his light machine guns. When his sections had been moved into position, Jimmy announced that he was going forward on patrol and invited me to join him. With the only alternative prospect of sitting on the ridge waiting to be attacked, I readily agreed, hoping to get a closer view of the enemy and to study his methods.

We moved forward, keeping clear of the track, until we came to the edge of a small copse looking across the dropping ground where we had landed to the village about four hundred yards away. The road on which Geoffrey had fallen wound back and passed just below where we lay hidden.

I searched the village with fieldglasses. Groups of men in shorts and black shirts stood around mounted machine guns, while their comrades hustled in and out of the houses. It appeared that there was a general search in progress and I applauded last night's decision not to leave Roberto there. I wondered if they had yet acquired knowledge of our presence. In a once Fascist country, there must surely be a few remaining sympathisers amongst the civilian population.

As we watched, the troops concluded their search and formed up into column. They seemed to be about a company strong and had two carts drawn by mules, presumably for transporting their mortars and other heavy weapons. Jimmy nudged my shoulder.

'Come on, we'll set an ambush on the road.'

We slipped back through the copse; once out of sight of the village we set off at the double to join the main party. As I staggered along, trying to keep up with the indomitable little Frenchman, I cursed my heavy marching boots and equipment.

Arrived at the top of the ridge Jimmy whistled a call for his section commanders. When they came running up he gave out a sharp string of orders and they went off returning a few minutes later each accompanied by four men armed with sub machine guns. Jimmy collected the groups around him and started talking again. While he was thus occupied I looked around for my British companions.

They were sitting together under a tree. Geoffrey was hard at work with a small drawing block and a heavy black pencil and he had already completed half a dozen sketches, chiefly drawn from memory, depicting various phases of our journey so far. With a grin he showed me one extremely uncomplimentary reproduction of myself when I had been sitting at the edge of the hole in the Halifax, glaring at the despatcher as he warned me we might have to turn back.

I explained the situation and told them that I was going down onto the road with the ambush party. Geoffrey wanted to come but I persuaded him that he would be able to see everything from where he was and he might have time to do a quick sketch. Then, with twenty men, we moved to a spot about half a mile below where the road wound through a small cutting.

It was a perfect place for an ambush. Thick bushes grew along the edge of the road and a wall of firs stretched to the gully. We deployed along both sides, picking covered positions within twenty yards of the road. When we came to withdraw we could follow through the trees for about two hundred yards and after that we should have to break across open country but Jimmy had arranged that the light machine guns above would give us covering fire when necessary.

I checked over my sten gun and settled down to wait. Jimmy estimated that the column would take around thirty minutes to arrive along the tortuously winding road.

Time passed slowly; it was now after ten o'clock and the sun glared down from a clear blue sky. The little white villages nestling into the rolling hills gave the countryside a peaceful look. Just below our position a farmer tramped slowly across his field, driving a herd of cattle before him, and farther afield I could see through my glasses peasant women, trotting in and out of their cottages carrying water and wood, with children running at their heels. The leaves of the trees beneath which we lay hidden were turning to their autumn tints, some still green, some coppery, some a glorious gold.

It all seemed so unreal. Why were we crouching, when all around was peace? I relaxed drowsily, reflecting that we must not fire; it would be sacrilege to desecrate the serenity of this pleasant scenery. I awoke to a nudge on my shoulder. Half conscious, my mind far away in happy dreams of the past, I stretched out an arm to brush her silky hair. Jimmy nudged me again.

'*Mon Capitaine*, they are coming,' he whispered.

By then wide awake, I rolled over and edged across to peer through the bushes. As far as the corner the road was clear but we could hear the tramp of heavy boots approaching.

I loosened the bolt of my sten, moving the gun to a ready position. On either side the Partisans crouched, invisible to the casual eye. It seemed that we had the perfect position. If everyone could be constrained to hold their fire, we should do considerable slaughter.

As I listened to the approaching footsteps my mind went back to Yugoslavia again. Things had been different there. My first battle had finished in slaughter but we had been the victims. Now we had the initiative and I intended to exploit it to the full. I felt a warm feeling for this ragged band who showed such aggressive spirit.

A soft whistle ... the men came up to a crouching position alert and waiting as the sound of voices talking Italian reached us; Jimmy whispered, *'Fascisti'*.

A group of men rounded the corner, marching in straggled formation across the road. I let them close. Surely they could not be Fascist troops, raggedly dressed as they were, without caps and with their arms carried anyhow! The leader wore a brown leather jacket. I relaxed as Jimmy burst into a roar of laughter and stood up for our would-be victims were Major Antonio and his ragamuffin band.

He related briefly that after searching the village the enemy had departed for their base. He warned me that they already knew of our arrival and would probably return when they had managed to round up some reinforcements. We climbed back to our main positions and Jimmy called in his men and sent out a party to collect some food. Having ascertained that he intended to remain in position till dark I unrolled my blanket and lay down to sleep.

But I was not to be permitted to rest that day. Within a few minutes we heard fighting again and an hour later the attack on our position started. Shells began to fall and we snatched an occasional glimpse of trucks moving along the road below. For a time we held out but, when the real attack developed, Jimmy gave orders to break away. Sending off a small party in the opposite direction with orders to show themselves occasionally, we slipped back to headquarters at the farmhouse and within a matter of seconds all evidence of Partisan occupation had been destroyed. I ran upstairs to see Roberto but the doctor had arrived and I found him busy setting his broken leg with a wooden splint. In a few words I explained the situation and took a last look round to make sure that nothing incriminating had been left in the room. Roberto was confident and cheerful as I wished him good luck and slipped out.

The Partisans had already left but a guide waited outside to show me the way. We set off down hill and a quarter of an hour later found the others resting in a small glade. Jimmy explained that he was waiting for patrols to report; he suspected that we had experienced only part of a concerted attempt by the enemy to surround us.

The day passed in a whirl of activity. The little Frenchman had prophesied correctly and rumours poured in of enemy forces in all directions. We dashed hither and thither, sometimes making contact and firing a few shots, then breaking away again. Buoyed up by tension my weariness had left me but Paul limped heavily, finding it difficult to keep up. Both he and Geoffrey were handicapped by their heavy packs and I urged them to bury their surplus equipment, warning them that if we got into a tight corner they might lose the lot; but they were determined not to be parted from their tools and refused to jettison anything. Towards evening the attack wore off. The enemy, finding us too elusive to catch even by day, had withdrawn to their billets for the night.

It was just getting dark when we heard a burst of intensive firing just over the hill and a wild-eyed apparition appeared carrying a letter. The newcomer wore a battle dress tunic with the Italian colours embroidered on his collar and I noticed that he did not carry the red star of the communists in his hat.

The news that he brought was excellent. His formation, a unit of the Badogliani, had cut off about fifty Fascists in a small village a mile away. They were barricaded in a school house and the Partisans had sealed all possible routes of escape but needed assistance to finish them off. He urged us to hurry because the Fascists would certainly attempt to escape as soon as it was dark.

We arrived on the scene just in time. The enemy had made an attempt to break out but had been repulsed with some casualties. While Jimmy deployed his men I climbed to an upstairs window of a nearby house to watch the proceedings.

The school was a narrow one-storey building about fifty yards long. By the flashes of fire coming from it, I judged that the enemy had three or four light machine guns, one of which was mounted in the roof of the porch. An open playground lay between my house and the building and on the far side was a church with a tall pointed steeple. The Badogliani had a considerable number of men, occupying posts in the houses and the church, and I gathered that others stood guard on the road leading in, against a possible relief attempt from outside.

On our arrival we had met the commander of the Badogliani formation. At an amicable conference with Jimmy he had suggested that his men remain in their present positions and open up heavy fire on the building while the communist formation closed in. At a given signal firing would stop while Jimmy led a grenade attack. I asked if they had demanded the surrender of the Fascists.

'But they would never surrender to us,' answered the Badogliani leader.

'Why is that?'

'Because we always shoot the Brigata Nera,' he answered naively.

It was absolutely true. I was to discover later that a Fascist was executed immediately on capture. Rough justice maybe but if, in their turn, they caught a Partisan, they were not above torturing him before handing him over to the firing squad. For obvious reasons the Brigata Nera could not take reprisals against the civilian population, so the Partisans lost no popularity by their ruthless policy. Any Germans captured, however, were treated as prisoners of war and held as hostages. I was rather amused to hear that on one occasion a number of German prisoners had been released in exchange for a truckload of salt, of which commodity the Partisans were badly in need at the time.

In a few minutes the action was over. Bottled up as they were in the dark, the enemy never saw the men creeping up on them. Half a dozen grenades burst simultaneously, tommy guns rattled and resistance was overcome. An occasional shot from inside the school signalled the cleaning up process.

By the time I arrived, the booty was being collected – four Breda light machine guns, thirty rifles and a small mortar were stacked outside the school.

It was then that trouble started. The two formations who had been excellent friends in adversity, were quarrelling angrily as to whom the loot belonged. The Badogliani claimed it as theirs, stating that they had cornered the enemy and would have finished the battle on their own if we had not interrupted! The communists loudly declared them to be cowards who fought from the safety of houses leaving the dirty work for someone else.

When things began to look really troublesome I intervened. Using Jimmy as an interpreter I told them to shut up and divide everything evenly and, surprisingly enough, they did not resent my interference and both parties agreed readily. They were soon allies once more and, with some wine stolen from a nearby cellar, we drank to our success.

By now I was completely exhausted and was relieved when Jimmy gave the word to set off for home. As we left the village and started through the woods I heard angry voices raised behind us. Apparently our rearguard were engaged in political argument again but I left them to it as I was, by then, interested in nothing else but a chance to rest.

It was eight o'clock when we reached the farmhouse in the woods where Paul and Geoffrey were already sleeping soundly in a hay loft. I went upstairs to visit Roberto who recounted his adventures of the day, relating how the enemy had passed by just above the house but, diverted by our decoy, had not stopped to search. His leg was comfortable and seemed well set.

After leaving him to sleep, I sat for a moment downstairs, smoking a last cigarette and thinking over all that had happened during the last twenty-four hours. The night was warm and still and the scent of hay hung in the air. I liked this green and fertile countryside; unlike the hard Balkan mountains, it was a human place. Most important I liked these people amongst whom by sheer chance we had arrived. They were aggressive and co-operative – the only two qualities which matter in a guerrilla and, thank God, they treated their politics with a sense of humour. I was sorry that we had to leave them soon. Stubbing out my cigarette I walked round to reassure myself that sentries had been posted. Then, climbing into the loft alongside Paul and Geoffrey, I was soon sound asleep.

*

It seemed less than a minute later when I felt someone shaking me. A voice penetrated through the cloud of sleep that had engulfed my exhausted mind and body.

'Get up, sir. I've brought a car for you.'

I pulled my blanket closer around me. What was this pest muttering about?

'Shut up, blast you. Go away and let me sleep.'

Then suddenly I realised what he had said. I rolled over, opened my eyes and sat up. Silhouetted against the dim light of the doorway I could make out a huge black figure.

'Say that again, slowly.'

The voice responded, speaking with a broad Scots accent . . .

'I'm William, sirr. I've come to take you to Nani.'

'Did I hear you say something about a car, or was I dreaming?'

'Yes, sirr; a nice little job it is. I stole it yesterday when we got your letter.'

'You mustn't do that sort of thing. You'll get sent to prison and I'll be an accessory after the fact!'

Pulling myself together I stuck out a finger and prodded the apparition. It was solid certainly, very solid. Rolling over I kicked Paul in the stomach.

'Wake up and tell me if I've got hallucinations. A large Scots lunatic seems to have got into this God-forsaken place!'

Paul grumbled, searching for his torch. A thin line of light picked out the now silent figure.

William McClellend was about six and a half feet tall, and almost as much across. His ferocious face and heavy jowl, extensively covered with a thick black stubble, was creased in a devilish grin, the effect of which was not enhanced by gaping voids in his yellow teeth. Beneath these terrifying features his broad chest was encased in an aged battle dress jacket, the shoulders of which were adorned with the faded insignia of the Scots Guards. A pair of shorts, ski boots and a slung sten gun completed this surprising picture.

William talked incessantly as we collected our kit together. He had been captured at Tobruk by the Germans and was sent to a camp near Turin. On the Italian capitulation he had escaped with some others to the Val d'Aosta on the French frontier and joining up with the Partisans there he had spent the time since wandering from one formation to another. During the last month he had been with Nani and when my letter arrived he had volunteered to collect us. Being by nature averse to walking, he had stolen the nearest available car because, according to his statement, the owner was a Fascist, and had driven over after dark.

Not without regret I bade farewell to Jimmy and his band. They were certainly pulling their weight and I felt I would have liked to stay to give them the support they so badly needed.

William advised leaving Roberto where he was for the present. He stated that the roads were none too secure and that we might have to abandon the car and take to the country. He told me that Mauri had a number of cars and captured German lorries and suggested that, when we had contacted him, we might send back a strong escort to collect the wounded man.

We found the car parked in the lane on the far side of the ridge above the farmhouse and, after twenty minutes violent jolting down a rutted cart track, we turned onto the road. William switched on the headlights, changed into top gear, and started talking.

The journey took two hours. For the whole of that time we were regaled with a constant flow of anecdotes as, detail by detail, William recounted his adventures with the Partisans. We heard how he had captured cars, raided Fascist cellars, abducted Fascist girls. How he had ambushed German staff cars and looted the pockets of their dead occupants; how when the Partisans were short of funds he had staged a bank robbery. In all their lurid details I am convinced that the tales were basically true, if only by virtue of the raconteur's forthright naivety in openly admitting, quite unconsciously, that every operation was planned with the idea of his own personal, or the Partisans' collective, gain. William came from Glasgow and I felt that he was a truly worthy scion of the Chicago of England.

Major Wilcockson, the author, Corporal Bert Farrimond and priest: Don Carlo, the Green Flames Brigade Commander

The mission: Hugh MacGlade (escaped POW), Peter Lizza (interpreter), Angiolino (Don Carlo's brother), Farrimond, the author

The barn near Albinea where Partisans hid 'Gordon' (Glauco Monducci) and the author after they were wounded in the attack on the German HQ in the Villa Rossi

I asked him if he had ever made any attempt to rejoin the British forces. He replied without evasion that, in the early days, he had made an attempt to get south but, finding the countryside hostile and lacking maps or contacts, he had been unable to travel further and had turned back to Genoa. I was not surprised when he went on to say that he enjoyed being with the Partisans and could see no reason why he should leave before the liberation.

I will give William his due: he was a bandit, not a Partisan, but he had certainly pulled his weight. His nefarious activities must surely have caused the occupying forces considerable worry and inconvenience and, whatever his intentions, he was doing far more for the war effort than he could have done serving as an ordinary private soldier. In the latter category too, I think his original ideas would have been a little out of place. One William in the mountains was an incomparable asset but thirty Williams in barracks would provide a problem with which I should hate to be faced as a platoon commander!

These views were confirmed later. He was well known amongst the Partisan leaders; in fact, on a number of occasions, he had been offered the command of sub-units but he always preferred to remain on his own, temporarily joining whichever formation happened to have the most adequate stock of food at the time. Nani described him as an oddity but stressed that everyone admired his daring and initiative. They certainly took note of his advice; this truly remarkable Scotsman was a throwback to border days.

We followed a tortuous route, twisting and turning, climbing, descending. Sometimes our driver turned off the engine and headlights to coast past a dangerous spot. At one moment we would be merrily bowling along a main road, suddenly to pull up and turn off across country, bumping along farm tracks or even open fields, to rejoin another road further on. William seemed to know every track and every gate and he picked out his way unhesitatingly, never overshooting or turning back, never halting to look, his monologue continuing without pause and without encouragement. Eventually we turned through white gates down a gravel drive and drew up before an imposing mansion. William stopped the car, climbed out and ran round to open the door.

'Nani is staying here, sir. I'll take you in. Then I must take the car into the woods and hide it.'

We went inside to a pleasant hall. Despite the warmth of the night a log fire blazed merrily in an open grate at one end of the room which was full of heavy, ornate furniture arranged around the walls. William whistled and an answering hail came from above.

Two men came into the room from a door in the opposite wall. One, who was small and grey with twinkling eyes, walked across with his hand held out and greeted us in Italian, introducing himself as Giuseppe, owner of the house. His companion who was tall, thin and aquiline carried himself with a slight stoop but his step was that of an athlete. His hair was dark and straight, his eyes jet black, set in a face tanned almost black by the sun. If he had been dressed differently he might easily have passed as a Pathan from the frontier of Afghanistan.

Speaking English slowly but grammatically, he introduced himself as Nani, commander of the Garibaldini division.

Nani was indeed a striking figure: dressed plainly in a khaki shirt and shorts, his sunburnt arms and legs bare, he carried no insignia or badge of rank. But the most astonishing thing about this influential leader was his age. Although his eyes showed a depth of intellect and full maturity he looked no more than twenty-three at the most and I later discovered that he was only twenty-one, though his compelling personality commanded absolute obedience from men his senior by twenty years.

William bustled off outside and Nani suggested that we might be hungry. Agreeing readily, we followed him to the next room where food lay ready. He sat at the table with us, while Giuseppe fussed around. I had already decided to be absolutely honest with Nani so, telling him why we had come and where we wanted to go, I demanded his help.

He listened carefully and when I had finished he sat thinking for some time.

'Of course I'll do everything within my power to put you in touch with Mauri. I must admit that I would far prefer that you stay with us and help my division. We Garibaldini have received little Allied support whereas the Badogliani receive much supplies. However, as you say, you are a soldier and you have your orders.'

'Thank you.'

Ignoring my remark, he went on.

'Unfortunately we have no transport at this moment. The car you arrived in tonight was only captured this morning and I have no stocks of petrol. Even if I had, it would be unsafe to undertake the journey in one small car without escort. You could march to Mauri's headquarters but that again is tricky because you must cross the plains and it is a long journey. If you would be disposed to remain here temporarily I could send a courier to Mauri and ask him to send an escort over for you.'

I agreed to his plan at once. Nani promised to despatch a letter as soon as it became light and we went on to talk about other things.

We soon fell to discussing the favourite subject of all resistance movements – politics. But I was very impressed by the open and honest way in which this communist leader talked about his own and other parties. This attitude seemed to be general wherever I went in Italy. Partisans were quite dispassionate in their views and, apart from minor bickering, there were no serious quarrels between groups of different sentiments, whereas in Yugoslavia one had only to mention the other political faction to be treated to a display of propagandist invective worthy of the Great Doctor Goebbels himself.

In northern Italy the resistance movement was composed of Partisan groups of various political creeds – the Badogliani, the Garibaldini or communists, the Action Party, the Social Democrats, the Christian Democrats – to name a few. All these troops came under the direction of the Committee of National Liberation in the nearest big town, to which Committee they each elected a representative member. The Committee worked in secret, representing themselves to the occupying forces as ordinary peaceful citizens and, apart from direction and co-ordination of the Partisan effort, the Committee undertook to obtain and distribute funds.

Nani stated that numerically over the whole country the Garibaldini were by far the largest party but, owing to their dispersion and the Allied policy of supporting the strongest group in any particular locality, they had received little or no material help. He was in no way bitter about this, recognising that, provided the arms were despatched and someone used them, the final object of assisting the Allies to the full would be attained but he complained that, whereas his men, all veterans, were fighting with inadequate equipment, the Badogliani had received more arms than they had men to use them. Rather than hand over the surplus to their rivals they had recruited new men, till the state was rapidly being reached where there would be a glut of Partisans in the mountains reducing mobility and rendering the already difficult food situation impossible.

His argument was very sound. Half a dozen daring guerrillas can achieve far more than half a thousand bad ones. However good its material, when a resistance movement becomes an army it is inevitably vulnerable, losing mobility and becoming very difficult to supply.

Nani stressed that he did not want to increase his numbers in the field but he asked for modern weapons with which to equip his present forces. The surplus would be cached till the day when the Allied armies approached and, then, only issued to sympathisers to be used in the general uprising. Wisely, he foresaw another winter in the mountains and intended to keep his forces small until the hard days were past.

Although I should have liked to do so I made him no promises that night except that I should put forward his case. As we finished our preliminary talk, William returned to report that the car was hidden, and we were led upstairs to a comfortable bed.

As good as his word, Nani sent off a courier at dawn. When I awoke and came downstairs I found him already hard at work poring over a map as he prepared a report on all his forces and enemy locations in his area for me to take away. I settled down to read over what he had already written and to ask questions.

It was a glorious morning. Through the window the sun shone brightly, glistening on the dew-soaked open countryside. The house, which was situated on the top of a crest, had been built on a ledge overhanging an almost precipitous thickly wooded slope overlooking the plains a couple of hundred feet below. Behind the house a plateau stretched back for some hundreds of yards before it broke up to join the rolling country beyond. What a wonderful base this place made! – For an attack, it was close to the enemy's life line, the roads of the plains but secure in defence with that steep forest in front and Partisan country behind. I noticed that Nani had dispensed with all guards, remaining here alone except for his host.

The day wore on quietly until noon when, just as we were sitting down to an appetising meal, a peasant came in to warn us that he had sighted an enemy column about two miles away behind the house. Grabbing a bottle of wine and some food off the table, we went out together to investigate. We followed the road by which we had arrived the previous night across the plateau till it swung across, hugging the contours of the ground. In front the ground fell away across a valley to a village perched like a fortress on a ridge about two thousand yards distant. The peasant pointed out the direction from which he had observed the enemy to be approaching and Nani explained that the column was probably heading for that village where a Partisan detachment was based. We sat down under the cover of some bushes to watch for further developments.

We had not long to wait. Within a few minutes of our arrival, mortar shells started to fall on the top of the ridge opposite us and we saw the Partisans double out from the houses to mount a machine gun in a commanding position. During the next two hours we were treated to a demonstration which brought back memories of a young officers' tactical course in England. Sitting in comfort nibbling my lunch, I felt like an umpire at a training camp on Salisbury plain as, through field glasses, I enjoyed a grandstand view of the action.

Little black specks appeared crawling over the crest as the enemy scouts edged forward. They halted, checked by machine gun fire, and a runner doubled back. Then we saw a party of signallers arriving with a telephone and a few minutes later shells were directed towards the machine gun position. Forced to withdraw, the Partisans doubled back covered by fire from the village and the enemy column wound up into view. Again they were halted and the same process repeated, as the Partisans forced the enemy to deploy at every place where they could harass the advance.

As it entered the village we obtained a wonderful view of the column. It appeared to be a company of Brigata Nera and comprised about two hundred infantryman supported by a section of artillery armed with two outdated mountain guns. The guns and transport wagons were drawn by oxen, thereby considerably reducing the mobility of the troops. Realising this, the Partisans drew the infantry into short skirmishes, breaking off contact before the sweating crews could get their weapons into action.

Geoffrey was delighted at this performance. Staring through his glasses and sketching rapidly, he drew some excellent action pictures while Paul, muttering journalese, scribbled busily as he concocted a colourful account. After a while the column passed out of sight and, as we were by then convinced that they were not heading in our direction, we returned to the house.

I received a letter from Mauri the same evening and he gave a rendezvous to which he promised to send transport to collect us at noon the following day. William said that he knew the place which was on the edge of the plains about five miles from our present position.

After a good night's rest we bade farewell to Nani and our host and set off on foot. William led the way, keeping amongst the wooded foothills and heading towards the south. Avoiding all roads, we passed only an occasional peasant who stared at us oddly, asking no questions but hurrying on with frightened glances.

Around eleven o'clock William turned sharply to the left; we followed him, making our way steeply downhill, until ten minutes later we joined a dusty track leading to the main road which skirted the edge of the plains. At the junction William called a halt, stating that this was the rendezvous.

As we had three quarters of an hour to wait, William suggested that we should hide ourselves while he went off to forage in a village about three hundred yards distant along the main road. He slipped a peasant's cloak around his shoulders and slung his gun beneath, out of sight. I walked back with Paul and Geoffrey around a corner of the side road and sat down by the ditch. Geoffrey was busy with his pencil and paper so, asking him to keep watch, I turned on my back and drowsed in the sunshine, my senses lulled by the hot sun and gentle breeze murmuring in the crops.

Some minutes later Geoffrey leant over and whispered:

'There's something coming up the road.'

I sat up to listen. Far in the distance there was the faint throb of a motor cycle, cruising slowly, alternatively ringing clear then dying away as its rider negotiated the bends of the road. Then the throb was joined by another and further away I could hear the rattle and rumble of some heavy vehicle. It was not yet half past eleven – early for our escort to arrive and that heavy rumble sounded more like a small tank than any private car owned by the Partisans. Geoffrey gave voice to my feelings:

'I wonder if it's our escort or a German convoy?' he asked.

'I'm not sure. We'd better keep under cover.'

We crouched in the ditch, our heads below the level of the low hedge, with our guns ready. Paul knelt behind me, a revolver in each hand. Laughing, I asked him:

'Can you hit anything, cowboy?'

'I can if it's close enough in front.'

'Well don't forget in your excitement that I'm on your side.'

The rumble of traffic drew close till, with a roaring of engines and banging of doors, it halted at the junction of our lane. Very suspicious by now, we crouched down well out of sight.

The sound of voices came from the road. Then footsteps sounded, walking towards us.

A dozen men rounded the corner. One glance at them set our minds at rest. They could be nothing else but Partisans. Furious that they should have found us huddling ignominiously in the ditch, I climbed out summoning what little dignity I could muster and stalked forward to greet them.

At the road an astonishing sight met our eyes. Expecting a clandestine journey in one or possibly two small cars, I was amazed at the effrontery of this Partisan show of force.

In front were two motor cycles; a small one and a heavy German model complete with side car and mounted machine gun; behind these were parked three vehicles: a huge open diesel-engined lorry, a gleaming limousine and, in the rear of the convoy, a small armoured car! But it was the Partisans themselves who made the picture. About forty of them, every man armed to the teeth, they wore brightly coloured squares of parachute wrapped around their heads and knotted at the nape of the neck. Sashes of similar material around their waists served as holsters for pistols and knives. Dirty, their clothes ragged, they might have walked straight out of a scene from Treasure Island.

William had by now returned carrying food and wine in a basket and he was greeted effusively by the Partisans who appeared to know him well. Their leader was keen to get started; so we climbed into the car, settling ourselves comfortably on the upholstered seats.

The Italians piled into the lorry, clambering onto the roof and the bonnet when the back was full and, with a roar of engines, the convoy moved off. Behind us, bumping and crashing over the rough road, the armoured car raced to keep up.

After a short distance we turned off the main road. Following lanes and tracks the route twisted and turned through the fertile plain. Sometimes we halted while the motor cyclists went on ahead to see that some dangerous point was clear. Then we turned onto a major road and, after following it for a few hundred yards, turned off again on the other side. On these occasions the armoured car would go ahead taking up a commanding position until we had gone through. Once, when we rattled over a level crossing, I was interested to see that the permanent way was rusty and obviously disused and William explained that guerrilla and bombing attacks had rendered the railways useless to the enemy.

We reached the foothills on the far side of the plain without incident and, as we climbed into Partisan country, we were halted again and again by crude wooden barriers erected across the road.

Towards evening we turned off the road down a rough track leading to some old farmbuildings. In the yard were parked two other cars and a pile of empty containers and parachute material betokened the presence of the unit headquarters. The escort leader opened the door informing us that we had reached our destination and that Major Mauri was inside.

The sentries at the door intrigued me. They were all boys of not more than sixteen years of age and were dressed in very tight shorts, khaki shirts and yellow scarves. I noticed others who were similarly dressed wandering around and, on enquiry, heard that they were Mauri's bodyguard. In common they were all youthful. One of them escorted us upstairs to a room furnished as an office, where a man rose from the table to greet us.

Mauri was a striking figure. Of medium height and build, he was about forty years old, with wavy hair greying at the temples. He was remarkably good-looking and had penetrating light blue eyes. His well-muscled legs were bare and he wore a three-quarter length rich fur coat hanging level with his tight-fitting abbreviated shorts which gave the impression that he was naked but for the coat. Without being requested to do so he spoke in carefully phrased but eloquent French. His mouth was full lipped and sensual – he lisped slightly.

'I am very glad you have arrived safely. I am sorry I was unable to come to meet you myself but I trust the escort were helpful.'

'Everything was arranged excellently thank you, *Monsieur le Commandant*. I am only anxious that we may continue our journey to join Major Temple as soon as possible.'

'I have arranged to conduct you tomorrow myself. We cannot go this evening because it is a journey of thirty kilometres and we have to obtain a further supply of petrol. I have arranged for you to stay tonight in Marsaglia, which is a village about two kilometres from here where we will dine together.'

Mauri clicked his fingers and a boy of his bodyguard came into the room. Ordering brandy, he returned to his desk.

'If you will excuse me, I must finish some work that I have to do?'

'Certainly,' I answered, 'but, while I remember, I must just ask you one question. Why did you not put out the fires for our aircraft the other night when we dropped?'

He answered suavely, 'Ah yes, we had notice that you would be coming but a company of Brigata Nera had pushed up close to the dropping ground and I thought it wiser not to give the signal.'

Outside the french windows there was a little verandah; Geoffrey was leaning over the railing watching the mechanics at work on the armoured car parked below.

'Geoffrey, what do you think of the great man Mauri?' I asked.

'He's got a wonderful face. I'm going to ask him to sit for me.'

'Yes, I quite agree he's very handsome. But what was your impression of his character?'

Geoffrey thought for a moment. 'I don't know. He's very striking but there's something odd about him.'

'I couldn't agree more. I wish I knew what it was. All this show – his men dressed up to look like angels and pirates. He's got a large force under his command, but yet he was put off arranging our reception by a small force of Fascists. There is something odd about him; at the back of my mind I know what it is but I can't grasp it yet.'

Geoffrey was silent, staring at the yard below. I was thinking of other things when he replied:

'Although I hated his politics, Nani didn't use scent!'

*

We were treated to a banquet at Marsaglia. Mauri had invited many of his officers to meet us and when we arrived they were already in festive mood. These commanders were all well-educated and worldly, most of them being ex-officers of the Italian Army. Their manners were charming, their poise excellent but, watching them, I wondered if they were as well-qualified to command as Nani, Jimmy and the other natural leaders who, on their own merits alone, had risen to power in the ranks of the Garibaldini. The failure of the Italian Army in the desert and in Eritrea was largely due to the inefficiency of the officers. Would these, who had failed so dismally in a disciplined army, succeed in the far more exacting task of leading a guerrilla force? They would be ruthless enough, of that I was confident, but had they those essential qualities of determination and initiative?

We left at dawn the following morning. Our convoy was similar to that of the previous day except that, owing to shortage of petrol, we had dispensed with the armoured car. In its place at the rear, I rode with Mauri in a captured reconnaissance car in which was mounted the latest model quick firing German machine gun. Again we were accompanied by a lorry load of decorative pirates, though this time the yellow silk scarves of Mauri's youthful bodyguard were predominant.

The journey was quite uneventful. We passed through the same barriers and once in the plains drove through the side roads, heading south towards the imposing wall of the Maritime Alps. We skirted close to Mondovi, a town which, Mauri informed me, contained a garrison of upwards of a battalion of Brigata Nera. Then, turning towards a cleft in the range in front of us, we followed a road up the course of a river till we halted just short of a small town at the foot of the mountains. A patrol went on ahead to ensure that all was clear and, on receiving confirmation, we drove into the market place.

As soon as the citizens had reassured themselves that we were not the dreaded Fascist or German forces, they turned out in force to give Mauri a vociferous greeting. In Marsaglia I had remarked upon his popularity but I was surprised by the exuberant welcome he received here now. I wondered why the civilians showed this particular liking towards the man. It might mean that they preferred his politics to those of the Garibaldini or perhaps that he did little to worry them. If he were a very active guerrilla, causing frequent retribution to fall upon their heads, surely they would not welcome him so readily.

Villanova was an attractive little town, sheltering beneath steep mountain walls. The river rippled merrily alongside the street, passing through a lock to a mill. The white stuccoed houses were well built and clean and the inhabitants proudly displayed the marks of bullets on the stone walls, received during a battle in which an enemy force had been ambushed the previous week. We had been met by guides from the formation to which Temple was attached and after a few minutes halt we climbed into our vehicle and followed them out of the town on the winding road into the mountains.

After twenty minutes stiff climb the road ended in a small village. This was the Headquarters of the Badogliani formation to which Temple was attached. Nestling into the side of the mountain, it had only one route of approach – the road up which we had come. This road was heavily barricaded and holes had been dug in the surface, ready for mines to be set there when necessary. The Partisans who met us were well armed but less flamboyantly dressed and more efficient looking than Mauri's men. Watching them greeting Mauri's men, an intriguing question suddenly formed in my mind and I started to laugh aloud. Geoffrey wanted to know what I was laughing at:

'Could it be possible' I spluttered. 'Mauri – could he be queer?'

Geoffrey stared, not following my thoughts.

'That odd look of Mauri's. Those young boys in his bodyguard – half naked. His own odd clothes, general flamboyance and the scent. It's unusual in an Italian and he is without doubt an outstandingly great commander and a tough customer but many of them are very interesting – I wonder?'

But the thought was interrupted. Bounding towards us in corduroy shorts, his brown face creased in a grin, came Neville Temple.

CHAPTER THIRTEEN

Journey from Pino

We shook hands warmly.

'Hullo, Mike. I'm glad you've arrived. How's things?'

'Fine. We were dropped in the wrong place, that's why we're late in arriving.'

'I'll say you were. You gave us a lot of worry. The morning after you dropped they came up on the wireless to say that the plane hadn't returned. Mauri reported you hadn't dropped to him and we all thought that the plane must have crashed. Base had you posted as missing for twenty-four hours.'

'And the aeroplane?'

'Oh, that had to land short of petrol north of Rome. They got back two days later.'

I was silent. If we had been reported missing for however short a time, Gwen must have known. It was all right now but what hell she must have been through the poor darling. I wished that she would go back to England and get away from the atmosphere of this job. It was such fun for those on operations but hell for our loved ones who had to wait for news behind the scenes.

For a time we talked about Andrew. It seemed that he had been captured on patrol in Southern France, only a few miles from the American liberated zone. I asked about the operator,

'That's a bit of a mess-up. When Andrew was captured he had already made contact with the Americans and his operator went to join them. He couldn't get back here, so there's no operator for you but that doesn't matter because I've more work than I can cope with here so I'll be glad of your help.'

I introduced Geoffrey to Temple, who already knew Paul. Finally I produced William, now shaved and smart, who brought off a parade ground salute.

'This is a professional bandit,' I explained. 'He's been pretty useful to us and he'll serve as my interpreter if there's nothing else for him to do.'

Temple told me about his Partisans. They were about five hundred strong and were commanded by a man called Cosa. Cosa, an ex-officer of Alpine troops was uninspiring in appearance but a very able commander. His formation was based in Val Ellero, the valley at the mouth of which this village, Prea, was situated and so far all enemy attempts to gain access to the valley had been repulsed.

Temple was very enthusiastic about his troops and he recounted their exploits in ambushing convoys and destroying enemy communications. Like Mauri's, they had captured a number of cars which were used for long distance attacks in the plains as far as Turin.

The dropping ground was located on a plateau some four thousand feet higher into the mountains. Temple had established his Mission Headquarters in a mountain hut about half way to this ground and an hour's march from Prea. A telephone cable connected him to the reception party and to the village.

A hard climb brought us to the hut, called Pino after a single colossal pine tree which grew in the yard. It stood three thousand feet above sea level and commanded a wonderful view across the plains to Turin, shimmering in a heat haze. Beyond, seemingly less than a stone's throw away, the mighty Alpine bastion outlined the borders of Switzerland and France. The Matterhorn, like a gigantic spire, pointed its peak towards the sky. To the west Mont Blanc showed up rugged and crude, the white of its snow-covered cap broken by grey windswept rock. A squadron of American Thunderbolts cruised around the sky, black specks against the snow on the distant mountains, then swooping down to be lost from view as their camouflaged wings toned in with the chequered countryside. We heard the rattle of their guns and an occasional white puff showed where some convoy or fortification had drawn the attention of the hovering airmen.

Close to where we stood, a thin grey figure sat hunched up on a stump of a tree. A map lay open on the ground in front of him and he held a field glass in his hands. Temple pointed to him.

'That's the admiral. He's aircraft observation officer.'

'Explain!' I protested.

'Poor old man. He joined the Partisans, but he's much too old for active work, so I took him on to sit up here on fine days when the fighter bombers are out. He keeps a list of targets which we hear about from Partisan intelligence sources and as they are bombed he ticks them off. Each night we send out chaps to see if they've been effectively destroyed or not. Then we're able to wireless through a list of outstanding objectives which gets sent on weekly to the Air Force.'

'Is he really an admiral?'

'Ask him,' said Temple.

Pino was the home of a very happy party. Apart from Temple, there were his wireless operator Farrimond, two American pilots, who were working as cypher clerks until such time as an escape route to liberated territory could be arranged, the admiral and a section of Partisans under an Italian subaltern whose duty it was to provide orderlies and guards for the Mission. The party was completed and, on occasions nearly exterminated, by a pair of mules who were inaptly named Aurora and Bella. They were neither beautiful nor docile but what they lacked in sweetness of disposition they certainly made up in liveliness of spirit.

I soon found myself engulfed in the daily whirl of Mission activities. Temple's time was taken up organising and directing the very comprehensive intelligence and sabotage activities of the Val Ellero Partisans. He was also in contact with the Committee of National Liberation in Turin and disappeared sometimes for days on end, dressed in various odd disguises, to keep clandestine appointments with mysterious agents. I took over from him the routine jobs of arranging for the reception of supplies by parachute and training the Italians in the use of explosives.

The autumn days were hot and dry, the nights cool. Marching daily to Cosa's headquarters in Prea, and climbing to the dropping zone at night, I felt my muscles hardening and was filled with a sense of physical well-being. Under our instructions the Partisans took shape, learning the use of their weapons and acquiring discipline and experience till, in a short time, they showed signs of becoming a trained and efficient striking force. Occasionally the enemy made weak attempts to push up into the valley but with the mountainous country favourable to us, our well-placed defences were too formidable for their second line troops and the situation on the front prohibited the withdrawal of the Alpine Division which they needed if they were to round us up. I looked forward hopefully to the day when, with the Allied armies pushing forward, we would be able to sweep down to clean up the plains.

Supplies were our only worry. The weather, so perfect here, had been bad in southern Italy and few sorties got through. There was also a shortage of aircraft and our allotment was small. Listening to the news broadcasts, we heard of large-scale support of Tito and his forces and presumed that many of the loads which might have come to us had been diverted there. Apart from purely selfish preference, I wondered if it was a wise policy to stake so much on the possibilities of the Yugoslav Partisans. From my experience of the Slavs I had to admit that they were more virile and better soldiers but I wondered whether, in a confusion of politics and civil war, they were actively or potentially as helpful to the Allied cause as these very amenable Italians.

The Italians were not particularly warlike and only desired that the war should finish soon so that they could get back to their music, wine and lovemaking. On the other hand they realised that, having declared war on the British and lost, they now had to work their way to some form of recognition as a free country after the war. Towards this end, they were ready and willing to carry out whatever orders they received through their liaison officers, unlike the Yugoslavs who, nationalistic to a degree, scorned interference or direction and busied themselves with their own private civil squabbles, to the detriment of their effort against the common enemy.

I passed many interesting evenings talking to the admiral about the Italian outlook on the war. He was a proud old man and had been a very important person in the Navy having commanded the Italian Fleet in the Adriatic and Dodecanese. Before the war he had commanded a squadron which had been sent to help the Falangists in Spain, and he told me many interesting stories about that rehearsal for total war.

Paul and Geoffrey were spending most of their time in the village with the Partisans and, when Temple was away, I passed many spare moments talking with the wireless operator. Bert Farrimond was the ideal type for his job; a dour Lancashire miner in civil life, he would never give up a task as hopeless. Sometimes when conditions were bad and he had difficulty in contacting base he worked away for hours, determinedly tapping out his call sign and never letting up till he got an answer. He only complained when there was not enough work to do and then he could be very tiresome. I found him to be a kindred spirit when he confided that his favourite peacetime recreation was wildfowling. He also confessed to having been a poacher of no mean repute and he described many ingenious and highly scientific methods which he had developed. He was a sportsman by nature, loved the life in the mountains and was in no hurry to return to civilisation.

I had been at Pino around three weeks when one evening, as I was just on the point of going to sleep in the hay loft which served as a dormitory, the admiral came in.

'There's a message from Major Temple. Will you go to the Partisan Headquarters immediately?'

I pulled on my boots and, running down the mountain path in the bright moonlight, I reached the village about half an hour later.

I found Neville at the inn; he had just returned from one of his clandestine expeditions. Dressed as he was, he could never have been recognised as an Englishman. There were two civilians with him. I shut the door after me.

'Hullo, Mike. Sorry to drag you out at this time of night. We've got to make an important decision.'

He introduced the two strangers. One was a professor from the University, who passed under the *nom de guerre* of Salvi[1]; the other was a lawyer by name Piva. Neville went on:

'As you know base are very keen to find out everything about the Liberation Committee and these two are members of it. They've volunteered to go to Southern Italy and report if we can get them out.'

'How are you proposing to do that?' I asked. 'By air?'

'Well, we've got no landing ground prepared, as you know. Mauri is building one in his area but God knows when it will be ready. This information from Turin is red hot and they also know a lot about enemy dispositions and weaknesses. We can't wait for the air trip. They'll have to walk out through the lines.'

'Into France?'

'Yes,' answered Temple. 'As they're going we must send the American too and I think our friends from the Press Department might join in the party. They've seen enough, and they can't get their work published while they stay here and, frankly, I'm rather bored with them. That makes six in all. Now Salvi and Piva are damned important and I don't want them to fall by the wayside. It's going to be a tricky journey because there are no guides who have been through before and the front is always changing. We'll give them an escort, of course, but I want someone who knows the ropes to command the party.'

As Neville paused, I realised what was coming:

'Would you like to go?' he asked.

It had never occurred to me previously that this contingency might arise. All my plans had been based on the assumption that I should remain with the Partisans until the liberation. But this suggestion opened up a new train of thought. I could see Gwen again. How I'd missed her and longed for her these last few weeks. Previously I had

---

[1] His real name was Professor Giovanni Bessone

been reconciled to an enforced separation but, now that it was possible to go back for a short time, I felt that I'd go through anything to do so.

Neville was talking again.

'You can take the party through to France. Make for the coast. We'll listen to the news later, but I think Mentone is in Allied hands by now. If you're with them they won't get held up by Security and you can beg a plane to take you to Southern Italy. You can report on everything we've been doing to the chaps at base and chivvy them up to send more supplies. Then come back again and drop with the first sortie.'

'All right,' I replied. 'I think it's an excellent idea. But I've got a little business to transact in Bari, so I'll take just one week's leave before I come back.'

Neville laughed.

'I'm almost jealous. In any case, if the sortie position doesn't improve, you'll certainly be held more than a week; but come back as soon as you can.'

'Don't worry about that,' I assured him. 'I want to be in at the kill. When do we start?'

'Tomorrow morning,' said Neville.

Our departure was delayed for twenty-four hours by the arrival in Prea of a party of escaped prisoners of war. Temple wisely decided that, rather than keep them hanging around with the Mission, we should take them with us and, as they had been marching all night, it was necessary to allow them a day to rest and recover their strength.

When, finally, we set out, our strength was sixteen persons. Apart from the two Italians, Paul, Geoffrey and the Americans from Pino, there was an Australian, two British, another American pilot and a Frenchman - a truly cosmopolitan crowd. Three Partisans were enlisted to act as guides and, at the last moment, I decided to take William, knowing that he would always make himself useful as interpreter or in other directions.

We left Prea at dawn and Neville came to see us off. As the men lined up I was unable to prevent myself doubting the feasibility of shepherding this unwieldy group over an unreconnoitred route through the enemy lines but Temple set my mind at rest.

'Don't worry about that, Mike. All you've got to be responsible for are the Italians from Turin. If you decide it's impossible to go through as one group, go on ahead and leave the others to fend for themselves. If necessary, they can always come back here.'

'All right. I'm glad you said that; we've a long way to march and I've a feeling there'll be some lame ducks amongst us long before we arrive at the other end. Don't fuss yourself about the Ities, they'll be in Rome hobnobbing with the Pope before the week's out.'

We went on to talk about the arrangements we had made for our reception at the other end. A signal had been sent asking base to warn the American forces along the French frontier of our arrival. We had told them to expect us around October 2nd, four days ahead.

'Goodbye, old cock and good luck. We'll expect you back within a couple of weeks.'

'Yes,' I answered, 'and see that the fires are put out properly next time. I'd hate to be stolen by Major Antonio again!'

Our route lay due south into the mountains. We followed a bridle path up the valley, climbing steadily all the time. I had left my pack and other superfluous equipment with the Mission, carrying only my sten gun, ammunition and a rolled blanket. The days were still hot and dry, so I wore only a khaki shirt and shorts, relying on good weather throughout the journey.

At the head of Val Ellero we halted to refresh ourselves with goat milk drawn from a herd grazing by the path. In front of us the ground stretched away, rising gently till it came to the foot of a steep ridge about four miles away. The top was lost in heavy cloud but I judged that we were now about four thousand feet above sea level. The pass which we must cross in the afternoon was about seven thousand feet up and after that there would be a good three hours' march downhill, to the first habitation where we could spend the night. I summoned the guide, telling him that we must push on as quickly as possible until we were over the highest part of the mountain.

Our troubles commenced in the early afternoon, as we started the stiff climb up to the pass. The sky, which had been blue when we left Prea, turned to a dull grey and snow began to fall. As the fine flakes, driven by an icy wind, stung my bare legs, forming minute icicles which clung to the hairs, I regretted my optimism in presuming fine weather. Already some members of the party were finding the going heavy, particularly Geoffrey, who had fallen earlier in the day, bruising the bottom of his spine. He had been relieved of his arms and haversack by one of the Italian guides and he struggled gamely to keep up.

It was here that I had trouble with Paul; things had been deteriorating between us for some time. The reporter was marching beside Geoffrey at the tail of the column, which had closed right up.

North Italy: The route from Prea to Mentone is indicated by the broken line

We were negotiating a particularly steep slope at the time, which necessitated the use of both hands and feet, when I suddenly heard the shrill of a whistle behind. Hooking an arm around an out-jutting rock I turned to look round. The column was closed up behind me and a rough check of heads showed four short amongst whom were the two press men. Telling the guides to lead on to a ledge a hundred feet higher up I scrambled back down the path. Sitting on a rock smoking cigarettes were the missing four. I was livid.

'What the devil are you doing back here? No halt has been called.'

The reporter answered tartly, 'Geoffrey's lame. I gave the order to stop.'

'I know perfectly well he's lame,' I protested, 'but you'll keep going till I give the order.'

Paul was determined. 'I'm an honorary captain', he pointed out, 'and as such I will not place myself under your orders.'

This had to be stopped at once . . .

'I don't care a damn what you are or what you write. While you're with the party you'll do as you're told. Make up your mind now; do you want to go on or back?'

Geoffrey was already struggling on ahead followed sheepishly by the other recalcitrants. Paul and I glared at each other but he realised that I was serious. He had endured enough of the rough and ready resistance life and his career as a newsman depended on his getting his story out soon. He could not afford to wait until the liberation.

At the head of the pass we came through the cloud, out under a clear blue sky again. To the north one could see, as usual, perfect fine weather with the plains bathed in sunshine. To the south ahead a thick, dirty grey belt covered the earth, with here and there a snow covered peak peeping through. Where we stood, the snow was nearly two feet deep and I was thankful that our start had not been longer delayed. A week later it would have been impossible to cross the Maritime Alps by that route.

At noon on the second day, we saw the sea for the first time. Twenty miles away and over six thousand feet below the blue expanse of Mussolini's Mare Nostrum stretched to the horizon. Moving parallel to the coast and looking like a toy in the bath a destroyer cruised serenely along, intermittent white puffs obscuring the line of the hull as she shelled the coastal road between Ventimiglia and San Remo. Never an answer came from the shore. Reaching the end of her traverse, she swung round to sail leisurely back again; unharassed by aircraft or opposing naval forces, it was an exhibition of British naval power.

I called a halt to watch the bombardment. It was vitally important to find out how far the Allied troops had pushed forward along this coast and I hoped that the shell burst might give some indication of their position. But west of Bordighera the shells were falling out of sight in villages inshore and it was impossible to judge accurately where they burst. We should have to rely on local information after all.

The following evening, tired and footsore, we reached Pigna, a small town on a by-road about fifteen miles distant from the coast. It was situated at the head of a steeply sided ravine which opened out into a valley running to the coast. In the other three directions the town was shut off by impassable precipitous slopes which made it into a natural fortress. We were welcomed by a formation of Garibaldini Partisans, who informed us with great pride that ever since the capitulation they had held out in Pigna against all enemy attempts to dislodge them. The bridges on the road had been blown and, on account of the encircling formation of the mountains, the Germans were unable to bring artillery to bear on the place which was the last Partisan outpost before the battle zone.

As Pigna was to serve as our jumping-off place, I called a conference of the local Garibaldini leaders and told them of my plan to cross through into France. Though protesting that they were willing to help, they appeared to be very sceptical of the possibilities. They declared that they had established no contacts with the Allied forces and that the line was moving daily backwards and forwards, rendering useless any reconnaissance of enemy positions. Again, the ground was so broken and precipitous that cross country travel was impractical and it was only possible to march along tracks or mule paths and these would certainly be mined or patrolled.

Though many of these Partisans had been resident in Ventimiglia before the war, all declined knowledge of the countryside for fear of being forced to guide us. Labouring under the language difficulty of William's rough and ready interpreting, and with my temper aggravated by our hosts, it was some time before I could elicit the vital information concerning the locality of the danger areas on the route to Mentone.

It seemed that there were two in particular; the front line itself, wherever that might turn out to be, and the main road running north from Ventimiglia to Cuneo. This road, following a cleft through the mountains, comprised the main enemy line of communication and presented a serious problem. It had to be crossed but the paths of approach on both sides were said to be few and far between and the Partisans assured me that they were all heavily guarded. Only in the coastal areas, where the country flattened out, would it be possible to reach the road without following defined tracks. But this small area of level country would surely be packed with enemy artillery and reserves.

After much argument, I managed to obtain a promise of the services of a Partisan guide who would conduct us as far as the main road. After that we should have to fend for ourselves, choosing our route as best we could and keeping westward parallel to the sea until we reached the Allied forward positions.

Of one thing I was certain, it would be sheer suicide to try to stumble through with a large party of tired men. The front line area was, as far as I could estimate, about ten miles in depth and all of it wicked going, which would have to crossed during one night. We should have to move as a fighting patrol, travelling fast and avoiding observation and, as far as possible, contact with the enemy.

After three days' hard marching, at least half our number were already physically exhausted and not equal to the task. Two alternatives lay open to me; to rest for two days at Pigna or to split the party and carry on with the fittest men. The choice was obvious . . . Even if we were to rest, the column was too large and cumbersome and we should have wasted vital time and already we were one day behind schedule. Fortunately, the two emissaries were in excellent condition; hardened by perennial holidays in the Alps, they had stood the march well. I decided to take two others as well. William was fit, but I did not feel justified in taking him. He was probably the most reliable of all the men and I felt happier leaving him to keep an eye on the others. The Americans were all tired, so I detailed one of the British, Fred Dobson. He could speak a little Italian and was keen to come. The fifth man was an Italian, Biagio, whom we had collected en route.

Biagio had an unusual and rather chequered history. He was a trained wireless operator and had been sent in about a year previously to make contact with the resistance movement. After some weeks of freedom he had been captured by the Germans, escaping four months later. He was not aware that we knew of his activities whilst he was in German hands, when it was suspected he had used his radio to transmit false intelligence reports to the Allies. Temple had been warned about the man and told to arrest him if possible.

Footnote 1986.

'Biagio' was Italian Navy W/T Sgt. Secondo Balestri. The Gestapo tried to 'turn him round' but, whilst operating his set under German control, he used a remarkable mathematical memory (and the failure of his captors actually to monitor his supervised transmissions) to alter a coded group from 'I am in good hands' to a warning message 'I am in German hands'. Subsequently he substituted the word NON for ALT (Italian telegraphese for STOP) and relied on the security check system and these specific warnings to alert his British control. After his escape from the Gestapo British security were anxious to check the facts and that he had not been released to become a double agent. Under interrogation in Rome he demonstrated his ability to alter a coded message in course of transmission thus substantiating his story, although to be doubly sure security kept him on ice until the end of the war. In September 1945 he was awarded a Certificate of Merit by General Alexander and recommended for decoration.

*

When we found him, Biagio had seized this opportunity to get back to the safety of liberated territory. Wanting to keep my eye on him, I refrained from mentioning the fact that his alleged collaborationist activities had been discovered, and encouraged him to accompany us.

I called a conference to explain the plan:

'As many of you are exhausted, I have decided it is quite impossible to carry on as we are tomorrow. I shall go ahead with a small advance party of five. The rest of you will remain here for two or three days whilst the advance party will leave at dawn tomorrow. We will take a guide from the Garibaldini and one of the Badogliani Partisans as courier as far as the road. If possible we will cross tomorrow night and send back the two Partisans to show you the route. If we are captured, you're bound to hear about it from Partisan Intelligence sources. Wait for three days and, if you hear nothing, follow on the same route. Morton will be in charge of the rear party and William will remain to help.'

There were no dissidents. Tired as they were, the members of the rear party were only too glad of a chance to rest.

The morning was misty, sure forerunner of a hot day, when we assembled ready to move off. The Garibaldini had agreed to take us the first few miles in an old truck which they kept at Pigna and a mechanic was fussing around trying to coax the engine to start. Paul and Geoffrey were up to see us off.

I shook hands with them . . .

'Well, goodbye; we'll tell the American army you're coming through. Perhaps they'll polish their bayonets, so that you give them a good write up.'

Paul laughed. 'That'll be the day. They might be a million miles away for all the use they are at the moment.'

'You'll get through all right.' I told him.

But Paul was sincere when he answered. 'Well, thank God, I'm not trying today; I couldn't walk a step.'

'That's the worst of you correspondents,' I answered. 'You don't do enough PT.'

'Oh, shut up and push off you bloody thug.'

The engine started up, firing spasmodically. We piled into the back of the truck and ten minutes later we were out of Pigna, following a winding road which climbed up the steep slope from the town. After an hour's drive, the road ended at a bridge across a ravine, which had been destroyed by the Partisans. We got out and went on on foot following a motor road cut into the mountain side. This road, like many others in the vicinity, had been built some years before the war under orders of Mussolini's government and led up to the rear positions of the frontier defences. I was astounded at the impregnability of these now deserted blockhouses and underground fortifications which were only the second or third line of defence of the frontier ten miles ahead. If the German army were pushed back this far they would certainly be able to put up a very stubborn resistance to further advances. I wondered why Mussolini had gone to such colossal trouble and expense to build this Maginot Line. He must certainly have envisaged war with France.

At midday we climbed to the top of a steep ridge and the guide announced that the main road lay in front. We stood at the edge of a hundred foot cliff at the bottom of which the ground sloped away for two miles to a valley. Ventimiglia lay out of sight behind the hills to the south but we could observe a good stretch of the road in front.

What we saw was not reassuring. As we had been warned in Pigna the country was a mass of ravines and peaks and beyond the road the ground rose steeply for some miles to the French border, a line of mountains culminating in cliffs of grey rock which, from our position, looked impassable. The white puffs of bursting shell fire appeared between the road and the crest but they were scattered around the countryside and gave no indication of the demarcation line. Similarly the noise of battle which drifted towards us echoed and re-echoed around the hills till it had no directional significance.

Salvi read my thoughts.

'It's going to be difficult.'

'Very,' I answered. 'But, as there's no one round here to ask, we must just push on and see what happens.'

After a halt to rest our aching muscles we looked around to find a way down the cliff. Salvi found a cleft down which he assured us we could climb. Too heavy and clumsy for rock climbing, the next half hour was hell for me. With our weapons slung across our backs we lowered ourselves slowly, clinging by our finger nails to such crevices as there were.

The Italians led the way, picking their footholds quickly and surely. Dobson and I followed cautiously, overcome by nausea every time we looked down. It was over half an hour before we reached the bottom and the nervous tension and the strain on tired muscles made my legs shake as I stood looking incredulously at the descent we had accomplished.

Soon afterwards we struck a mule path which we followed moving cautiously down the side of the valley till we found ourselves in a small wood 200 feet above the road. The guide informed us that Fanghetto, a small village, lay a few hundred yards ahead. One glance showed me that there was no other way of reaching the road except by the path on which we were standing and, worse still, I could see no route up the steep slope on the far side of the road. Already trucks were passing all the time. With the coming of darkness traffic would be very heavy indeed and we could not hope to march unmolested along the side of the road while we searched for a route into the mountains on the far side.

We had two hours till darkness. The guide was in civilian clothes and carried identity papers. After a few moments' hesitation he yielded to our demand that he should go into Fanghetto to reconnoitre a way across.

An hour later he was back again and the story he told showed the impracticability of any attempt to cross there. The village was full of Brigata Nera, whose task it was to patrol the road. Even if we succeeded in slipping through unnoticed the river was fast and deep, the only bridge across was heavily guarded and there was no track into the mountains on the far side except for an enemy supply road half a mile to the south.

There was no alternative. With heavy hearts we turned back. Disappointed at our failure, I stumbled along with my body aching from weariness as we toiled back up the steep path.

We reached the cliff as night fell. Realising that it would be hopeless to attempt the climb in the dark, we looked for cover for the night, finding a deserted shepherd's hut where we devoured the scanty rations which we carried and, without water to quench our thirst, huddled together for warmth to sleep.

We started back up the cliff at dawn. Coming down had been bad enough; climbing up was more terrifying still. Gasping for breath I joined Salvi sitting on our vantage point of the evening before.

We smoked in silence, both thinking the same thoughts. We could not turn back now. Even if we did return to Pigna and sent out men to look for a route, our chances would be little better. As the Partisans had failed to make contact with the Allies so far, there was little hope of their succeeding now and time was so precious that we could not afford to wait. I asked the guide whether he could suggest an alternative route.

'You may be able to get through to the north.'

'What do you think, Salvi?' I asked. He answered in French, indicating the guide with a curt nod:

'He thought we could get through here – he knows nothing and has no cause to worry overmuch as he has only to come as far as the road with us.'

On the face of it, it seemed that Salvi was right. After this failure it would be crazy to go northwards for, if we failed to get through there, we should have to trek all the way back again. But what alternative was there? Only the enemy-infested area, where the valley broadened out near the sea. The sea? . . . I looked towards San Remo where our old friend the British destroyer was again harassing the coastal road. Why had I not thought of that before? The sea was British and from Bordighera to Mentone could be no more than two hours' rowing time. I questioned the guide eagerly. Did he know of any boats that we might steal. He thought for a long time, finally answering:

'I know a fisherman in Bordighera. He owns three boats but the Germans have taken away the oars.'

'Could any more be found?' I asked.

'I expect so but not at night. There is a curfew after seven.'

After discussion and some argument we worked out a plan. Our Badogliani courier would return to Pigna to the Partisan commander there, ordering him to send a civilian by bicycle with a letter to the guide's fisherman friend at Bordighera. The letter, which was written by Salvi, offered the fisherman 20,000 lira or £50 if he could get his boat ready and come to meet us at a rendezvous in the wood above the town that same afternoon.

To Salvi's question: 'And if he doesn't turn up, or gives us away?' I gave the only answer:

'We'll have to take our chance on his betraying us. If he doesn't turn up we can't wait another night. We'll just have to risk it and try to get through near the coast.'

With our plan irrevocably settled, I felt cheerful and strong again and we set off soon afterwards marching southwards along the ridge above the road. The going was easy with a slight downhill gradient all the way. We avoided paths, keeping to the wood, for fear of meeting an enemy patrol till by midday we could see Bordighera about five miles in front of us and, passing a deserted vineyard, I called a halt for lunch.

We had little left in the way of rations but the rich black grapes slaked our thirst. After the bad luck that had dogged us I felt optimistic that things would go right from now on. The others were cheerful too.

The rendezvous was a sandpit in a small wood about two miles from the sea. Since our halt at the vineyard we had moved with care, keeping spread out and hurrying over open ground so that we might not be observed from the road below. At the sand pit, we came across a family of gypsy charcoal burners. Mistaking us for a fascist patrol, they were guarded in their speech at first. When we enlightened them, however, they became very helpful and offered us food and wine.

It was a welcome invitation but before accepting I drew the father aside and, using Dobson as interpreter, asked him about the enemy dispositions. He led us out of the pit to a small knoll from which we could look around.

To the west the road ran parallel to the foot of the ridge on which we stood and the river divided into two parts some miles to the north, one branch running alongside the road. Beyond there was flat ground for about a mile and then the other branch of the river. There the plain ended and the ground rose steeply to the frontier range which stretched to the south as far as the sea. In the V formed by the two branches of the river there were two steep rounded hills, each about five hundred feet high and covered with dead scrub.

The gypsy pointed out enemy positions hidden behind the southern slope of these hills and he explained that others were deployed on the further side out of sight from where we stood. All along the road there were signs of enemy fortifications and the movement of horse drawn limbers revealed the position of a well camouflaged battery just below us.

We were in an unusual position because, while the field artillery was concentrated beside the road to the west in front of us, the heavy pieces were to the east behind the ridge on which we stood and every now and again we could hear the deep whistling murmur of a passing shell, followed closely by the roar of a gun. In some strange way we had managed to penetrate the enemy's rear defences in broad daylight without opposition and without even knowing that we had done so. I questioned the gypsy about enemy patrols. He seemed surprised at the question . . .

'But they are passing all the time. However, you needn't worry. They always come either at dawn or in the afternoon and one went through just before you came. There should not be another today.'

We sat in the sand pit, waiting to see if the fisherman would come. To pass the time I busied myself with map and note book, compiling a report on enemy dispositions, carefully marking in the exact location of the artillery positions with notes as to how they could be identified under their camouflage by the surrounding natural features. That report might be invaluable to the Allied counter battery and bombing intelligence staffs if I could get it into their hands. The afternoon wore on whilst my companions dozed in the sun, taking turns to patrol the entrance to our hideout. By four o'clock I was beginning to get anxious and I questioned the guide but he assured me that there could be no mistake in the rendezvous as this was the only sand pit in the area.

An hour later, with the sun dropping behind the frontier range to the west, it was obvious that something had gone awry. Perhaps oars for the boat had been unobtainable. Perhaps the fisherman had decided that the risk was too great. I called my companions and led them to the place whence we could see the battle front.

'I don't think there's much hope of the boat plan coming off now. We'll pick out a route before it gets dark.'

The flat ground of the river delta looked ominously full of enemy troops. Low-lying and criss-crossed by tracks, it was bare of trees and hedges which might have afforded us cover. On the other hand the two knolls which rose incongruously between the river tributaries, as if some absent-minded giant had dropped them by mistake, were steep-sided and covered with dense vegetation. If we could cross the river and road we might take temporary refuge in the scrub until we could discover a way to get forward.

In consultation with Salvi I drew up a plan: the gypsy had agreed to guide us as far as the river. After crossing the road we would make for Mount Pozzo, the northernmost of the two small hills in the delta, from the summit of which we should be able to pick out a route across the western branch of the river and its parallel road beyond to take us into the mountains on the far side.

'And our objective after that?' asked Salvi. I looked towards the range marking the frontier. Somewhere over there Allied troops held their positions. Even with field glasses it was impossible at that distance to see a path over the rocky crest. I chose a peak which was unmistakable by virtue of its triangular shape.

'We'll make for Mount Grammondo. There's a full moon tonight and it will serve to keep our direction.'

'What time do we start?' The frontier was a full ten miles away. Two thirds of that distance would be a tortuous climb into the mountains.

'As soon as it's dark. We must reach the Allied front before daylight.'

Back in the sandpit I wrote a letter to Paul explaining our plans and the route we were taking. I advised him to investigate further the possibilities of obtaining a boat for his own evacuation. I had made two copies of my report on the enemy defences and I enclosed one in case we failed to get through. As we were no longer in need of his services I gave this letter to the guide and, paying him off, told him to return to Pigna.

As the stars came out in the darkening sky we prepared ourselves for the journey, checking our arms and ensuring that our equipment fitted so that nothing might rattle. Our gypsy friend spoke to his wife in a strange tongue. Crawling into their tent, she appeared with a flask of strong cognac which she pressed into my hands, wishing us good luck.

Apart from my sten gun, Salvi and his companion were armed with sub machine guns. Biagio carried a rifle but Dobson had only two grenades – little enough should we run into trouble. I gave the final orders:

'No talking or whispering. Our aim is to get through without a fight if possible. If we bump into a patrol, no one will fire unless I give the order. Keep closed up all the way. We are few enough to avoid observation and we cannot afford to get separated.'

My particular worries were two in number. Crossing the valley we could be sure that any challenge would come from the enemy but once in the mountains we might easily run across an Allied patrol. At night, patrols shoot first and ask questions afterwards and any protestation of nationality might easily be regarded as a trick. The other and greater danger was mines,

With a silent prayer I moved into place behind the gypsy as he led the way out of the sandpit along a winding footpath down the hill. As the moon was not due to rise till nine there would be three hours of complete darkness. All the better as, in that time, we should be able to cross the valley. In the dark I could just make out the phosphorescent shimmer of the river below.

Our footpath ended in a muddy sunken lane. The gypsy whispered:

'The road is about 100 metres ahead.'

I slipped some money into his hand and waited till, turning back, he had disappeared from sight. Then, with the party closing up and hugging the hedge, we moved silently forward.

The sound of heavy footsteps came from the road in front. I crept forward to the junction and knelt in the shadow of the hedge, as a solitary soldier paced slowly past. Continuing down the road, he exchanged a few words in German with a companion who was standing about fifty yards to the left and started back towards us again, passing so close that I could have touched him.

Sentries . . . I was wondering how to deal with this situation when I heard the tap of hooves and the rumble of wheels up the road to the north. I whispered to the silent figures beside me:

'Get across at the double immediately after this column has gone past.'

It was a train of ammunition limbers which, in less difficult circumstances, would have been a lovely sight. The horses jogged along slowly, their heads well up, their manes flowing. Above the musical jingle of their harness, the rattle of wooden wheels made a deafening noise.

As the last limber passed, I sneaked forward over the road. Doubled up and bunched together we ran swiftly across the open field on the far side of the road and slipped down over the bank of the river. As no alarm came from behind, it appeared that the timely passage of the column had covered any noise we might have made.

We waded the river one at a time. It was wide but, mercifully, shallow and doubling across a small open space we found ourselves at the edge of a thick maize field. The sound of voices, and the clank of metal from the darkness on our right, betrayed the position of one of the field batteries which I had observed through glasses that same afternoon and a moment later the roar of a gun confirmed this supposition. To the left, amongst a shadowy group of houses, a light flashed out as a door was opened. The dark shape of Mount Pozzo rose a few hundred yards beyond the railway in front. Keeping to the edge of the maize we crept forward slowly. Every few minutes the nearby battery fired a ragged salvo and a few shells were coming over from the Allied guns in reply. None came close enough to worry us and we were glad of this diversion to cover the noise of our movement.

The railway, which was long since disused, was unguarded and a few minutes later we were amongst the scrub at the foot of Mount Pozzo safely over the first danger zone. It seemed only a few minutes since we had left the sand pit but in reality two hours had gone by. It was now eight o'clock. In an hour the moon would rise and we still had another river to cross.

A road snaked its way up the steep side of the hill. Keeping a straight course through the scrub we were forced to cross it again and again. It was about half way up that, as we stumbled on to the road for the fourth time, there came a clatter twenty yards to our left. Two soldiers, messengers presumably, free-wheeling silently around the corner on bicycles, had seen us and, dropping their machines jumped into the ditch.

For a moment I thought that they would let us pass for they carried only rifles. I longed to yell to them, 'Don't fire, we won't hurt you', but as we dived across the road a shot rang out. Keeping to the scrub we doubled forward up the hill and I could hear the Germans, loath to follow us, remounting their bicycles and pedalling off frantically.

We wasted no time in reaching the top of Mount Pozzo. That one shot would probably have caused no alarm but those messengers' report telephoned forward might mean that others would be watching for us ahead.

From the crest we looked down to the other branch of the river. A by-road from the south ran parallel to it and across a bridge directly below us. On the far side a large village, almost a town, which I remembered from the map as Torri, nestled into a cleft at the foot of the mountains beyond. As far as I could see to either side of Torri the range rose precipitously out of the valley. That cleft was our only way up towards the frontier and we should have to cross the river opposite the village.

The further side of Mount Pozzo was steep and we were forced to keep to a path going down. It brought us out amongst some deserted farm buildings directly opposite the bridge. The road was just ahead and, creeping forward silently, I looked for signs of the enemy. Two glowing cigarettes fifty yards away to our left dispelled any hopes that the road might be unguarded and the sound of horses stamping and neighing betrayed another artillery position. The moon was up now, large and bright, and it was obvious that we could not hope to wade openly across the river without being observed.

The burning question turned on whether there were troops in Torri? I could see no sign of sentries on the bridge. It seemed too much to hope that it could be empty but demolished houses and piles of shattered masonry indicated that the village had been heavily shelled. Under daily bombardment it was possible that the Germans might avoid such an obvious target as a billet for their forward troops.

We waited, listening for a few minutes. From in front there were no signs of movement, only murmurs of conversation from the position to our left. I signalled the others to close up.

'We've got to cross that bridge. If we wade the river they'll be suspicious. We'll have to march across openly, and hope that they take us for one of their own patrols.'

I walked out onto the road and, turning to the right, strode along towards the bridge. Behind us now the Germans were talking and laughing and I held my breath, waiting for their challenge which would spell the end of our attempt. But the ruse worked and three minutes later we had crossed the bridge and were in the village street, diving for cover into the first doorway. We had been lucky again. Avoiding the streets and creeping through back gardens and alleyways we passed without challenge. The village was completely deserted save for some ducks and a pig, whose noisy escape made our hands fly to our guns.

Beyond Torri the slope was terraced into vineyards, tier after tier, like a gigantic ladder. Loath to use the paths, we scrambled up the walls, tripping and stumbling over the wires which held the vines erect.

We caught an occasional view of Mount Grammondo far ahead, its rocky peak grey and forbidding. Shells were bursting between us and the peak and had set a group of pines ablaze. Occasionally a machine gun spluttered but it was impossible to judge from which side it came. After the vineyards ended the steepness of the slope forced us to use the paths which, twisting and turning, divided frequently. On these occasions, we chose the one which showed least signs of use, keeping always towards the west.

It was two in the morning when Salvi tapped my shoulder. Sitting down, he murmured: 'I can't go on.'

We had climbed about half way from the valley to the frontier. It would be dawn at six and we had to be across the crest before then. Salvi was doubled up and obviously in pain.

'What's wrong?' I asked.

'It's my stomach; I have a dormant ulcer; the walking must have aggravated it.'

For half an hour we waited. Then I told him firmly, 'You must come on.'

He hesitated for a moment, then got to his feet reluctantly. We went on at a slower pace. It was soon afterwards that our narrow footpath finished at a track junction. Only one path led to the west and mule droppings showed that it had been used recently.

We were in a narrow ravine when Dobson whispered; 'There's someone following us.'

Halting for a moment I heard the sound of voices behind. There was no other route as the path was cut into the mountain side. Hurrying on at a fast pace, a few minutes later I stumbled over a strand of wire.

It was a thin red telephone cable running alongside the track. It obviously led to a field telephone. Salvi was excited. 'That's not German wire. Theirs is always black!'

I was sceptical. 'The Americans can't be as far to the east as this. We've only passed through the enemy artillery area. Their infantry must be ahead.'

That damned wire dogged us wherever we went. Twice we turned off on to smaller paths, only to meet it again further on, and I knew that we were to have trouble soon. It was near the crest that we came into a small copse. The wire was with us again and around a corner we came upon a pile of equipment lying beside the track. Some blankets, a steel helmet, a leather ammunition belt, a Mauser rifle. Enemy stuff. They must be close, for the blankets were still warm. Handing the belt and rifle to Dobson I signed to the others to come into line and crept forward through the trees.

We each saw them in the same instant; the wood had thinned out to a few scattered trees; ten paces in front, with their backs towards us, stood half a dozen Germans. To one side a signaller knelt, talking into the mouthpiece of a field telephone. The others were staring ahead at shells bursting on the crest. It was an artillery observation party. Unaware of our presence, the enemy stood grouped close together with their helmets and arms lying on the ground. I rose quietly to my feet, my companions following suit, bringing their automatics to bear on the men in front. As, warned by some instinct, one of the men turned around, I pressed the trigger of my sten.

Taken completely by surprise, they were a wonderful target and half of them fell in the first few seconds, the others diving for cover. As a grenade, hurled by Dobson, burst amongst the running men I dashed forward out of the wood along the path now clear in front of us. The ground lay steep and open for half a mile to the rocky cliffs which topped the crest ahead.

Every machine gun in the area had opened up and the next half an hour was hell. The alarm had been raised by the noise of our fire. Clambering, slithering, diving behind rocks, we strained to reach the crest.

Salvi, who had fully recovered, led the way. A born mountaineer, he spotted a crack in the rocks and started climbing up it.

We were fifty feet up, with a sheer drop below, when the barrage came down. A hail of shells burst around us, splinters whistling and whining as they ricocheted past. Holding on by our fingers, unable to duck behind cover, we climbed frantically to escape from the hail of flying metal.

We reached the top, gasping, and staggered to shelter amongst the rocks. Behind us red flashes twinkled from the guns in the valley. In front, silhouetted in the moonlight against the phosphorescent sea, lay Allied-held Mentone.

We rested half an hour until the stars faded in the greying sky. We were through the German lines and I knew it would be safer to approach the Allied positions in daylight.

All was quiet when we set off but, crossing the path which ran along the ridge, a strand of wire barred our way. With a silent prayer I stepped across. If mines had been laid on this front this was where we would find them.

Not knowing the location of the forward posts, I planned to march straight for the Mentone road and wait there for passing traffic, but that turned out to be unnecesary. We had covered no more than three hundred yards downhill when a burst of machine gun fire cracked warningly over our heads. I threw myself flat, all restraint gone.

'Don't shoot,' I cried. 'Don't shoot! We're British.'

The voice that answered was sweeter than any I have ever heard. A harsh accented voice, but speaking English:

'Put that gun down; advance one and be recognised.'

CHAPTER FOURTEEN

Fleshpots Revisited

At a luxurious hotel by the sea in Mentone which served as Brigade Headquarters, I asked to see the commanding officer. Half naked, our thin drill clothes torn and blackened by the burnt scrub through which we had scrambled, our boots battered and disintegrating, we contrasted strangely with the immaculately groomed staff officers just coming downstairs to start their morning's work.

The colonel came at once. A tall, handsome, middle-aged American, he was in charge of the coastal section held by a composite American and Canadian special brigade.

In the operations room I told the story of our journey through the line. The colonel followed closely as I traced our route on a map firing pertinent questions, while two intelligence officers noted my replies. He was delighted to hear of our encounter with the observation party. It appeared that they had been unable for some time to locate that particular post, which had been worrying them considerably, directing accurate fire on their forward positions.

When I came to our crossing Mount Grammondo, the Colonel remarked tersely, 'You were lucky, that's the only stretch on the front which isn't mined.'

The next few hours passed in a whirl of activity. After a hurried breakfast, we were hurled into staff cars and driven to Nice, where we were met by a British liaison officer with the FFI. Having bathed and dressed in a borrowed GI uniform, I was taken to see the general in command of the American army in Southern France. A further more searching interrogation was followed by a hurried lunch in the Free French mess, when Salvi had to be rescued from the political tirade of a drunken Maquisard, and by two o'clock, bundled together into a small saloon car, we had left Nice and were on the long road to Avignon.

For the first time I had an opportunity to think over the momentous events of the past 24 hours. Resting in that sandpit at Camporosso while we waited in vain for news of a boat – lying in the ditch as the gun limbers trotted past – the clash with the bicyclists on the road up Mount Pozzo. My spine thrilled as I recalled that tense moment marching across the bridge into Torri, waiting for that challenge which never came. Again and again I lived through that wonderful second as the observation party crumpled under our fire. The nerve-racking climb up the face of Grammondo, so clear in my mind that I seemed to hear again the shells cracking and whining amongst the rocks. That view of Mentone in the early dawn. It was so vivid, so real, that my exhaustion disappeared, as I felt the relief I had known at the time.

Came a sobering thought: what of the rear party at Pigna? I did not regret for a moment that we had left them behind. They had been physically exhausted and could never have completed that march under peaceful conditions, even if they had been fit. With a party of sixteen men, we could never have crossed the valley without detection. But how would they fare now? We had been lucky, immensely lucky and, even with knowledge of the route, the odds were against a second successful attempt. Yet there was no way to warn them and, even if we could do so, no other suggestion to make.

After a time I fell asleep, utterly exhausted, green dragons chasing each other through my brain: Salvi playing football with an emancipated gypsy with Mihailović as referee; Paul scrambling up the slopes of Grammondo and asking the American colonel for his autograph; the church in Prea, Gwen and I standing by the altar being married by a bespectacled parson in a blue suit, who looked like Neville.

When I woke up we were rattling down the cobbled street of a brilliantly lighted town which the driver announced to be Avignon. Having dispelled the guard's suspicions, induced by our gait and dress, that we were nothing more unusual than a hilarious party of GI's, we were admitted to the hotel which held the Allied headquarters in the town. A charming grey-haired American colonel promised us an air passage to Italy the following morning and after a further lengthy interrogation we were given an excellent dinner and a bed for the night.

From Avignon by car to Marseilles. A mail plane waited on the runway ready to take off. As we climbed into the air setting course from the town across the beaches of golden sand and out over the still blue sea I looked down and recalled the last time that I had flown over this coast. How different it had been then as we huddled in the narrow fuselage of a Halifax with parachutes on our backs thinking that the war would be ended before we returned from that one way journey.

I wondered what they were doing now at Pino. As it was after ten o'clock Bert would have finished his morning schedule and decoded the messages. Neville was reading them now, perhaps, anxiously scanning them for news of our safe arrival. The admiral would be sitting on that tree trunk with his field glasses and maps while the Thunderbolts searched the plains. Or perhaps they were fighting in the valley, whilst the enemy tried again to blast out our hornet's nest. The first thrill of arriving in free territory had not yet worn off but I knew that I must go back soon. While there were yet Partisans in the mountains I could not be content for long unless I were with them.

We stopped to refuel at Corsica, landing on one of the many aerodromes in the narrow coastal belt to the east of the island. As we circled the runway I could see squadrons of fighters parked on the ground, those same aircraft which we had watched daily circling over Mondovi and Turin. Take that Thunderbolt, for instance, roaring up the runway. Perhaps in fifty minutes time the old admiral would be watching it as it circled and swooped over Pino. Fifty minutes to Pino but days of sweat and fear to come back.

After a brief halt we took off again for the long trip to Naples. We crossed the coast near Rome, where St Peter's looked like a doll's house below, then southwards over flat drab country till, at dusk, we circled the great harbour of the town. At the aerodrome we were told that, as there were no planes to Bari that night, we should have to wait until the following morning to continue our journey.

Searching for a telephone, I was directed to an office building marked 'Security'. Inside sat a hard-bitten American sergeant, his feet on the table, his jaws moving rhythmically.

'Good evening, sergeant. Can I use your phone?'

Without answering he pointed his thumb towards the instrument in front of him. As I moved to pick it up he suddenly jerked upright and, lowering his magazine, regarded me curiously.

'Say, who the devil are you?' he enquired.

There were no badges of rank or nationality on my brand new 'combat jacket'. I explained that I was a British officer and produced my pass.

'OK, sir, carry on; lift the receiver and turn the handle sharply,' he instructed, resuming his former position.

'Hullo, is that Force headquarters? Give me the signal office, please.'

The line buzzed and a feminine voice came softly through:

'Signal office speaking . . .'

'Is that the planning officer? It's Michael here.'

A faint gasp came down the line.

'Darling,' I said. 'It's Michael; I'm in Naples.'

The American who had lowered his magazine when I first spoke now got slowly to his feet and, with a look of incredulity on his tanned features, he lumbered awkwardly out of the office.

It took some moments before Gwen would believe me and the conversation was necessarily protracted. When I finished, I found the sergeant listening through the door.

'Thank you,' I said. 'Sorry to have disturbed you.'

He didn't answer but as I walked out of the building I felt his eyes on my back.

The English are all mad, anyway.

Gwen met me at the airport. In the first moment I realised just how hard it would be to tear myself away again. I knew that I could never taste real happiness until we were together always, without that shadow of impending separation hanging between us. I was torn between my feelings for her and the knowledge that whilst the war lasted I could never be content unless I were in the mountains doing the job which I knew and loved and I longed for some solution but could see none.

'What's the matter, darling?'

'Nothing,' I said, 'Except I love you far too much for my comfort of mind.'

She smiled happily. 'But isn't that a good thing?' Better to tell her now, the disillusionment would come harder later on.

'It's wonderful, darling, but it makes things harder when I have to leave you.'

She clutched my arm, gripping hard, as I went on, 'I've got to go back almost at once.'

Though she took it bravely, she was badly shaken.

'But why should you go, always you? Why can't you be given a staff job? Let someone else take your place. You've done your share.'

'No one has ever done his share,' I answered. 'I've had a wonderful war so far. I've never sat for months in a trench in the rain waiting for the order to go forward and be killed. I've had some excitement. I've known fear but it's all been interesting and adventurous. I've never had to suffer the stagnation and the butchery of the ordinary soldier's war. Those are the men who deserve a rest.'

Gwen understood only too well; she knew it was hopeless to argue.

'Well,' she answered. 'I can't stay here in this atmosphere always, knowing a little about you but never enough. I'll try to get them to send me back to England.'

Lost in the first happiness of reunion, I had forgotten my four companions, seated disconsolately on a pile of baggage, waiting patiently and watching the scene of activity around them. Salvi had a sentimental faraway look in his eyes and when I introduced him he remarked gallantly, but unaffectedly:

'Now I understand, Madame, why the Captain would have fought the devil himself to get through.'

We drove through Bari, taking the road to the south, reaching headquarters an hour later. An officer was waiting to take Salvi and Piva away. They were to be rushed through security and all the other formalities and flown to Rome after debriefing. A somewhat different welcome was waiting for Biagio but, impressed by his excellent conduct throughout our escape, I resolved to put in a good word for him in my report. Dobson was taken off to a rest camp. After three years in captivity he had not yet woken up to his new found freedom and stared vacantly at all around him.

When I called on the chief to make my preliminary report he handed me a signal from Temple, which had arrived that morning. It was addressed to me personally.

> Well done. Everything fine here. Return soonest. Good hunting.
> Neville.

We discussed when I might go back again.

'Not for a time at any rate.' Our chief was adamant. 'There's no hurry. You're the first of our agents to come out from that part of the world and a lot of people want to see you and talk about it. In particular we want to discuss the possibilities of supplying arms overland or by sea as our allotment of air sorties is still very inadequate.'

'Well, to be honest,' I replied, 'I wouldn't mind staying a few days but I want to get back fairly soon.'

'We'll talk about all that later. I expect you've had enough for today. You'd better buzz off now and come back in the morning.'

It was four days later that I was lunching in the hotel at Bari when I was told that headquarters wanted me on the phone. I had been there that morning, so I was surprised to get the call.

'Is that Lees? Can you come down this afternoon?'

'Yes, certainly,' I replied, 'but why?'

'I can't tell you now but it's important.'

Begging a lift outside the hotel I arrived soon afterwards. When I entered the Chief's office his face was serious and he handed me two telegrams without speaking. The first, from Nice, was excellent news:

> Morton and Long with four others arrived by boat at Mentone this morning.

I read the other which advised us that there was a build-up of enemy troops and that the dropping ground was under threat. They advised that I should delay my return until things settled down. Reluctantly I accepted and my bosses suggested that I should make a short trip to England with Gwen, leaving her there, and make a report to London HQ.

I never returned to Pino. On 16th November Neville Temple was killed by a lorry during a heavy attack by German Alpine troops. With the winter coming on and no prospect of an Allied advance before the spring the enemy had diverted troops to wipe out the Partisans who, previously of only nuisance value, had recently become a very real threat to his rear. Declaring an amnesty for all who wished to leave the mountains, surrender their arms and return to civilian life, they threatened to wipe out mercilessly, as *franc tireurs*, any who remained.

The Allied command anticipated bad weather conditions and, realising that it would be impossible to supply large forces under these conditions from the air, they directed the resistance commanders to remain quiescent but to preserve the Partisian organisation with an active nucleus around which they could rally for the first blow in the spring.

Farrimond was safe in hiding and would be evacuated as soon as Mauri had completed work on his airstrip which he was preparing.

CHAPTER FIFTEEN

Arrival in Emilia: Fools' Paradise

It was December 1944. After a few weeks leave at home, I received orders to report to a certain address in London where, I was told, I should receive further instructions. After wandering through a maze of passages and finding no one who had heard of me or was in the least interested in my future, I finished up in the office of a bucolic-looking colonel who admitted to signing my letter of recall. He proffered a box of expensive cigarettes and glanced through a massive file which I recognised as my personal dossier.

'You must report back to Italy at once,' said the colonel. 'I have no idea what you are to do there but they've asked for you back.'

'For an operational job, sir?'

'I think so,' he replied, yawning as he rose to open the door.

I reported to headquarters in Italy on Christmas Eve. Engrossed in celebrations no one was particularly helpful but I finally managed to elicit the information that I was not due to fly for a week at least and that if I wished to go to the restcamp I would find the other members of my party there and could have a look at them.

The rest camp was near Brindisi. We turned off the main road up a white cart track which led to a farmhouse surrounded by poplars. As the truck pulled up in the farmyard a figure slouching in the shadows wandered down to stare idly at the newcomers. As I got out of the car I recognized Farrimond.

He had an interesting story to tell. He explained that a few days after I left them at Pino, Temple had organised a grand attack on Alba, a town second in importance only to Turin in that province and a centre of Fascist sympathies. The expedition had proved a tremendous success and Alba had been captured. Incensed by the effrontery of this action, the enemy had mustered a large force and, using tanks and a mountain division, had driven the Partisans into the hills around Marsaglia. Then, attacking from the south as well, they had cut off the Partisans' line of retreat into the mountains. It was during this fighting that Temple had been killed. Fortunately for Farrimond, who went into hiding, the airstrip had almost been completed before the enemy offensive and, in answer to his request, an aeroplane had been sent to pick him up a few hours before the enemy over-ran the field. I asked him what he had been doing since he came out.

'Well sir, I've had some leave and I'm just waiting around for orders.'

'Do you want to go back to North Italy again?' I asked.

He thought for a moment, 'I don't know; it all depends on what I'd have to do.'

My wireless operator had already been detailed but I could always arrange for that to be changed. I knew Farrimond was a good operator and a reliable man. It would be far better to take someone I knew and could trust.

'Would you like to come in again with me, Bert?'

Farrimond was silent for a moment. 'I'd go with you, sir, if I went with anyone, but I've not been out for long. When are you going again?'

'In about a week, I think. Don't make a decision now. Think it over and let me know tomorrow. I don't want you to come if you're not keen on it.'

Farrimond came to see me that same evening to say that he wished to accept my offer.

Christmas passed like any other day. With so much to think about the celebrations seemed superfluous and I was glad when the holidays finished and I could find someone willing to give me a brief. We were detailed to take the place of a Mission that had been in for about six months and was coming out for a rest. They had been working in the mountains west of Bologna only a few miles behind the enemy front line. We were to be dropped by daylight to a pinpoint some miles to the east, where an officer who had already been there for some months was to meet us and provide us with guides to reach our destination.

I was to organise and supply a Partisan formation known as the Reggiani Division. Our tasks were to organise sabotage, particularly on the roads close to the front, to provide up to date intelligence about the enemy front line and to prepare and organise the Partisans for the coming spring offensive.

I was delighted with this mandate. Operating close to the front line we would be in action all the time and we should be working in close co-operation with the Allied army. A forward base for supply aircraft had been established somewhere near Florence. This would ensure adequate supplies and if, as appeared to be the case, we were to drop in broad daylight so close to the enemy front, the Partisans must be in considerable strength. A glance at the map showed the mountains to be high and broken – ideal in fact for Partisan warfare – and in all respects the possibilities appeared unlimited.

As I still knew only a few words of Italian, I was given an interpreter, a young Italian-born Canadian who passed under the name of Lizza.

After a few days spent in collecting our equipment and testing our wireless, we flew to the advance base near Florence. We were booked to drop the next day and I was kept busy learning all I could of the base headquarters which would be responsible for our supplies and instructions. I met the staff officer detailed to look after our interests at base and I was pleased to discover that he had spent some time himself on operations of a similar nature before becoming chained to a desk. I hoped that this would give him a realistic approach to our problems and that, in spite of his rather effeminate manner and limp and clammy hand, he would foresee our difficulties and, understanding them, help us along.

The man 'in the field' always condemns those at base, often unjustly and invariably proclaims that he was 'let down'. This is easy to understand, as he is living in a small world of his own, with his own pressing problems overshadowing everything else. He is also often in discomfort and sometimes danger and he has ample time to work up and magnify grievances. On the other hand, the man at base was far too frequently inclined to become bound to office orders and to relegate outspoken demands for supplies or support to his pending tray, classifying them as hysterical outbursts to be dealt with at leisure. Agents in enemy territory were far too often regarded as symbols on a map and as pawns to be used in a struggle to satisfy personal ambition.

We were woken at five. The sky was overcast and a freezing cold wind blew from the north. I was thankful for my warm flying suit, as we walked out onto the aerodrome. Our stores had all been packed and loaded into the aircraft the night before. We were to fly in a Dakota, accompanied by two others which were carrying supplies to the same pinpoint.

As we climbed into the aircraft it struck me how different was this departure from the others I had experienced. At Brindisi and in the desert there had always been an atmosphere of drama – a strange tension reflected in the manner of the players. In a fatalistic way the gaping hatch of the Halifax had been symbolic, as a doorway to another world. But today, settling back comfortably in a bucket seat, looking through the window at the fierce glare of the sun on the tarmac, I felt as if I were just taking a trip to pass the morning. With no feelings of apprehension or even pleasurable excitement, I thought only of minor commonplace things.

Turning out over the sea, we re-crossed the coast just south of La Spezia. Intermittent flashes from a hill near the town, betrayed the position of a light flak battery whose shells were bursting futilely some thousands of feet below us. In perfect formation and without changing course, we cruised serenely on towards the mountains. Two of the escort of four Mustang fighters which had been circling above us broke away and hurtled down to attack the German gunners, causing them to regret their impulsive action. Below us, on our right, white puffs of smoke outlined the battle zone down amongst the rugged barren mountain peaks.

We flew on a zigzag course, probing the way through the range and following the lie of the land. Often the snow covered peaks towered a clear thousand feet above the aircraft until we had crossed the highest ridge and could see clearly to the distant plains and the great river Po. Soon afterwards a voice shouted, 'There it is' and looking through the doorway I made out a pattern of red dots on the snow-covered ground below.

While the escort circled high above the Dakotas sank lower, banking around in a tight turn and changing to 'in line' formation. The red dots grew, until they resolved themselves into salvaged parachutes spread out on the ground, the 'breathing hole' showing as a tiny white dot in the centre of each patch of colour. Other small specks became figures fussing around the dropping zone or standing waving at our plane.

As the aircrew fixed their safety straps and stacked the packages alongside the door, I checked my parachute harness and adjusted the bag strapped to my leg. This bag weighed about sixty pounds and contained all my personal kit. It was fitted with a quick release device whereby I could let it down on a twenty foot rope from my waist, as soon as the parachute opened.

We made three runs to drop supplies. The despatchers worked hard to stack the heavy packages by the door so that one hard shove precipitated the whole lot out together at the exact moment of crossing the pattern below.

When all the stores had gone, moving cumbrously on account of the heavy bag on my leg, I positioned myself in the doorway with Farrimond and Lizza just behind. Holding onto the webbing lifeline which connected the parachute to the aircraft, I glanced at the pin to satisfy myself that it was properly secured. The floor tilted as we banked around, slowly righting itself again. Then that unmistakable note like the flutter of a settling pigeon's wings warned me that the engines were throttled back and the red light flickered on the wall.

The red turned to green. Pulling forward with both hands on the side of the doorway I swung my legs outside somersaulting backwards as the tail of the aircraft flashed past my head.

The 'chute cracked open jerking my head violently backward so that I could see the soft cream silk billowing out. It was lovely material and I made a mental note that I must save a length to make up into a scarf for Gwen. I reached down to my knee and released the bag paying the rope out slowly so that it could not jerk away. I heard a shout from above: 'Are you trying to catch a . . .' but the rest of the remark was lost as, with the added weight of the bag, I fell rapidly clear of the others.

The ground was coming up fast. I slipped my hands up the webbing straps and pulled them down to my shoulders. A group of men on the ground, dancing and gesticulating around a red parachute like cannibals at a cooking pot, drifted away to one side and I felt the upward jerk as my suspended bag hit the earth. As I released the webbing straps my feet hit the branches of a tree and toppling over I fell to the ground beneath.

I stood in a stream about twenty yards from the small field in which the signals had been laid out. Bert and Lizza had fallen into trees almost alongside but with the help of a crowd of Partisans we managed to extricate them uninjured.

I was informed that the British Mission were in a village which we could see about half a mile distant. A Partisan in battle dress, wearing the insignia of a lieutenant of the Italian army, offered to accompany us.

We were standing on the southern side of a large open valley which sloped down towards a river. The sound of gunfire denoted the battle zone on the far side of the high mountain range to the south. The ground around us was covered in a layer of snow no more than a few inches deep and the paths that we followed were deep in mud. The valley appeared to contain well-populated villages and great black farmhouses were dotted around the slopes. The track to the village was thronged with peasants jostling along with mules towards the dropping zone.

As we rounded a bend in the track a tall figure came into view. He wore thick lensed glasses and carried a Tommy gun, and was obviously British.

'How do you do,' he called out. 'I'm Wilcockson. I'm so sorry I wasn't there to meet you but nobody warned us you were coming out of the plane.'

Feeling a little surprised that base had omitted to signal our arrival, I explained who we were and what we'd come to do. Wilcockson issued orders for our equipment to be collected and led us back to his headquarters.

Wilcockson was staying in a village called Gova, a small place of only about two hundred inhabitants. In peacetime it had been a popular winter sports and mountaineering centre and boasted two large hotels which were now used as Mission and Partisan headquarters respectively. As I looked at the commodious room with comfortable beds and fitted washstands I reflected that, if my area were in any way similar to Wilcockson's this promised to be a very comfortable form of guerilla warfare!

Bert was delighted at finding that electric power, from which he could work his wireless set, was laid on to the hotel and on enquiry we were told that light was relayed to nearly all the mountain villages. This was a godsend as it meant that we should be able to dispense with our elaborate and bulky charging equipment.

I gave Wilcockson the latest news from base and, in return, he explained the local set-up. He was acting as Liaison Officer to a group of Partisans known as the Modenesi who controlled this part of the mountain south of the town of that name. The division which I was destined to join bordered on his and was known as the Reggiani after their nearest town Reggio about forty miles north-west of Bologna. I was delighted to hear that the Reggiani headquarters were at a place only five hours' march from Gova, so I should be able to reach it in less than a day's march.

'And where are the nearest enemy troops?' I asked.

'The plains are thick with them, of course,' he replied. 'They also have garrisons along the motor-roads through the mountains. The nearest garrison is about two hours' march from here.'

That sounded a little too close to permit of daylight drops.

'But surely they know about the Partisans and that you are getting all these arms by parachute. I'm surprised they allow you to exist so close to them.'

For answer Wilcockson pulled out a map to show me that the garrisons were so dispersed that it was impossible to establish a headquarters further than three hours' march from any one.

'Don't you worry about the enemy,' he went on. 'They sometimes send up patrols of Brigata Nera but the Partisans here always beat them off and they've not got the troops to spare for a full scale attack on us. We've had no trouble for months.'

I remembered hearing similar words once before but being a newcomer to the area I proffered no advice.

'Well, see your patrols are active tonight, because I'm allergic to Germans. Wherever I land they always seem to cause trouble within a day or so!'

We made our plans over an excellent lunch. I decided to visit the Reggiani Division's commander the following morning to seek out a suitable spot for our headquarters leaving Farrimond at Gova where he could test out his wireless. As soon as he had established communication satisfactorily he would come to join me.

I was not unduly impressed by the Partisans I had seen on the dropping ground and around the village. Slovenly in appearance, few had the physique of those I had met further north. On the other hand they were numerous and extremely well armed and, if they had succeeded in surviving so long, they must be well organised. I wondered when the fine weather would break. With only a few inches of snow on the ground their mobility had not yet been hampered. The real test would come when the heavy snow fell.

Wilcockson had told me that the Reggiani Division consisted of four brigades; three Communist and one from the strongly right wing Christian Democrat group known as the Fiamme Verdi or Green Flames. It sounded an odd combination but political animosity was weak in these parts and it appeared to have worked out all right in practice. The commander was an ex-army colonel who called himself Monti[1]. Wilcockson stated that he was pleasant but rather easy going. To assist him in controlling the communist brigades he employed a political commissar who passed under the pseudonym of Eros. I was astonished to hear that Monti used a staff of over fifty officers and men to control the division which was around two thousand strong; it sounded a rather clumsy and unwieldy headquarters for a guerilla formation.

Sitting in the hotel at Gova that night it was difficult to accept the

---

[1] His real name was Colonel Augusto Monti.

fact that we were surrounded on all sides by enemy-held territory. The drop had been accomplished so smoothly and comfortably and now we sat listening to the news and drinking some of the excellent local wine, of which Wilcockson had accumulated a very good cellar. A servant in a black dress and a smart white apron quietly laid the table for dinner, as we discussed things remote from our present environment. While I talked of my leave in England to Wilcockson Bert was engaged in a forcefully worded argument with the other operator about the respective merits of two football teams and Lizza chattered in Italian with the other interpreter.

Dinner was served by the maid with the assistance of a uniformed orderly. It was an excellent meal: spaghetti cooked in wine and grated cheese, bully beef camouflaged to belie its reputation, an omelette made with real butter. Marsala, which had preceded the meal, was followed by a sparkling red wine and, to finish, we opened a bottle of Sassolina from Wilcockson's cellar. It is a strong sweet liqueur prepared from aniseed, and is made in Sassuolo, a town in the vicinity.

As the plates were cleared, we blessed the luck which had brought us to this land of plenty where we could get a better meal than could be obtained anywhere in liberated territory.

*

When I awoke at dawn and went to take down the shutter, I saw that my premonition had been correct: the winter had set in with a vengeance. Furiously driven snow whirled against the window panes, forming a thick icy crust and sometimes blotted out even the houses immediately across the village street from view.

Dressing up as warmly as my wardrobe permitted I went downstairs to see what it was like outside. The front door was already blocked shut by a huge drift and I had to find another exit on the lee side of the house. Feeling the icy blast driving through my clothes and burning my exposed ears and face, I realised that this was no casual snowstorm but a real blizzard that might last for several days.

The snow was already more than three feet deep and some smaller huts were almost obscured by drifts which had piled up against them. To move in that weather would have been almost impossible and Wilcockson counselled postponement of my trip to the Reggiani. I was adamant, however, and, waiting till ten to see if the blizzard would abate, I started off with a guide.

We struggled along for half an hour, taking it in turns at making the tracks, sinking to our thighs in the powdery snow. Finally, after turning first uphill then down, the guide announced that he couldn't find the way and, not without relief, I agreed that we should turn back before our tracks became obliterated. When we reached the hotel, our clothes were stiff with ice and crackled like cardboard when we pulled them off. We spent the rest of the day sitting tight by the fire. No patrols went out, no couriers came in but that was of little consequence for it was clear that as long as the blizzard lasted there could be no movement of troops.

Farrimond succeeded in contacting base on his wireless during the course of the day. Sitting in a comfortable chair with his equipment laid out on the table, he was in excellent humour and remarked that this was just the sort of job which suited him. I certainly agreed about the comfort but I had misgivings as to what might happen now that heavy snow had fallen.

I awoke next morning to find the sun streaming through the windows of my room. The deep blue sky over the blinding white glare of newly fallen snow formed a bewitching picture. Dressing quickly and consuming an enormous breakfast of fresh eggs and bacon I packed up my kit ready to start. We were fortunate in that some peasants had preceded us making a track through the snow but, even walking in their footprints, the going was very heavy and I found myself hampered by the short pace one was forced to take. We halted only once but it was evening before we arrived at Colonel Monti's HQ.

Monti had established himself at a place called Febbio which was a village situated considerably higher than Gova, tucked away into a corner of the mountains which surrounded it on three sides. Apart from the route which we had followed, the only other approach lay along a track up to a narrow pass in the mountain range behind the village. I guessed that by now the pass would be an almost impossible route except for men on skis.

Colonel Monti had established his headquarters in the priest's house, a large well-built stone building on the edge of the village. From a number of rooms opening off the hall I heard the clacking of typewriters and the chatter of women's voices. Orderlies darted about carrying piles of paper and there was a general atmosphere of busy industry about the place. I felt, however, that this type of office might have been more suitable to a big business concern than to a supposedly mobile Partisan headquarters.

Monti was a man of about fifty years of age. He was tall and goodlooking and his greying hair had started to thin back from his

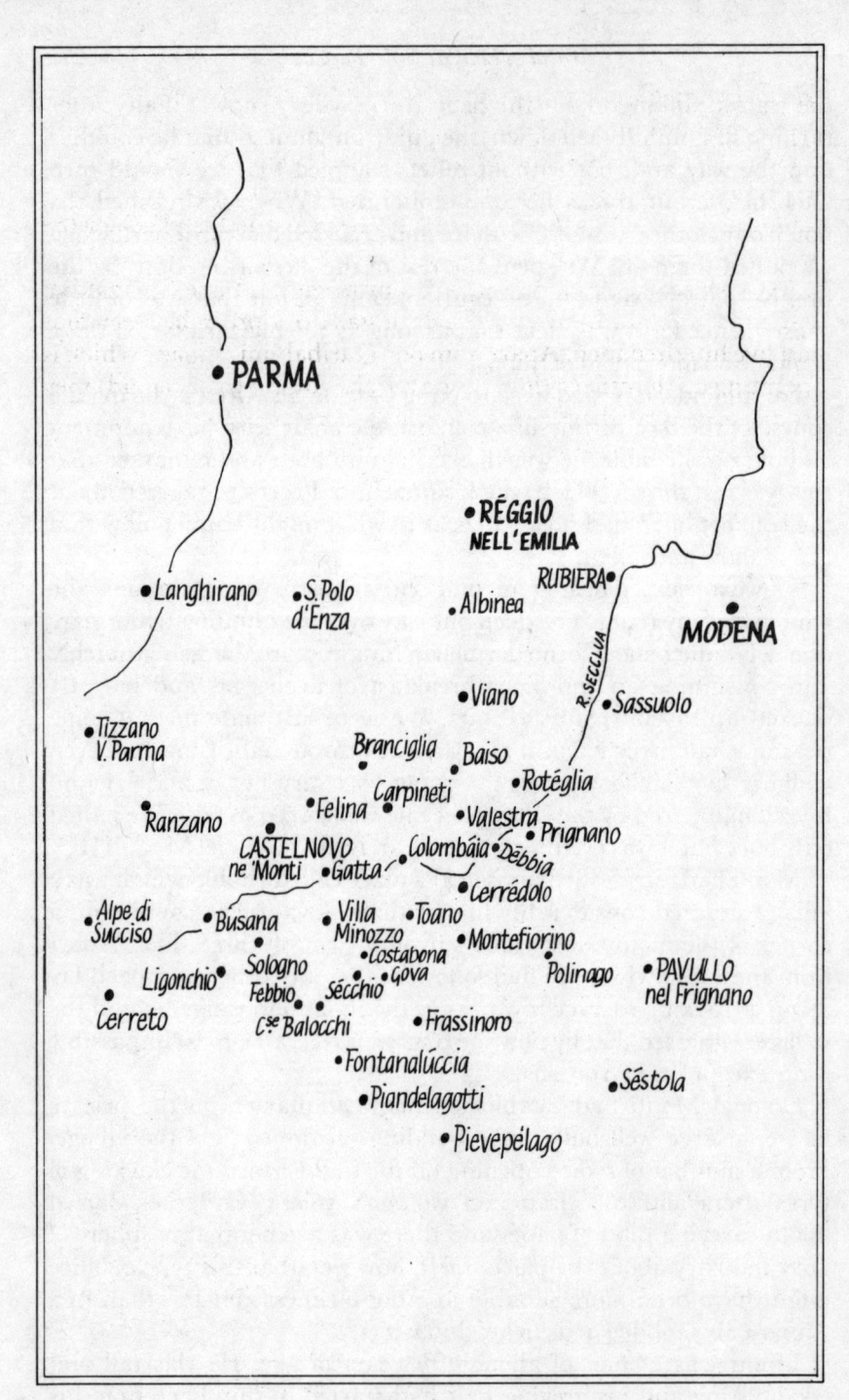

EMILIA
Reproduced from *Echoes of Resistance* by Laurence Lewis
© D.J. Costello (Publishers) Ltd

fine forehead. Gentle in his movements, he had charming manners and a quiet voice but he made little impression of that forceful personality which is essential to a commander of irregular troops. After an exchange of compliments I asked him to tell me something about his division, its achievements in the past and his plans for the future.

'As you know', he said, 'we have four brigades, three Garibaldini and one Christian Democrat. Each brigade comprises between four and five hundred men. Apart from one Garibaldini Brigade which is operating on the other side of Route 63 (the Reggio-Spezia road) they are all concentrated in these mountains around here.'

'And what about defence?' I asked.

He replied with the same careless confidence:

'Oh, that is secure; the south is protected by the mountains which are now impassable, except at one place, Civago, where we have a strong garrison. Our eastern flank, where you came this morning, is protected by the Modenesi division. The Green Flames hold all the paths along the river Secchia to the north and the Garibaldini brigades are deployed to guard the approaches off Route 63.'

As I had not yet seen the country I offered no comment and, marking his dispositions on a map, I listened as he went on to explain other things. Monti stated that he had received a considerable quantity of supplies from my predecessors but that all the arms dropped had been of light calibre. Now he wanted heavier weapons - mortars and medium machine guns. He also asked for more clothing and food. I was surprised to hear this because I knew that huge stocks had been delivered and, apart from air supply, the division employed a Quartermaster's staff of over sixty men to collect food from the inhabitants for distribution to the Partisans. The country was potentially rich, the Germans had taken little and there seemed little real reason why outside help should be necessary.

When I asked about their sabotage activities, Monti became embarrassed in his replies. He tried to change the subject with accounts of intelligence collected and a propaganda news sheet which the commissariat distributed weekly, urging a general 'go-slow' movement among the Italian workers in the towns. Pressed to be more explicit, he admitted that little offensive action had been taken during the last few months. He offered excuses, many of which were very feasible but I was worried to find that apart from their inactivity in the past the Partisans had no definite plans for the future or even for the part they were to play in the coming spring offensive.

During that evening I met most of the personalities who directed the Reggiani Division. Miro, the second in command, was a quiet but forceful character, a Communist; like many of his brethren I had met before, he was never parted from a heavy leather coat even in the warmest of surroundings. Marconi, a huge hearty doctor with a great black beard, who had done sterling work in the early days in helping British prisoners-of-war to escape. Eros, the political commissar, not very aptly named, was an ugly stunted little man, though earnest and genuine in his ideals. Petro, the quartermaster, an individual to whom I took a dislike, probably quite unfairly.

The most unusual person present was the Christian Democrat Brigade commander, a Roman Catholic priest, Don Carlo. Don Carlo[1] had taken to the mountains soon after the capitulation and fought as a Partisan ever since. He had crossed the lines twice to elicit Allied support for his formation, returning each time to carry on his active command. It was rumoured that he received grants of money from the Pope with whom he had been in touch before the Allies captured Rome. He was reserved in his manner, almost shy, but he had great charm and a sense of humour. He was I think, without exception, the best advertisement for the clergy that I have ever encountered.

At first sight these Partisans appeared to have everything: the men, the arms, a perfect terrain; good for defence yet close enough to the enemy's lines of communication to enable them to carry out continual harassing operations. Outwardly it seemed the perfect set-up but I had a feeling that underneath all this there was something wrong. These men were living in the mountains, not fighting in them.

The present inactivity might have been excusable if they had prepared vigorous plans ready to be put into operation when the time was ripe. This demand for more arms when those they had already received were not in constant use; for more food when the country could provide all they needed; for clothing – a luxury in irregular warfare; this attitude of mind that it was sufficient that they remain in their mountain stronghold not worrying the enemy too much, lest he exact retribution. I felt that here was the perfect example of what happens when guerillas receive help from outside and no longer have to fight for each meal and each round of ammunition. The bountiful Allied supplies had engendered a complacency in the Partisans and I

---

[1] His real name was Don Domenico Orlandini.

worried about how I could best get them going. To break up their apathy, they needed a jolt.

They got it, not from me, but from the enemy, and much sooner than I had feared.

CHAPTER SIXTEEN

The Reggiani Regroup

I started back for Gova early in the morning with Don Carlo, who was rejoining his brigade at Costabona, a village on my route and had agreed to accompany me to point out the features of the countryside. It was another glorious day and the track which we followed had been well trodden by supply mules so that the going was easy enough even though the snow lay deep on either side. We walked slowly, halting often, so that I might study through field glasses the features which Carlo named. Mount Cusna lay behind us, the white expanse of its broad humped back unbroken by trees or buildings. To the left, Mount Prampa obscured the curve of Route 63 which encircled its further side. In front beyond Villa Minozzo, a village which had been twice burnt by the Germans the previous summer, the river Secchia wound towards Castelnovo nel Monti, a small garrison town on the road. 'What's the strength of the garrison?' I asked.

'About three hundred men normally,' answered Carlo, 'but I hear that a battalion of Brigata Nera arrived there last night.'

'Have you any idea why they've reinforced the garrison?'

'Who knows; they might be going up to the front but Fascist troops are not normally put into the line.'

Carlo appeared unworried by this development and went on to point out other places of interest and we were both astonished when we reached Costabona to find Wilcockson in the main street with all our wireless equipment and kit loaded onto two mules.

'Hullo, are you moving home or something?'

Wilcockson stared aghast. 'Good God, haven't you heard the news? The Jerries put in an attack last night on the Modenesi who have split up and gone into hiding. They have captured Gova this morning and we only just managed to get out in time. You're a bloody Jonah, you are! Your arrival has broken our luck.'

The news came as such a surprise that it was some minutes before the full significance of the situation came to me. The Modenesi had gone underground, leaving the eastern flank open.

The next few days showed the futility of Monti's command. Panic reigned supreme and the Partisan resistance was chaotic. The enemy pushed on from Gova marching unhindered into the Reggiani positions from the east. At the same time the Brigata Nera attacked from Costabona across the Secchia and a battalion of Austrian ski-troops by-passed Civago and swooped without warning on Febbio. As the Modenesi had done the Reggiani soon gave up the uneven struggle and dispersed, some sneaking away in civilian clothes to the plains, others crossing Road 63 into the mountains on the further side. We escaped by the latter route leaving Costabona the following day.

It was a nightmare march. The information service had completely broken down, leaving us in ignorance of the distance to which the enemy had penetrated, so that we were forced to avoid the beaten tracks and struggle through the deep soft snow. We crossed the river at dusk in full view of Costabona and to add to our difficulties it was here that one of the mules chose to decide that it had had enough and refused to go into the water. Persuasion, blows and curses proving useless, we took off the load to see if that would change its humour. As it remained adamantly immobile, I climbed into the wooden saddle to ride it across but even that course failed and we were forced to leave the brute. Wading through the icy water up to our waists, we reached the far bank and marched on, loaded down by the extra equipment. When last I saw that mule, it was standing motionless by the water laughing at our retreating backs!

The enemy made one great mistake. They forgot to shut the back door and on the night we crossed over the road was left unguarded. It ran along a high ridge and the approach was so steep, and the going so difficult, that we could never have crossed it if a patrol had been there. With the moon shining on the snow, our dark clothes showed up for miles and, as we were unable to move at faster than walking pace, we could have been mown down by a couple of men with a machine gun. Fortunately, the road was empty and, after twenty hours marching, we reached the safety of the mountains on the further side, where we heard that Monti and his staff had also escaped across the road, but by a different route from the one we had taken. In Ranzano, the village where we had halted, I watched the headquarters column straggling past. All vestige of morale had disappeared and officers and men alike stumbled along with their arms packed on to mules. Many were lame from frostbite, for which there could be no excuse, as they all had good boots and spare socks. The only bright spots in this demoralised army were provided by the sight of the women couriers who, unlike their male counterparts, were fit and cheerful, showing no signs of strain.

During the next few days, we learned the full situation. As a division, the Reggiani had disintegrated; a few of the sub-units had spilt up and gone home. But, surprisingly enough, the majority had escaped intact and were hiding in various other mountain areas, in the foothills and in the plains. The central supply had of course ceased to function and it was a foregone conclusion that the enemy would discover and loot the food dumps we had left behind. The information service was useless because, since the first day of the attack, the enemy had stopped all roads into the mountains and not even civilians or women were allowed to pass by.

There was one bright side to the otherwise gloomy picture. The Partisans had suffered few losses and an unconfirmed report stated that the Green Flames guarding the Secchia River had inflicted heavy casualties on the attacking Brigata Nera before they were outflanked from the east. There was no news of Don Carlo but nobody worried much as he well knew how to look after himself. I was glad, on reflection, that the showdown had come so soon. The enemy had deployed a full division against the area and it was unlikely that they would be able to spare that number of troops a second time. This push must have been organised some weeks previously and timed to start after the first heavy snowfall so as to catch the Partisans immobilised. As the build-up for a big attack, as this one had been, needed a great deal of planning and preparation, I felt sure that we could now count on immunity for at least a month or two, in which to gather our strength for the spring.

I looked forward to the opportunity of forming a guerilla force in my own way from the experience which I had gained in Yugoslavia and in the Maritime Alps. It would have been difficult to rectify the old organisation, seemingly excellent but actually weak, but, now that the enemy had obliged by destroying that for me, we should be able to start afresh and, for the first time in my experience, with ample raw material and reserves.

I already knew that Monti realised that he was unequal to the task of commanding the Reggiani Division alone and, now that they really needed the material assistance I could give them, I felt sure that they would be amenable to my directions. Fortunately the Italian Partisans unlike the over self-conscious Yugoslavs, were fully aware of their military shortcomings and only too glad of the presence and advice of the British officers attached to them.

I had a long interview with Monti, explaining to him that I intended to take an active part in the reorganisation of the Reggiani and the direction and planning of sabotage operations. As politely as I could, I hinted that I was not satisfied that the command was sufficiently dynamic and that, whilst he remained as figurehead and attended to the administrative side, I would deal with everything else.

To my surprise Monti, putting my insinuations into words, fully agreed with me. He explained that there was a very strong movement, particularly amongst the Garibaldini, to unseat him and instate Miro, the second in command, in his place. We became firm allies at once, because nothing would have been further from my plans than to accept Miro as commander of the division. He was an intractable type with pronounced communist ideas and politics, the one diversion which it was essential to avoid.

It was two weeks before the enemy withdrew. With the usual Teutonic lack of imagination, they combed our area thoroughly, burned and looted a few villages and departed, never thinking to pursue us or to set an ambush against our return.

We were by no means idle during this period of waiting. Farrimond was occupied in compiling and despatching lists of the stores, chiefly explosives, which we should need, while I set about organising a sabotage squad and a private intelligence service. To lead the squad, I recruited a young officer called Gordon[1] from Monti's staff. He had been in an Alpine division previously and was well trained in mountain warfare. He was strong, intelligent and active, and proved to be an ideal choice. I armed him with a letter of authority and told him to go off on a search around the scattered units and not to return till he had collected the forty best men in the division.

His formation was to be equipped from the first supply drop with everything they wanted and they were to be trained in all forms of sabotage. When they came to prove themselves fully trained I intended to send them off by sections to instruct and lead saboteurs from the Partisan brigades and to use them collectively for any special operations for which we might need special troops.

I appointed a Partisan called Kiss to organise the intelligence service. Goodness knows how they chose their nicknames but this one was certainly unfair. Kiss was about thirty years old and of nondescript appearance except for a pair of huge penetrating grey

---

[1] His real name was Glauco Monducci.

eyes. With these, his slow meticulous voice and secretive manner, he was an Oppenheim choice for the part of master spy. Though the Partisans had a comprehensive intelligence service, bringing in regular reports of enemy activities in the towns and on the roads leading to the front, I preferred to have another independent source as a check on their veracity and also to have my own couriers standing by ready to go out after any specific information that I needed at any time.

Kiss had lived in Reggio before the war and had many friends amongst the inhabitants there. He himself had been twice taken prisoner by the Germans, each time escaping, so he knew their ways well. He set about establishing contact with the most reliable of his acquaintances in the towns and in the villages along the main roads. We were most keen to obtain regular traffic reports. From the number and type of vehicles passing and their unit signs, it was a fairly simple task to trace the identity of any enemy divisions moving to or from the front. This information was vitally important to the Allied command and it was our ambition to be able to signal full details of the identity and strength of units on the move before they reached their ultimate destination. These reports would serve to check up on the Partisan rumours, which were abundantly plentiful but often unfounded or grossly exaggerated.

Kiss was adamant in insisting that we should employ only young women as couriers. He insisted that men were always liable to be captured in a sudden round up for slave labour and deported to Germany, whereas feminine charm, apart from its value in extracting information, could often be relied upon to counteract suspicion on the part of over-conscientious sentries. For my part, I had been convinced already that the few Partisan women I had seen were worth a dozen men apiece.

Later, many times over, I had cause to remark on the bravery of those girls. Unfortunately their courage sometimes verged on foolhardiness, as was illustrated at Pavullo.

On this particular occasion we had received a signal from base, asking us to find out urgently the identity of some enemy troops who had been reported to be in Pavullo, a town near the front line. Strictly speaking, this town was not in my area but in that of another British officer who was attached to the Modenesi. However, in view of the urgency of the matter, I gave orders to Kiss that he must find out the information at all costs. Twenty-four hours later two girls came back with all I wanted to know and, having signalled it through to Base, I forgot the whole affair.

Three days later I received a good humoured letter from my colleague, protesting that though, in principle, he had no objections to us spying on his Germans, as our reports would serve to confirm one another, his own agents in Pavullo were complaining that the activities of my couriers had aroused a spate of enemy counter-intelligence investigations. It appeared that the girls had been saving time in carrying out their enquiries, by accosting German soldiers in the streets and demanding to know the details of their units!

While waiting for the enemy to withdraw, I wandered around getting to know those of the Reggiani units which had escaped to Ranzano. They were mostly Garibaldini, as the Green Flames had dispersed in the plains, and were very discontented with the arrangements that had been made for receiving and distributing stores dropped by aircraft. It appeared that my predecessor had always elected to live with Don Carlo at his headquarters and had chosen a dropping zone there. The Garibaldini were convinced that the Green Flames, who were charged with the task of managing the dropping zone, had always looted fifty per cent of the stores before collecting them for distribution. They also told me that the allocation had always been half to the Garibaldini and half to the Green Flames which was hardly fair in face of the three to one assortment of brigades. This story was borne out by their ragged appearance and obsolete arms and Monti later confessed that some of the Green Flames Partisans had been equipped with as many as four sets of clothing and boots whereas many of the Garibaldini went barefoot. This situation had caused serious bad feeling between the two factions. Whatever one thought of their politics, it was essential to be fair in distributing stores if one was to get the best out of a mixed resistance movement.

The day before we left Ranzano, Gordon reappeared with a first instalment of twenty men. Though ragged and poorly equipped they were still an impressive gang of toughs. There was one man whom, I particularly liked and whom I later appointed as second in command. He was a wiry little Emilian called Rubens, who had spent the years before the war as waiter-doorkeeper of an apache dive in Paris. Another, a Sicilian, had been captured by the Fascists and taken to their HQ in Reggio to be beaten up. Seizing his moment, he had broken loose from his torturers and jumped clear through the glass of a second floor window, miraculously escaping unharmed. The brutality of his treatment had, however, left its mark, and his only thought in life was to exact revenge. He became a very loyal saboteur.

Gordon had somehow acquired arms for all his men, including two Bren guns. This was reassuring, as I would not be able to take a drop before journeying back to our own territory. This we intended to do right away since the girl that Kiss had sent off with instructions to let us know when the area was clear had come back to say that, apart from spasmodic patrolling, the enemy had retired to the plains leaving our area clear.

The march back was uneventful. Nearly three weeks had passed since the heavy snow-fall, the tracks were well beaten down and the going was fairly easy. Expecting trouble at any point from Road 63 onwards we moved as a fighting patrol with our one mule which carried the wireless set in the middle of the column. I had put Gordon in complete charge, travelling as a passenger myself, and I was impressed when we reached the road by the masterly manner in which he deployed his two Bren guns ahead to secure and hold the crossing. Slipping over quickly I felt a thrill of expectation knowing that now, back again in our own territory, we were free to start organising for the colossal task ahead.

At the first village below Castelnovo we were mistaken by the villagers for a Fascist patrol and their embarrassment when, having 'Viva'd the Duce', they realised their error, was highly entertaining. Without much difficulty we extracted the information that, though there was still a fairly strong garrison of troops in Castelnovo, the mountain villages were now free of the enemy except for the occasional small patrols of which we had already heard and of which we had no fear. We were heading for Costabona where I hoped to be able to contact Don Carlo and possibly Luigi, one of the Garibaldini brigade commanders, and, halting for a few hours in the early morning, we arrived at noon the following day.

On the road to Costabona I made a new acquaintance who later proved to be a very loyal friend. We were marching through a small village near the line, when we encountered a group of Partisans wearing the red star of the Garibaldini. Speaking in execrable Italian I was enquiring about the local situation when an extraordinary individual approached. He was of medium height, very round-shouldered and he walked slowly, leaning heavily on a long Alpenstock. A pair of protruding blue eyes blinked through thickly lensed spectacles in an unshaven red face and a drip hung on the end of his hooked nose above a permanently open mouth. After listening for a moment, he addressed me in excellent, but pedantic English the words forcing themselves upwards through his overgrown adenoids.

'How do you do, sir. Allow me to introduce myself. I am Frits Snapper, Reserve Lieutenant, late of the Royal Dutch Army.'

I struggled to control my laughter. While I had met men of almost every nationality in the mountains never before had I encountered a Dutchman or one such as this.

'How the devil did you get here?' I asked.

Lieutenant Snapper drew himself up to his full height vainly endeavouring to gain an extra two inches by straightening his back.

'I have the honour, sir, to have been attached for some months to the Reggiani Division in an honorary capacity.'

That was too much. I sat down in the snow, shaking with laughter. Frits appeared quite unperturbed.

'You're such a tonic, you'd better stick around. Will you do me the honour of joining my mission temporarily, in an honorary capacity?' I asked him.

Tears came into his great soft eyes. 'That, sir, is a compliment which it gives me the greatest pleasure to accept.'

At Costabona I found Carlo reinstated and by great good fortune Ramis and Luigi, the Garibaldini Brigade commanders, were there too. The latter pair had spent the last two weeks in the foothills, sleeping out in the cold woods by day and creeping into the villages at night. It transpired that Carlo, in his quiet way, had never left the area. Taking refuge in disguise with a local priest, he had passed himself off as a servant when the Germans visited the house.

My arrival was most opportune, because the troops were dribbling back and Luigi, Ramis and Carlo were just getting together to make some form of plan, in the absence of Monti and his staff. We settled down to work at once and it was well into the evening before our conference was finished and I could leave for the place where we were to stay. I had chosen a village called Secchio, situated between Costabona and Febbio, which was in a central position less than one hour's march both from Carlo's HQ at Costabona and Luigi's in a village near the Secchia river, Minozzo. Ramis worked very closely with Luigi, so I could always get in touch with him through the latter and, though divisional HQ which was to be re-established at Febbio would be two hours' march away, I hoped to be able to arrange some form of signal system for passing urgent messages to them.

Secchio was little more than a group of houses perched upon the side of the valley formed by a tributary of the Secchia river. A good track led over the ridge behind to Gova and the Modenesi territory, which was round about three hours' march away. The valley led up to Febbio, nestling under Mount Cusna with a sheltered open space in front of it where I intended to establish the dropping zone. It was an ideal layout and with properly organised defences I hoped to make it into a perfect Partisan base.

Carlo had come up with us and he introduced me to the village priest, Don Pedro, who was a thin timorous little man, but a great patriot. Though realising the danger to himself, he immediately offered to accommodate my Mission for as long as we liked and put his entire house at my disposal. His mother, who looked after him, was a sweet old woman and in time she came to treat us all as her own children, attending to our wants with tender care. Gordon billeted his men in a building which had previously served as a village school, while Kiss guarded the morals of his courier girls by accommodating them in an isolated farmhouse a few hundred yards away from the village.

I had been outside with Bert, fixing our wireless aerial from the house to the steeple of the adjacent church, when I came in to find the two priests enacting a scene most unfitting to ministers of the bible. They sat in the dining room and on the table in front of them stood a bottle and two glasses of wine. The bottle was nearly empty and Don Pedro was on his feet, his face white with fury, shouting at his guest, who was shaking with laughter. Fearful that we might have committed some indiscretion which had brought on this tirade, I asked Carlo in French what was the cause of this outburst.

'Well, you see,' he explained, 'during the summer when we had very few arms a supply sortie was arranged for my brigade near this village. Don Pedro was very keen to have his own Partisan command and, as the sortie came at night, he sent out the inhabitants to steal the containers and they got away with six Bren guns. He secretly organised a small force from amongst his parishioners and went off to ambush trucks passing along the Reggio road. By pure chance some of my men saw them go and followed. As was not surprising with untrained men, he bumped into an enemy patrol and, in the ensuing fight, they were badly beaten and his men threw down their arms and ran away. Pedro was saved from capture by the Green Flames who intervened to help and, putting him under arrest, brought him back to my HQ where I reprimanded him for stealing our arms. He gets furious when he's ragged about it since he's very self-conscious of his failure as a Partisan chief.'

To cap this story, I heard another about Don Carlo himself. He always made a practice of dropping his guise as a Partisan to say Mass for his men on Sundays. One such day, as was his habit, he was at the altar with a pistol under his cassock when a courier rushed into the church and gave him a message to say that Fascist troops were approaching the village. With a calm worthy of Drake, Carlo dismissed the messenger and, turning to his congregation, detailed a small patrol to contact the enemy. Then, resuming his office, he finished the service before going into action.

Of such was the calibre of the village priests in the mountains. They were all friendly and some were very helpful. Another I met, Don Vasco of Febbio, had a specially constructed dummy loft in his house, where he had hidden escaped prisoners of war for months when the Germans were in the village. Though I tried to make him accept a reward or at least payment for the expense he had incurred on their behalf, he would accept nothing more than a couple of silk parachutes to distribute to the poor in his village.

*

The enemy gave us the month's grace we needed and by the middle of February the division was on a really active footing. When Monti returned about three days before our arrival at Secchio I called a conference to outline my proposals. The plan was to form a stronghold in the Secchio Febbio Valley as a base for attacks upon the enemy communications. We decided upon a perimeter of outer defence similar to that which the division had occupied previously, except in that the eastern flank would be protected by our own units independent of the Modenesi.

Each brigade was allotted a certain zone, with instructions to dig positions along the perimeter line but to keep the majority of their men in reserve so that, if the enemy broke through anywhere, we should not be outflanked as had happened previously and so that we should always have men to draw upon for sabotage and other such work, whilst still keeping the base intact. Each brigade was allotted a certain area in the plain and along the enemy held roads, in which they were to carry out regular sabotage and ambushes in accordance with a central plan. In spite of bitter opposition from Monti, I insisted that the headquarters at Febbio should be cut down to half its present strength, completely dispensing with the quartermaster's department and allowing the brigades to obtain their own food. This was an excellent incentive to them as the best food and wine were obtainable only in the plains where they would have to fight the Germans to get it. In return I promised to provide the Partisans with heavy machine guns for the perimeter and with food and clothing for the men.

To organise the dropping ground near Febbio we recruited a force of about fifty men in equal numbers from each brigade. This was designed to deter the men of any particular group from hiding containers that they found and thus getting more than their fair share. To take charge of this force Monti produced a wonderful old ruffian called Scalabrini who had spent seventeen years of his life as a miner in America. Apart from his stock of oaths, of which he was rightly proud, I could never understand a single word of the pseudo-English which flowed volubly through his matted beard. In his turn he refused to understand my Italian and, as he scorned an interpreter, we conversed mostly by facial expression and intonation, with sometimes remarkable results! On one occasion, before we received the first sortie I warned the old man that if one container was missing, he would be shot! He was quite unperturbed by this threat and I understood him to affirm that a great number of other people would be shot before they got away with a single pair of socks.

He was right. On the morning of this sortie I was still on the way to the dropping zone when the planes appeared over Mount Cusna and started to circle the ground. As the parachutes fluttered down the rattle of machine guns, sub-machine guns and rifles broke out in all directions. Imagining that the enemy had broken through at Civago and were staging a perfectly timed attack I started to run towards a small hillock from where I could see what was happening.

As I reached the top a whistle sounded and the firing ceased. Then a gaunt grey figure walked out into the open space where the stores lay scattered around. The old devil had posted his men all around this space and, without warning anybody about it beforehand, had given them orders to open fire indiscriminately *pour décourager les voleurs*. At his signal they ceased fire but remained in position until he had personally noted every package dropped. Then and only then could the collection go forward. This method, though somewhat expensive in ammunition, certainly paid dividends. We never lost a single container in two months of supply dropping.

In my own little stronghold at Secchio things were going really well. Gordon had forty men by now, all perfectly equipped, well disciplined and trained. Sections from this force were already going out to the brigades and the first convoy ambush had been successfully carried out the previous week. If all went well now squads would be

(Left) Doctor Chiesi, who attended 'Gordon' and the author when wounded and hidden in the Reggio suburbs, at the 1949 Italian celebrations *(Right)* 'Gordon' and the author in the bullock cart which, with a false bottom, was used to move them to a new hiding place. Italy, 1949

The author with Gordon Lett, the British consul in Bologna in 1949, and previously British Liaison Officer in Rossano Valley, who also hosted SAS sabotage troop. The photograph is taken in front of the Villa Rossi.

In March 1949 the author was invited to become a free citizen of the city of Reggio. The ceremony was preceded by a mass in the chapel of the Villa Rossi, celebrated by Don Carlo, and the unveiling of a tablet on the wall of the villa to the SAS who fell in the battle, Lt Riccomini, Sgt Guscott and Corporal Bolden

(Above) The Villa Rossi, of the attack on German

(Centre left) The entrance gates of Villa Rossi, Albir

(Bottom left) Gianni Farr leader of the Garibaldini attacking Villa Calvi, with 'Gordon'

pouncing upon the enemy at different places every night.

Kiss, too, had accomplished marvels. He had numerous agents in Reggio and the bigger villages busy compiling reports which they handed to the couriers whom he sent down to them at regular intervals. In the latter capacity he had twenty-five girls in his employ though there were never more than three or four in Secchio at any one time. The mass of intelligence which came in from our own and Partisan sources was so voluminous that I was often up till dawn, checking the facts and condensing them into messages to be despatched by Farrimond in the morning.

Bert was very pleased with life. Working his set off the electric light he had none of the worries and troubles of batteries and charging engines. A few days after we arrived at Secchio, before things really got under way, he half jokingly complained that I gave him too few messages to despatch. He regretted this statement later when he was often working fourteen hours a day coding and working his set. But he was working under ideal conditions and we lived in great comfort and fed well.

Frits Snapper spent part of his time with the mission and the rest organising our courier service through the lines. This service was based on Civago, where the messengers followed a tortuous route through the German lines to the forward Allied positions. The couriers were not Partisans and they worked on a purely commercial basis, charging two pounds ten to carry a dispatch for delivery in Florence or to guide one refugee through. Since they often made up parties of refugees, taking through as many as a hundred at a time, it was a not unremunerative business.

A special courier could be despatched with urgent mail for which the charge was twenty pounds but otherwise any dispatches waited at Civago for the regular bi-weekly service. Frits was well in with the guides and I used him to see that my interests were properly attended to. It was a constant wonder to feel that in enemy Europe I could sit down and write a letter with absolute confidence that it would be safely delivered to my base in Allied territory within three to four days of sealing it. The enemy front line posts were widely dispersed. The guides knew the exact location of every position and every minefield and they seldom came to harm on their journey. Their greatest fear was the weather for, far from any refuge in a sudden blizzard, they might easily have perished.

Frits also made himself useful as an interrogator. He spoke German and French, as well as Dutch, English and Italian and I used to call him in to question the prisoners whom the brigades always sent to me before placing them in the compound which we kept for them at Febbio. He was excellent at this job, barking out queries at the terrified individuals, who were expecting far worse things than death at the hands of the Partisans. Though many of the prisoners, who were mostly German garrison troops, were stupid and ignorant, they all talked and sometimes we found one who was able to give useful information.

Frits was an extraordinary character. Charming and abundantly endowed with learning, he was in some ways almost simple, as was shown by his own account of how he joined the Partisans. From anyone else I could never have believed the tale. It started in Holland in nineteen forty, after the Germans had over-run the country and the Dutch army was disbanded and ordered home. Frits then lived for some months as a civilian, doing, as he put it, a 'little annoyance' to the Germans with his colleagues in the Dutch underground movement. He soon became discontented with his lot and resolved to escape to England to join the Dutch forces which he heard were forming there. So, accompanied by a friend, he set out for Switzerland which he succeeded in reaching without any great difficulty. But once there, he found himself stranded, as the few aircraft flying to England had room only for very important persons but none for such as Frits.

After a year of waiting his money ran out and he conceived the fantastic plan of crossing into Italy, with the idea of joining an Italian ship sailing to Tunisia and escaping to the British army fighting there. One dark night, together with his friend, without passes or papers, he slipped across the frontier near the Simplon. The plan fell through because Frits in his patriotic zeal had omitted to take account of the fact that neither of them spoke a single word of Italian! As was only to be expected he was picked up by the Fascist police and charged with being an Allied spy. The charge was dismissed because the judge was unable to convince himself that the Allies could be stupid enough to employ a spy who did not know a word of the language of the country in which he was spying. So Frits escaped execution, but was interned. After the capitulation, the Germans took over the internment camp where he was held, whereupon he went to the Commandant telling him a long story of his hate for the Italians and love for Germans and the Commandant immediately released him. Frits promptly took to the mountains to demonstrate his real feelings in a very decisive manner.

*

In preparation for the part we were to play in the coming spring offensive I had instructed Kiss to discover the location and details of all likely targets within striking distance. These were to include all enemy headquarters, centres of communication and any hidden dumps, camouflaged against air attack. In particular I was interested in an enemy headquarters at a place called Villa Spadoni on the edge of the Reggio plains. We had received various reports about this place but each contradicted the previous one and, apart from the suspicion that it housed a headquarters of importance, we could be sure of little else.

Gordon had recently recruited a couple of Germans into his sabotage squad. They were men who had deserted from the enemy forces for one reason or another and were trained and well-disciplined. Not surprisingly, they were extremely useful for accompanying the saboteurs when we called upon them to confuse the enemy sentries. One day one of them returning from a raid brought in a young Austrian sergeant who, he stated, wished to join the Partisans.

This new recruit, Hans, was an Austrian who had been serving in the 4th Parachute Division near Bologna. He looked promising enough but I was not really interested in him until, whilst outlining his story, he remarked that he had deserted from the Villa Spadoni where he had been stationed in charge of an armoured car. Not to waste this stroke of good fortune I interrogated him very closely indeed. Hans was adamant in his statements however much I questioned him. Villa Spadoni was an artillery headquarters with a colonel in command. It was a comparatively important target but he was convinced that somewhere in its neighbourhood was another place far more important, possibly even an Army Command. He had no idea of the location except that it was somewhere in that area. Fearing possible Partisan attacks the Germans guarded their secrets well but I was determined to get details of this mysterious headquarters, so I sent for Kiss and repeating Hans' information insisted that he find out more even if it meant neglecting all other intelligence.

I was standing beside the table in our room. The sunshine streamed through the windows over Bert's shoulder onto the cypher pad. He started to write out the message: 'Please report on possibilities of using force...'

There was a knock at the door and Kiss walked into the room.

'Excuse me, sir, I've gathered that information you wanted.'

This was excellent news.

'Well done, how did you do that?'

Kiss permitted himself a slow Oppenheim smile. 'Well, one of the couriers whom we employ is a very beautiful young lady.' He smiled and, true Italian that he was, a dreamy look came into his eyes. 'She is not averse to love. Last night she returned from Castelnovo where she was visiting the officer in charge of the garrison troops there. She obtained this information.' He handed over a slip of paper.

> There is an important German headquarters at Villa Rossi in Botteghe. It is the HQ of 273 Corps and serves as forward headquarters of the XIV Army. General Feuerstein is living in the villa. Last week Marshal Graziani visited him there.

Bert drew my attention to the pad in front of him. He had finished decoding the message; he picked it out with his pencil.

> Please report on possibilities of dropping a force of British SAS parachutists in your area to carry out attacks against enemy lines of communication.

I looked at the two messages side by side. Without hesitation I snatched up a form and wrote a short note: 'Excellent idea. Send as many as you can'.

'Get that one off at once, Bert.'

CHAPTER SEVENTEEN

Sizing up Botteghe/Albinea

The following day the enemy made his first attempt to probe our new positions. It was a ghastly failure for him and a triumph for Luigi's brigade. Hearing firing down by the river soon after dawn I set off for Costabona to see Don Carlo who had reported that his troops were engaged. I had covered no more than a fraction of the journey when a mounted orderly arrived with a message from the Green Flames to say that two companies of a Fascist police battalion had advanced from Castelnovo and were attempting to cross the Secchia. The message written by the commander on the spot was confident in tone and stated that no assistance was required.

After considering turning back to Secchio and forgetting the incident, it suddenly occurred to me that a good blooding could do a lot for Partisan morale and would teach the Fascists a lesson. Accordingly I turned left and hurried down a little valley to Minozzo arriving about forty minutes later. The firing was still intense along the river-bank below and I found Luigi standing by at his headquarters uncertain what to do. As there had been no reports of concurrent enemy advances from other directions it was fairly certain that this attack was purely a tentative action to ascertain our strength. It was therefore in our best possible interests to show them that we were very strong, so that they would leave us alone to get on with our preparations.

Accordingly I ordered Luigi to summon all his reserves and cross the river lower down between Castelnovo and the place that the attackers had reached. This would entail marching in full view of the garrison in the town but, as long as they had no spare troops there, which was a fairly safe bet, it would not matter much. Once in position, Luigi was to evade attack from the rear and, cutting off their escape, do his best to destroy the Fascist formations.

As soon as he was on his way I set off as fast as I could go towards the river to ensure that the Green Flames held out firmly, which was the first essential to the success of my ruse. I arrived to find a stalemate. The enemy, who were deployed on the far side of the river, were mortaring and machine-gunning wildly but with little effect. Every time they came into the open to wade across they were forced back by heavy fire from the Green Flames entrenched on the other bank. Worried lest Luigi might not get across there before they decided to retreat to Castelnovo to await reinforcements, I told Don Carlo, who had just arrived on the scene, to stage a mock withdrawal. From each post of half-a-dozen men, one or two ran back, showing themselves conspicuously as they did so.

Heartened by these signs the enemy increased their fire preparatory to making another attempt at crossing but, as the first Fascists started moving on the far bank, we heard the sound we had been waiting for, a rattle of sub-machine gun fire from down the riverbank. The Brigata Nera fought well; it was over two hours before a final grenade charge by the Garibaldini silenced their resistance. They knew as well as we did that the Partisans would take no prisoners. The attacking force was originally over two hundred strong, but only about fifty escaped with their lives.

Phil Butler came by parachute to take over as my interpreter and I sent Lizza off to the Modenesi mission. Butler, who had been working as a schoolmaster in Switzerland before the war, had learned Italian whilst wandering around these mountains during his holidays. Until recently he had been a lance-corporal in the Intelligence Corps and he understood the workings of counter-espionage organisations well. Apart from the value of his local knowledge, he was able to help by designing methods, in the light of his own experience, to outwit the German counter-intelligence. His manner was quiet and charming and he made a pleasant companion on the long marches which we made each day. Mercifully he was as strong as a mule which made him a great asset to me because, hardened as I was to the mountain country, I always marched fast and hated being held back by unfit companions.

There had been many complications delaying the delivery of the parachutists and, as at this time it looked as if they would probably never arrive, I planned to fill in the time by going down to the plains to have a look at the Botteghe headquarters myself. I had been formulating a plan to ambush General Feuerstein in his car, an operation which should not jeopardise our chances of success in a full-scale attack on Botteghe later. I also wanted to visit Gordon who was with ten of his men living in the foothills at the edge of the plains and carrying out ambushes every night on the trunk road between Reggio and Bologna.

I was expecting another officer to drop in as my second-in-command but, as planes were always dependent on the weather and other factors, I decided not to wait for his arrival and to leave the reliable Farrimond in charge much to the latter's gratification. Phil would come with me and, as we should be going right out of Partisan territory, we had to provide ourselves with civilian clothes. As before, I found this an almost insurmountable problem, finally compromising by wearing a moth-eaten pair of peasant's trousers and an Italian cape made like a cloak which covered my uniform jacket underneath.

Carrying sten guns fitted with silencers hidden under our clothes Phil and I left early in the morning taking a civilian guide from the boundary of Partisan country who was a member of the underground movement which operated in the foothills. Marching by tracks or lanes and avoiding the roads it was a journey of nearly thirty miles to our destination for that night, a village called Viano in a valley about a mile from the edge of the plains. Reaching the outskirts of the village about midnight, we encountered a broad motor road and crept along it, moving cautiously, as the German patrols often billeted themselves in Viano for the night.

Our guide led us to the house of the agent employed by Kiss for this area. It was a large modern building standing a little apart from its neighbouring farm buildings. No lights were showing behind the windows and, as we circled the house, we heard no sound of voices from within. While we stood back in the corner of a hedge the guide pressed a bell in the back door, using a pre-arranged signal, and a few minutes later a voice from a window above asked:

'Who is there?'

'Partisans,' answered the guide.

'What do you want?'

'We want to stay the night.'

The voice sounded agitated. 'Go away at once. I have nothing to do with the Partisans, and the Germans were in the village today; they may come back again.'

The interview wasn't going well. Before he could shut the window, I stepped out of the shadows:

'It is the English captain, open up please.'

After all, he was my agent and my voice implied no billets no pay. The window slammed shut! Two minutes later the door opened quickly and we slipped inside.

The agent was a rather handsome individual and, after

apologising for his original faux pas he set about making us extremely comfortable. I was astonished at the grandeur of his home which was beautifully furnished in excellent taste and with lavish arrangements. A bevy of servants, all in new uniforms, prepared and served us a tasty meal. Our host, though attempting to appear hospitable, was obviously concerned at the thought of the consequences to himself should the occupying force discover that we had visited his home. I had no fears in that respect because apart from our guide no one knew of our presence in the village and I intended to let it remain secret.

About an hour later we were going to bed in a very comfortable room upstairs. I was opening the window when I heard a suspicious movement in the bushes below. Whispering to Phil I told him to challenge. As there was no reply, he challenged again and I released the bolt of my gun with a rattle.

'Answer at once!'

A whisper came from below.

'It is I, your host.'

Very suspicious of him I ordered him into the open and asked him where the devil he was off to. The tone in which he answered convinced me that he was not lying.

'I am afraid to sleep in the house with you there, in case the Fascists come at dawn.'

'Where are you going?' I asked. 'I warn you that they know in the mountain where we are and, if you inform against us, you will certainly be shot.'

He seemed appalled at the suggestion that he might betray us.

'No, no, no, I am going to a farm in the woods,' he added miserably.

We contacted Gordon the following morning. He was hiding with his men in a little dell in the woods, about a kilometre from the village. They had attacked a convoy during the previous night, destroying two trucks and damaging an armoured car which ran over a mine they had placed. One of his men was missing but Gordon had reason to believe that he was only slightly wounded and hiding somewhere in the plains.

Gordon was in touch with the underground movement. I remained in the dell throughout the day while he sent out a courier, who had Fascist papers and could move freely, to summon the leaders to a conference. When they arrived towards mid-day I questioned them about their work and about the enemy dispositions – Botteghe in particular. Though owing to fear of reprisals their men were obviously doing little in the way of active work I realised their potential value as guides and agents to provide food and accommodation for the sabotage parties which we were sending down from the mountains. They could tell me little more about Botteghe than I knew already. Revealing nothing of my plans I questioned them on the possibilities of reconnoitring the place at close quarters and, after much demur, a young man volunteered to take us the same evening to a spot from where we could see the villa.

Taking Gordon and Giorgio, one of the German deserters, with us we left at dark and followed a tortuous route to the north, arriving three hours later at the place, a gaunt farmhouse which stood isolated on a small hill overlooking the plain. It was off the beaten track although roads into the mountains encircled it on both sides each about a quarter of a mile away.

So that no clue to our identity might slip out, Phil and I remained in the background while Gordon handled the farmer. This he did very thoroughly, if a little unkindly, uttering fearful threats as to what might happen in the case of the slightest disobedience. The wretched man was informed that we intended to spend the night and the following day as his guests and that neither he nor any member of his family was to quit the building on any pretext whatsoever. While Gordon and Giorgio took turns at standing guard we went into a hayloft to sleep.

The following morning was fine and clear. A faint mist hung over the ground at dawn but within an hour the hot sun began to clear it away. We stood on a small hill overlooking the plain which stretched unbroken to the river Po. Ten miles away to the north the white spires of Reggio shimmered in the haze whence, like a line of crawling ants, a convoy moved along the main road towards Modena which lay behind the hills to the east.

With my maps laid out in front of me I searched the countryside through field glasses, identifying each of the villages below. That sprawling mass to the right flanked by a river on the near side was Sundiano. Nearer, an isolated building with a bright brick roof – Villa Spadoni. But what was this small village, just below and slightly to the left, just a few cottages bunched together around a crossroads and three hundred yards beyond two large houses, the nearer built of bright red brick? That must be – Botteghe. Calling the guide to verify my deductions, I asked casually:

'Is that Botteghe?'

'*Si, Signor,* and that is the Villa Rossi.' He pointed at a large brick building. 'They say that a general lives there,' he remarked.

I drew a careful plan of the place: the two buildings, the little wood behind – that might be a good approach if it were not mined – the cross-roads cottage, presumably where the guards slept. Even through glasses I could see little sign of movement but that indicated nothing. It was only seven o'clock and the staff would not be working yet.

Around eight the roads which had previously been thronged with army traffic suddenly became empty. The reason was evident when, about ten minutes later, a flight of Thunderbolts roared over our heads and started to circle in search of targets. From then on, throughout the entire day, there were always Allied planes in the air, searching the ground for movement. The Germans put up little anti-aircraft fire and they had no fighter defence whatsoever but they apparently knew the hour of the first morning sweep and timed their movements accordingly.

We remained all day in our hayloft, watching through gaps in the eaves. A number of patrols and foraging parties passed along the roads around our hiding place but luckily none visited the building till evening came and we were free to depart.

I had been forced to abandon the idea of staging an ambush on the General's car because the few reports I could obtain of his movements indicated that he took a different road each morning and returned at various hours of the night. Sometimes, presumably, he never left his headquarters and, if we waited for an opportunity to come, we might waste many days, time that I could ill spare. However, I was elated at the success of our reconnaissance and I felt that if we could get the parachutists we should have every chance of making a successful frontal attack.

We left the farmhouse soon after dark rewarding our host materially for the anxiety he had suffered. Gordon was to remain around Viano for a few days longer, continuing with sabotage and trying to obtain further details of Botteghe. Wishing him good luck Phil and I took the road for the mountains arriving in Secchio twelve hours later.

A sortie had come in during our absence, bringing an officer who was to be my second in command. Smith was a sturdy Lancashire man, about thirty years old. He had previously been with Tito's Partisans in Yugoslavia, so we had a mutual subject for discussion which sometimes, under the influence of *grappa*, developed into heated political argument.

He had one bit of bad news for me: a message to say that the parachutists would not be dropped for some time yet. It seemed that base considered that their presence might bring on an attack against us which might disperse us and counteract our preparations. I was very angry about this as I considered that I was the best judge of the local situation and I knew that the enemy had no troops to spare for a large offensive. After our recent successful encounter on the Secchia, I was confident we could beat off all small-scale activity and I sent off a strongly worded message to that effect.

An attempt to destroy the headquarters at Botteghe, without the parachutists, would be a very hazardous operation. We knew that there were nearly five hundred of the enemy in the immediate vicinity whose task was to guard the place and other enemy troops with armoured cars and tanks were available at a few minutes notice. We should have to rely on surprise to make our attempt a success, and the size of the force which could be moved that long distance through hostile territory was very limited. I was sure that it was a feasible task, if we had a few seasoned British to stiffen up and encourage the Partisans, but I was afraid that without them there would be little hope of success.

While I was pondering this problem Kiss came along with more news about Botteghe. He had obtained information from a highly reliable source that the General went to church every Sunday for the early service at half past eight and that he was never accompanied by more than two soldiers who rode in the staff car with him and waited outside the church during the service. Kiss had a suggestion to make which, if diabolical in conception, was very sound sense. He stated that he knew the church well and that he had some years previously stayed at the priest's house, which was situated on the opposite side of the road from the front steps of the church, up which the General must pass. Kiss wanted to station himself in this house with a silent pistol and shoot the General as he got out of his car.

As the prospects of putting our first plan into action were dwindling, I decided to let him make the attempt. No harm would be done and Kiss was confident that there was every chance of success.

The first problem was how to get him into the priest's house unobserved. After considering many diverse means we decided that he must go disguised as a travelling priest himself and beg accommodation for the night. Then he would be free to move about whilst his host was absent at the service in the church opposite. At this juncture we took Don Pedro into our confidence and to my surprise the latter greeted our plan with enthusiasm and put his entire wardrobe at Kiss's disposal, even lending us his own identity papers which we altered to fit the case. Kiss left the mountains the following Friday as good a cleric as ever wore the cloth.

Whilst we were waiting anxiously to see what would happen, we had two great strokes of luck. A message came in on Saturday morning from base cancelling their previous decision and instructing us to standby to receive twenty parachutists under a captain who would be coming at once. The second fortunate event, was the arrival of a prisoner who had been captured by the Garibaldini. He was a private soldier, a nondescript individual and, assuming that he would know little of any importance, I left him with Frits who would give him the routine interrogation. I asked Frits at supper if he had found out anything of importance.

He answered casually; 'No, nothing much. He was in the signals corps. He said he was stationed as a place called Botteghe.'

No one but Kiss knew of my plans regarding the place.

'Where is he now?' I asked.

'I sent him off to Febbio to go into the prisoners' pen.'

'I'm afraid you'll have to get him back again at once. Go yourself and for God's sake don't let him escape.'

We pumped that man all night. I was prepared to use any method if he proved difficult but he talked quite freely. He had been the General's private exchange telephonist in the Villa Rossi at Botteghe. It was sheer fate that he should have fallen into our hands. He had been out for a walk near Viano when he encountered a patrol of Garibaldini who were returning from an ambush in the plains and, not being belligerently inclined, he had surrendered immediately.

That man knew everything. He told us the exact strength and location of the guards and the interior geography of the two buildings in which the headquarters were housed and he gave us a lot of first class intelligence about forthcoming enemy movements which he had overheard on the 'phone.

The only thing he was unable to tell us was the exact scope of command executed by the General at Botteghe. His postal address had been 451 headquarters but he affirmed that the General was in command of all enemy divisions from Bologna to the western coast.

To confirm the prisoner's reports I asked him the name of the general in charge.

'General Feuerstein was there until three days ago,' he answered.

'And now?'

'Well, that was the day I was captured but General Feuerstein was leaving to be replaced by General Hauk.'

Feuerstein was fortunate – I wondered if Hauk was unlucky enough to be a devout Catholic.

The planes came the next day, Dakotas, six in all; they passed over Secchio in formation as they circled down towards the dropping ground.

I had sent Smith ahead to arrange the reception but, since I had finished my morning's work, I slipped on my equipment and started up the valley after him.

The planes circled to drop their stores and then, as four of them, now empty, climbed away over Cusna, the last two straightened out for their run in and from each ten black specks shot out checking as the parachutes billowed open. It was half an hour later before I reached the ground. A couple of figures wearing red berets stood on the path ahead.

I accosted them.

'Hullo, glad to see you here. Is everybody all right?'

One, who wore the stripes of a sergeant, answered me.

'The captain fell on a house and broke his arm, sir, but the major's all right.'

'The major? What major?'

The soldier smiled as he answered . . .

'Major Farran, sir. We didn't know he was dropping either.'

I found Smith and Scalabrini with the rest of the newcomers. Smith was talking to a small young man with fair hair and blue eyes whose tunic was adorned with a long row of decorations.

'This is Major Farran, Mike.'

'How d'you do. No one warned me that you were coming, but it's just as well if the other chap is hurt.'

The blue eyes twinkled.

'No one knew,' he answered. 'In fact my chief would not give me permission, but I thought I'd come over in the plane to see the chaps jump. Well, you know how it is, I put on a parachute in case the plane crashed and then as I was standing by the door someone tripped over my feet and, bless my soul, there I was in the air. Well, a man on a parachute can't go upwards, so here I am.'

His left eye flickered in the suspicion of a wink.

'And we're going to have some fun too, by all accounts,' he added inconsequentially.

I smiled but before I could answer he went on:

'Of course, there's no way I could get out again, is there? I'm supposed to be doing a base job – chairborne!'

I gave him the lead he wanted . . .

'There's a courier service of course and we've never lost a man on it yet – but it's very dangerous, very dangerous indeed.'

'And we'll be liberated soon?'

'Oh, yes, very soon I expect.'

We both burst out laughing. Roy shook my hand.

'In that case I think I ought to stay. Now tell me all about this place you want to beat up. I'm itching to get at it.'

I was sitting with Don Pedro the following day when Kiss came in. Disappointment showed in his tired face, his black clothes were covered with mud and his dog collar was awry; he permitted himself a most unclerical oath . . . .

'The — never came to church.'

Don Pedro was shaking with laughter; I turned to him.

'General Hauk must be a bad Catholic – thus he was saved.'

'Ah, no,' said Don Pedro, who had a great sense of humour. 'It was because General Feuerstein was a good Catholic that fate intervened to save him. General Hauk did not go to church, it is true, but', and he turned to the window, indicating the group of parachutists outside who were cleaning arms in the sun . . . 'perhaps his life will not be spared after all.'

*

Roy had his own wireless set and he set to at once to get more men and special arms suitable for the task in hand. I had explained my scheme for attacking Botteghe, and he was already as interested as I was. Thanks to his good work three days later the force of twenty parachutists had expanded till fifty red berets were busy in our valley, sorting and preparing the mortars, machine guns, and even howitzers which had come from the air. The enemy left us to prepare in peace. They must have known of the parachutists but possibly they realised that they could do nothing to hinder us, since they had learnt their lesson on the Secchia two weeks before.

When the SAS first arrived I had racked my brains for some form of cover story to tell the local inhabitants so as to disguise our real intentions. After considerable thought and an animated discussion with Roy over a bottle of *grappa*, we struck upon the idea of putting to good use the controversial politics which had always cursed my existence with resistance movements. I summoned Frits and told him to disseminate the rumour that the newcomers with the red hats were a delegation of the British labour party to the Italian communist brigade.

Frits, who had been sharing the *grappa*, was slightly intoxicated when he departed to disseminate this crazily fantastic yarn. So well did he carry out his task that the morning after Roy arrived, two of his brigade commissars came to Secchio and accosted him, asking if it was really true that the gentleman disguised as an officer in charge of the party was the great Sir Stafford Cripps himself.

The enemy had been using a Russian division near Reggio recently as garrison and labour troops. These men had been captured during the German advance into Russia and, persuaded by promises of good pay and special treatment, had joined the Axis forces. They were organised into so-called Turkoman divisions and had been used primarily to fight the Partisans. They had acted with the utmost bestiality in this role. Illiterate and uncivilised to a man thay had looted, killed and raped, burning villages for the mere pleasure of it. The Partisans told terrible stories of how prisoners taken by the Turkomans were invariably tortured or beaten to death.

These men, observing the turn of the tide, were now deserting to the mountains in large numbers. The Partisans were all for shooting the lot of them but, though they were acknowledged traitors and murderers, they were still Russians and therefore of Allied nationality. I felt sure that, at the end of the war, their own countryfolk would bring them to justice and merciless justice at that, so, in the meantime, I determined to put them to some use. We had a number of bona fide Russians fighting with the Partisans, including three officers who had escaped from prisoner of war camps and had never thrown in their lot with the Germans. These men were charged with the task of recruiting an efficient force from the scores of Russian deserters who streamed into the mountains daily. Keeping the older soldiers who had brought their arms with them we sent the others through the lines and, within a week, we built up a force of a hundred Russians whom I directed to join Roy's troops to swell his command.

Gordon and his men were back at Secchio and rested; after a few days of preparation, we were ready for the great attempt.

On 21st March, base gave us permission to go ahead. There had been a lengthy interchange of signals beforehand and a good deal of fur had been flying on both sides. We were at Secchio discussing last minute details. It had been decided that our forces would consist of twenty SAS, forty Russians and forty Partisans half drawn from Gordon's men and half from the Garibaldini. Our fire-power was formidable. Each man carried an automatic weapon – twenty Brens and eighty sub-machine guns.

The plan in principle was that on arrival at Botteghe ten parachutists reinforced by Gordon's men would attack the Villa Rossi where, it had been reported, the General was sleeping. This left the other ten British and the Garibaldini for the other building, the Villa Calvi, which was used as an office block and where the staff were quartered. The Russians were to throw a cordon around the houses to prevent outside interference with our plans. I had handed over command of the operation to Roy, knowing full well that he had far greater experience of handling a force of that size and because his men, the parachutists, would bear the brunt of the attack.

'But you'll come along with us, Mike?' he asked.

'Good God, yes. I've lived for this day; besides I've done the recce and I hope you'll need my knowledge.'

Roy smiled. 'What will you do when we attack?'

'To tell you the truth,' I answered, 'I've got an urge to get that General. Don Pedro's asked me to punish him for not going to church on Sunday. I'll go with Gordon and my chaps to the Villa Rossi.'

We were sitting in Don Pedro's study. From time to time came bursts of laughter from Gordon's men outside who were being initiated into the mystery of the bagpipes. Roy, who was a great showman, had decided at the last moment to enlist a piper. In spite of my protestations that we had more than enough on our plate to permit any extra complications he insisted that the morale effect on the Germans of hearing a piper fifty miles behind the lines would easily outweigh any disadvantages. He signalled out his demand and Southern Italy was combed until a man was found who could play and owned a set of bagpipes. At one day's notice only he was bustled into a plane and dropped to Febbio. Now, only a few days later, he was ready to accompany us. Working with Roy made war seem like a hearty game. He heaved himself from his chair.

'Eat, drink and be merry, I'm going to the dance.'

In the schoolroom where his men were billeted Gordon had organised an impromptu dance with the courier girls employed by Kiss and we wandered round to join in. A few of Roy's men were already there, mingling amicably with the Partisans, and taking their

(L to R) Gwen Lees, Barbanera, Ken Harvey, Noris, chief stafetta of Gufo Nero, Roy Farran, 'Gordon', the author, Mario Crotti, in front of the Villa Rossi

Group including: Barbanera (Avv. Anibali) Alpi (Commander Allied Bn under Roy Farran), Gianni Farri (Cdr Garibaldini contingent attacking Villa Calvi) 'Gordon', Roy Farran (Cdr SAS and Albinea attack force), the author, Ken Harvey (led SAS stick in Villa Calvi), Gwen Lees, Sra Gianni Farri (who tended ML and 'Gordon'), Mrs Ken Harvey, Sra Alpi, Gorgio (Austrian member of Gufo Nero). Piazza Caduti Alleati. Albinea, 1985, following the naming of the square

In April 1985 a celebration was held in Albinea to name the square by the Villas Rossi and Calvi Piazza Caduti Alleati di Ville Rossi (Square of the fallen allies of Villa Rossi), during which gold medals were presented to representatives of the Partisans, the Russians, and the SAS and to Roy Farran and the author. The school in Albinea made a special study of the action and produced pamphlets in 1965 and 1985.

Mike and Gwen Lees revisit the mountains, 1949

turn to jostle around the tiny floor. Gordon played an accordion and was accompanied by Rubens on an old piano. I sat down in a corner to talk to Hans. He was alone and stared across the room with a melancholy look in his eyes. Our chances of success depended on Hans, for he was to march in front of our column so that in case of sentries challenging us, he could answer in their own language and try to pass us off as nothing more sinister than a routine German patrol.

'What's the trouble, Hans?'

He took little notice of my question, murmuring something noncommittal and scowling across the room. Obviously he was upset about something and I set out to find out what was the trouble.

It was some time before I could persuade him to tell the story. Apparently he had been overcome by pangs of conscience. Although loyal to the Partisans he hated the idea that he was to be an instrument for the destruction of so many of his own comrades. I asked him why he had deserted from the German army in the first place. In broken English he explained:

'I am an Austrian from Vienna. There will be many of my compatriots there tomorrow. Perhaps I shall have to kill them. But I must and I shall do it in revenge. I had a wife in Vienna but I shall never see her again. When I was away fighting at Stalingrad I had a letter from my mother to say that Trudi was going to have a child. I had not been home for two years.

'I went to my officer and asked for leave so that I might go to kill the other man but my officer was a Nazi. He would give me no leave nor any help in obtaining redress. He laughed at me saying that I should not be selfish about my wife. She had made some other soldier happy and done her duty by conceiving a baby for the Führer.

'That is why I fight my countrymen.'

In the morning we said farewell to Secchio. Don Pedro's mother kissed me tenderly and Bert shook my hand.

'Good luck, sir. Don't stick your neck out too much.'

'Don't worry, Bert,' I answered, 'I've too much to live for.'

As we were moving off, Bert asked suddenly; 'Can't I come with you, sir?'

Surprised, I answered, 'Of course not. You've got to stay here to work the set.'

'Yes, I know that,' said Bert, 'but I've had a feeling all morning that something is going to happen and I'd like to come.'

I laughed. 'Don't be a bloody fool. You'll be seeing a ghost next.'

We swung off down the path towards Costabona and the plains. The church – Don Pedro's home – that happy little village disappeared from sight as we mounted the corner of the hill. In front and behind the men marched slowly and evenly, singing as we went along.

CHAPTER EIGHTEEN

The Grand Finale: Down to Earth with a Bump

It was two days since we had left Secchio behind and we were hiding in Casa del Lupo or 'The house of the wolf', that forbidding farmhouse which once before I had visited with Phil. Our journey down had been by no means uneventful. Shortly after we had crossed the Secchia, refugees, pouring up towards the mountains, told us of a Fascist and German search of the foothills. Though we were confident that we could easily overcome any force that we encountered it was essential for the success of our plan that we should approach the plains unobserved. Lying up in the woods each day, we marched by night, keeping to paths and avoiding villages and two long marches had brought us to our destination just before dawn that morning.

The men were sleeping huddled together in the warm cowstalls. Roy was upstairs in the farmer's bed which had been placed at our disposal. At all four corners of the group of buildings guards stood around watching and nursing their Bren guns hidden in the shade behind opened windows. I prayed that no patrol would stray to the farmhouse that day but if one came we were ready. From the Germans wandering carefree along the nearby roads the house of the wolf hid its secrets well.

My whole body ached and I longed to go to bed. That malaria germ contracted in Yugoslavia two years before was active again, raising my temperature and sapping the strength that I would need when the night came; but I dared not rest. I knew that if I lay down now I should not be fit to go on again. I put aside the question of the long march back to the mountain, probably with wounded men to be helped along. There would be time to worry about that later. Sufficient only to see this attack a success and I should be content.

I went upstairs to wake up Roy. He mumbled in his sleep as I shook him. Then, opening his eyes, he jumped lightly out of bed, looking at his watch.

'Six o'clock – final orders at 8.30.'

'Yes I've told them,' I announced.

'Come downstairs and have some supper.'

We sat in the big kitchen sipping glasses of red wine. One by one the formation commanders walked in seating themselves in a circle around the hearth. The huge fire roared in the open grate throwing a flickering red light on the solemn men clustered around that gloomy room.

Roy stood with his back to the hearth with Phil interpreting beside him. In short sentences he explained the plan over again.

'We move off at 10.30. We should reach Botteghe soon after midnight. We will march in three parallel columns, the Russians, the Garibaldini and the Goufo Nero.'

The Goufo Nero was the black bat insignia worn by Gordon's men.

'Any questions?'

I looked at the ring of faces around the fire. Italian – Russian – German – British; features so different but in expression all the same. Quiet, determined and unafraid, thinking not of the morrow but only that we must succeed tonight. Two miles away, I thought, the General and his staff will now be dining in the Villa Rossi. Perhaps they are laughing as they talk and sip their wine. In the Villa Calvi the late workers will be locking away their files and packing up for the night. Soon they will go to bed to sleep and dream. Outside, the solitary guards will pace around stamping their feet to drive away the cold. Dream, drink, stamp, my friends while you still have time. Dream, drink and stamp as you have done over all Europe, treading on the peoples till even your friends, the Italians, rise in arms to strike you in the back. Live you blind fools while you may. Soon justice will come to Europe but it is for you we're coming tonight.

It was black as pitch in the yard outside. A last minute inspection was completed, to ensure that all hands and faces had been liberally blacked with soot, a word of command whispered and the column moved off into the night.

'There it is, Roy,' I whispered, as a small copse loomed up ahead. 'That's the Villa Rossi. Villa Calvi's to the left.'

We had circled around avoiding the village to approach from the Reggio side. Now we lay in an open field looking across to our objective two hundred yards away. It was ten minutes to one. The grass rustled as the Russians crawled past to take up their protective positions.

'All set, Mike?'

'All set.'

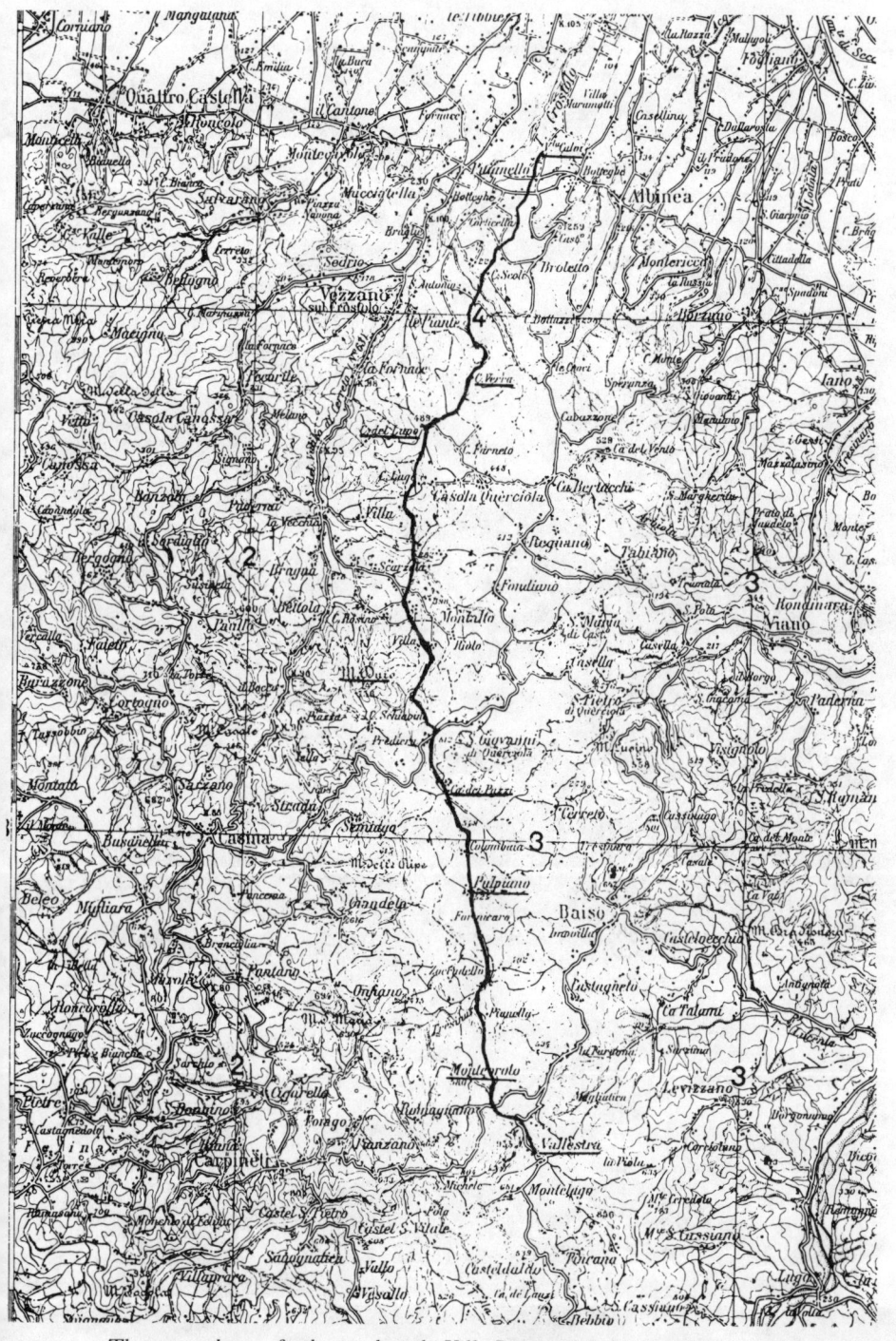

The approach route for the attack on the Villa Rossi and the Villa Calvi
This and the following two plans are reproduced from a pamphlet on the attack by courtesy of
the Scuola Media Statale L. Ariosto of Albinea.

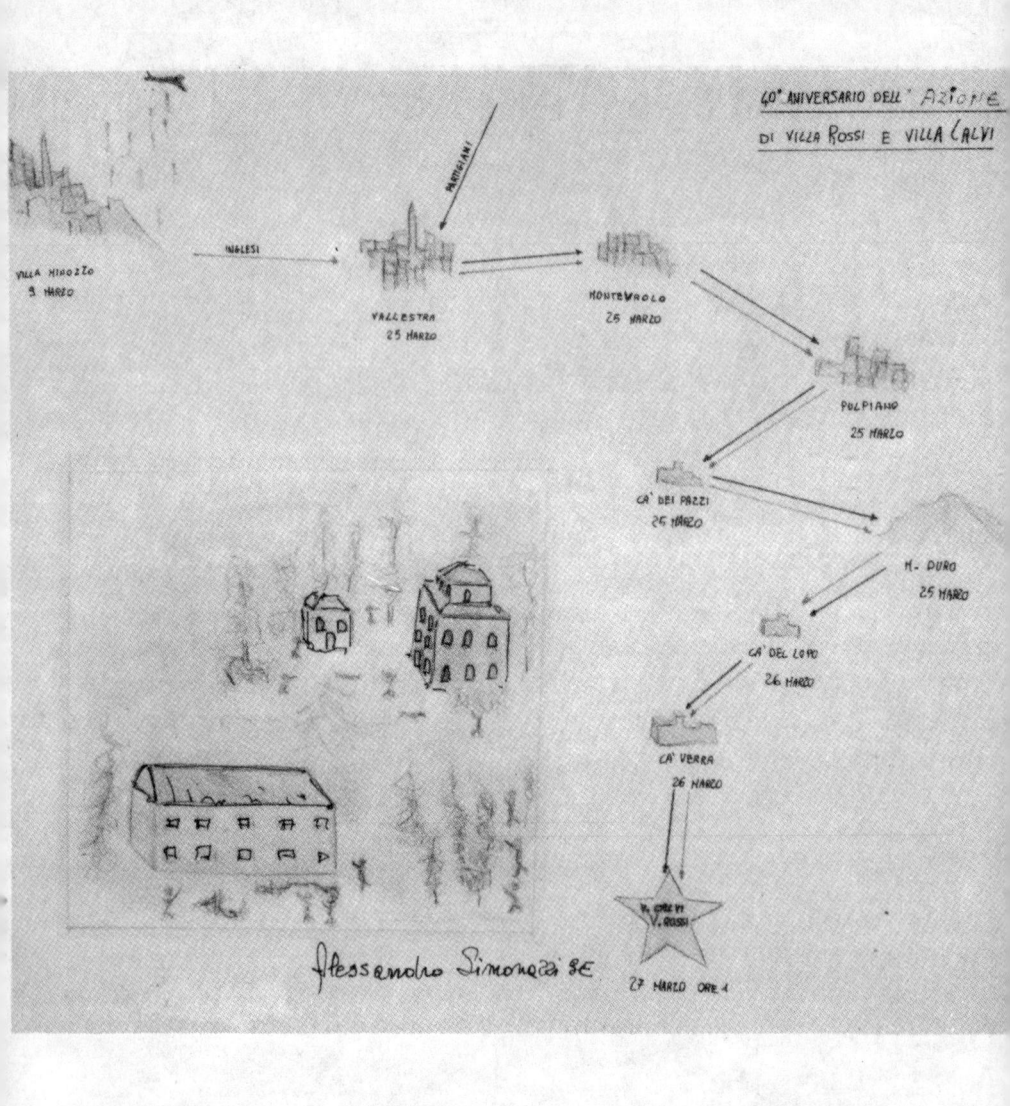

40° ANIVERSARIO DELL' AZIONE
DI VILLA ROSSI E VILLA CALVI

VILLA MINOZZO
9 MARZO

INGLESI →

PARTIGIANI ↓

VALLESTRA
25 MARZO

MONTEVROLO
25 MARZO

POLPIANO
25 MARZO

CA' DEI PAZZI
25 MARZO

M. DURO
25 MARZO

CA' DEL LOVO
26 MARZO

CA' VERRA
26 MARZO

V. CALVI e V. ROSSI
27 MARZO ORE 4

Alessandro Simonazzi 3E

1. *Area of concentration for the attack*
2. *Russian and Italian Partisans*

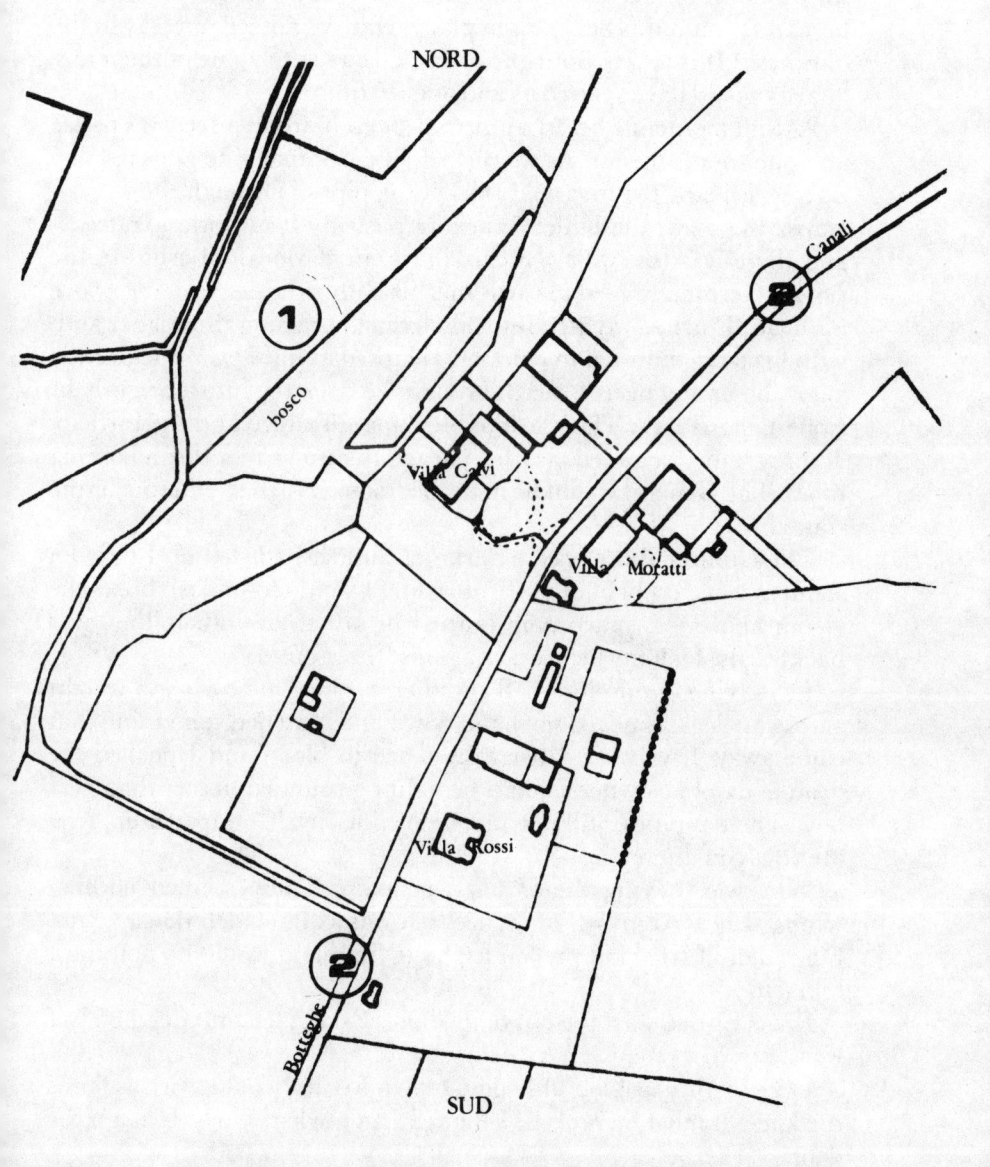

Plan of the Villa Rossi and the Villa Calvi

'OK. On you go, good luck.'

With Gordon and his twenty men I doubled forward towards the silent wood. Ten of the parachutists led the way in front. To the left, the other column ran towards Villa Calvi. We were nearer now – we were amongst the trees – we had got in unobserved. Doubts started to beset me: could this be the right place? Had we missed our way in the darkness? If this was Botteghe headquarters surely one of the many guards would have spotted us and opened fire?

At that moment I heard a guttural shout in front, a second's pause and one shot rang out. As we rushed forward, machine guns opened up and I heard the first wild skirl of the pipes. Through the wood – across the road, the bullets cracking past my head, into a gateway and there was the Villa ten yards in front. From the bushes to the right a German lunged towards me, his clubbed rifle swinging above his head. I turned my sten into his stomach pressing the trigger and, with his face contorted in pain, he collapsed at my feet. With Gordon following on my heels I raced through the doorway into a brightly lit stone-flagged hall. The crash of breaking furniture and the rattle of Tommy guns sounded as the parachutists cleared the adjoining room. The General would be in his bedroom. I turned and ran for the stairs.

The landing above was in darkness and as I started up I heard a shout of warning behind me. Unheeding I went on – a flash broke the gloom above – a sharp pain burned in my chest and, rolling over backwards, I felt my head crack against the ground.

I was lying in the outer hall and there seemed to be a heavy weight across my legs. I moved my hand down and clutched something that came away. It was a red beret drenched in blood and I pushed the dead body of its owner aside. The fighting sounded fiercer than ever now. The bagpipes, still playing, seemed to say, 'Get up, get up, why are you lying there?'

Why was I lying there? I felt no pain. There seemed nothing wrong. I heaved myself to my feet but immediately fell down again. Once more I tried but my left leg hung limp and would do nothing I told it to.

Boots rattled past me out of the door. Except for that dead body I was alone in the house.

On experiment I found I could crawl. My leg would work as far as the knee. It must be broken, I thought. I crawled slowly through the door.

'*Capitano, Capitano,* you are hurt.'

'Who is that?'

'Siciliano. Come away. We could not get up the stairs. We are going to burn the house down.'

He helped me onto my good leg. With my arm around his shoulder I hopped slowly back the way we had come. As we halted for a moment I glanced at my watch – one o'clock. All this had happened in ten short minutes.

Nausea came soon. Fighting against it I crawled and hopped alternately, slowly away through the wood towards the assembly point. Behind us the firing had died down but a fierce battle was in progress on the road where the Russians were holding up the enemy reinforcements which were trying to reach the house. Suddenly Siciliano exclaimed:

'Look, they are burning.'

I looked around. Both buildings were burning. It seemed that we had accomplished what we came to do.

At that moment came two long blasts on a whistle, the signal for withdrawal.

'Hurry, *Capitano*, hurry.'

It's hopeless, I thought, I'll never crawl thirty miles back to the mountains and they can't drag me that far. I must stay and take my chance with the Germans. I felt weak and faint; I couldn't care.

'Leave me here, Siciliano.'

'To be tortured and shot?' asked Siciliano, who knew only too well.

'Never.'

It was a nightmare journey. My arm around their shoulders, the Partisans and two of the SAS dragged me along till Botteghe lay two miles behind. Outside a farmhouse they let me lie down to rest and Siciliano leant over to speak to me.

'Gordon is here too, *Capitano*. His leg is broken. We are looking for a ladder to carry you on. We will take you where you can hide with friends.'

Three hours later we were carried into a barn.

Before the door closed I raised myself on my elbow to look into the distance where the sky was red above the burning buildings at Botteghe.

*

Gordon and I lay hidden on a bed of straw in that barn for three long days. Before leaving us, the Partisans built a heavy stack around the corner where we were lying and counselled the old peasant woman, who alone knew of our whereabouts, to absolute secrecy. Gianni, the Garibaldini leader, pressed my hand in farewell.

'*Au revoir, mon capitaine.* We must go now, but I shall send a message to my sister who is a nurse in Reggio. She will come to look after you.'

The following night I heard the door opening and voices whispered softly. A bale of hay was drawn aside and by the light of a lantern I saw the old woman with two attractive girls. The taller introduced herself.

'I am Gianni's sister. My friend and I have come to stay with you till they can get you away. You will have two more visitors tonight, Antonio is bringing a doctor.'

'Who is Antonio?' I asked.

'He is the leader of the resistance in Reggio,' she whispered, so that the old woman could not overhear.

The girl turned away and spoke to the peasant woman who bustled off, returning later with a kettle of boiling water. Together they set about preparing us for the doctor. Gordon groaned in pain as they tore away his trousers. He had been wounded beside me on the stairs of the Villa Rossi, and a bullet had passed through his leg shattering the bone.

'Where are you wounded, *Capitano*?' asked the girl.

'I don't know, I can't feel or move my leg; I think it is broken below the knee.'

They rolled up my trouser leg, stiff with congealed blood, but there was no sign of any injury. After minutes of searching we found a small hole in the hip and another under the leg above the knee. But I realised that, as I had been able to crawl, that part of the leg could not be broken. I wondered just what that meant. Apart from this damage, a bullet had passed through my chest, another through my left arm and a fourth through the calf of my right leg. As they worked, tenderly and efficiently cleansing and bandaging the wounds, I reflected how lucky I was to be still alive.

Antonio arrived with the doctor soon after midnight. The latter had obviously been forced to come against his better judgment. He glanced at our wounds, muttering all the while and insisting that he could under no circumstances come again. But, with the help of the girls, Gordon's leg was set in a rough wooden splint. Glancing at my leg, the doctor confirmed my fears.

'The nerve has been hit,' he said.

'How long will it take to get better?' I asked.

He shrugged his shoulders, as if washing his hands of the whole affair.

'Who knows – I can do nothing to help you. You should be in hospital.'

He was right! Of course we should be in hospital but what could we do in enemy country, unable to move, and fifty miles from the nearest Allied troops. As it was, we were lucky that the enemy had not yet found us. My hand tightened around the revolver lying ready underneath the blanket and Siciliano's words came into my mind. 'To be tortured and shot' . . . 'Never!' If the enemy came we would fight but it would assuredly be my last battle. I thought of distant England. Thank God they did not yet know of my plight. Gwen would be in bed now, curled up sleeping, dreaming perhaps of the future we had planned together. To me the future seemed very far away.

When the doctor had gone Antonio stepped out of the shadows. A small wiry figure, he wore a brown leather coat and a cap pulled over his eyes; slung across his chest on a leather strap hung a Spandau machine gun which dwarfed him.

'Well, Antonio, what's the news?'

'The Germans are searching everywhere for you,' he answered. 'You must move tomorrow, it is not safe here.'

'How can we do that?' I asked.

'Ah, we will find a way; we can do nothing at night because of the curfew and there are patrols everywhere since your attack on Botteghe.'

'Have you heard anything about that?' I asked.

A broad smile spread across his face and waxing lyrical he told us of the result. Ambulances had been on the road all day, carrying away wounded troops to hospital in Reggio. There was to be a formal parade at the cemetery and many graves had already been dug . . . Villa Calvi was badly burned and Villa Rossi had been damaged. The Germans were terrified and furious. He produced a cutting from the local Fascist paper, which stated:

> Last night a strong force of bandits attacked the garrison stationed at Botteghe. After fierce fighting they withdrew, after suffering heavy losses. It is believed that these brigands were British and some damage was done. The population must be made to understand that all armed Partisans will be treated as *franc tireurs*.

I asked the question uppermost in my mind:

'Did we kill the General?'

'I do not know,' answered Antonio. 'There are many officers dead and he has not since been seen.'

Antonio left, promising to return at midday. Giving us morphia injections, the girls took turns to watch. It was sometime later that I awoke from a fitful sleep as someone shook my shoulder. A hand was pressed tightly over my mouth and a voice whispered.

'Don't make a sound.'

Daylight filtered through cracks in the bales of hay which were stacked around us. Gordon, gun in hand, was sitting supported beside me. Outside I heard the sound of a woman wailing in the distance.

'What is it?' I asked.

A voice murmured, 'Fascists, they are searching the area.'

The Brigata Nera, those bloodthirsty devils, worse than their German masters. I knew that we should stand no chance if we were captured by them. But how could we resist with those two girls beside us? I struggled up on to one knee and whispered to them:

'Go away, for God's sake go away. Slip out by the back now while you've still got a chance.'

Gianni's sister answered with a smile, 'We are Partisans too and you are in my charge. Lie down and keep quiet.'

She raised her arm. There was a small revolver clenched in her hand.

Footsteps sounded in the yard outside and I heard a shrill voice raised . . .

'There is nothing there. It is only a barn.'

There was the sound of a curse and the weeping started again.

The door opened with a crash, letting in the bright rays of the sun. We crouched behind the hay, scarcely daring to breathe. For one terrible second there was silence, as the searchers glanced around. Then the door slammed shut again and the voiced died away.

Gianni's sister was crying softly without tears . . .

'Thank God, thank God; but we must get you away today.'

We were installed in a small house on the outskirts of Reggio. We had been transported the six miles from the barn, hidden away under the false bottom of a manure cart, and I could still smell the sickly stench in my hair from the liquid which had dripped down on us. Miraculously our wounds had not gone septic and mine were nearly healed on the surface although my leg was still completely paralysed and I could hardly move my body from weakness. Antonio had done wonders. Resistance men stood armed with machine guns in all the surrounding houses, to cordon off our refuge, and a small saloon motor car was parked ready in the yard in case we were forced to make a sudden getaway.

A nurse remained always on duty in our sick room and an ample supply of dressings and drugs had been stolen from the local hospital. Our host, a sturdy peasant type, was quite unperturbed at the danger of harbouring us and busied himself making us as comfortable as possible, bringing each day bottles of the choicest procurable wine. Gordon's father, who lived near Reggio, had been to see him, bringing toothbrushes, soap and other things of which we were in need.

On the seventh night after the action another doctor came. Gordon's leg had been troubling him and the nurse insisted that it be properly set in plaster. When the doctor had finished with him, he turned to examine me. His face was serious when the inspection was over. He pulled on his coat.

'Well?' I asked.

'The nerve in your leg is severed. If it is not repaired within ten days, it will die.'

'And what does that mean?'

'That unless you have an operation, you may never again be able to work that leg properly. Of course you could walk about with irons but it might never be normal.'

'Well, I can't get to hospital, as you well know. Can you operate on me here?'

He shrugged his shoulders.

'It would be impossible, there is no light or equipment, and you must lie absolutely still. No. I could not do it.'

Ten days to get into Allied territory. If I were fit and able to walk I would need all of that time. From here it was a good two nights' march to Secchio, a day to Civago and three days from there through the lines to Florence – if all went well and if I were fit. But crippled and unable to stand it was a hopeless prospect and though I racked my brains for a solution I could perceive none.

The following day one of the courier girls arrived from Secchio. She had been searching for us for days but Antonio had hidden us well. Except for the guards, who did not know our identity, not even the underground knew of our whereabouts. She carried a parcel of drugs, a large envelope containing my mail, which had been dropped in the last sortie, and a letter from Roy. Eagerly I tore open the mail. There were those envelopes addressed in that neat rounded handwriting which I had come to know and love so well. As I read the letters from Gwen, new determination and courage came to me. I must escape, and soon, so that we could enjoy the future together. She wrote happily knowing nothing of what had happened. If only for her sake I must escape.

I tore open the letter from Roy.

> Dear Mike... You don't know how sorry we all are about your rotten luck and will do everything we can to help you escape. Luigi has volunteered to take his whole Garibaldini brigade to bring you back from the plains. Then, when you get back here, you can hide somewhere and wait for the liberation which is bound to come soon. The couriers have also volunteered to carry you through the lines if you could stand the journey. Alternatively, base have wirelessed to say that if we can prepare a landing ground they will send in a light aircraft to fly you out. We can do nothing, however, till we know where you are and whether you are fit to move.

Roy went on to give the results of the action. It was rumoured that the attack had badly upset the German command, though it appeared that General Hauk had been away that night and had thus escaped. Don Pedro would be sorry! But our agents in Viano stated that thirty Germans had been killed in the two buildings. Of these a large proportion must be officers. Villa Calvi had been gutted and all the documents destroyed. Our own casualties had been three killed, all SAS in the Villa Rossi and a number wounded, but, apart from Gordon and myself, they had all escaped to the mountains.

> ... a good night's work (wrote Roy) and we are preparing for plenty more. The Partisans are in fine fettle. I only wish you were here to lead them still. Bert is prostrated; he wanders around Secchio murmuring, 'I knew it would happen. I warned the silly bastard!'

Nine days' grace. If I were to send the courier back tonight it would take two days for her to reach the mountains. Allow one day before Luigi could start. At best he could not be here in less than six days. Then moving slowly on stretcher my time would be up even before we got back to Secchio. Apart from that the Garibaldini could never hope to cross the ten miles of flat country from the foothills to Reggio unobserved and, once they were spotted, the enemy would bring up large forces along the motor roads to wipe them out. There would be no chance of success and it was not worth the risk to try it. A landing strip? I knew that there was no suitable ground in the Reggiani country but I remembered that a plane had landed once before to rescue an injured American pilot in the mountains near Ranzano, the village whence we had escaped during the enemy push in January. There was an Englishman there, a liaison officer. If I could get to Ranzano, he might be able to help. I looked at my map, about ten miles across the plains and twenty over the foothills into the mountains. But how could I hope to move thirty miles? I thought of a cart but all carts entering the mountains were searched at the German check points to ensure that they carried no arms or ammunition for the Partisans. We could not hope to avoid that search. If we could once get into the mountains the rest would be easy but those check points formed a seemingly insurmountable problem. Antonio came that evening. I told him what had happened and asked if he could help. He thought for a long moment, then a sly smile came over his face. . .

'I can't promise but I have an idea.'

'What is it?' I asked.

'I will say nothing but tomorrow I will return.'

The hours dragged slowly by. Lying near the window I watched as the dawn came and the sun rose into a blue sky. Aircraft engines rumbled above. They must be the daily morning fighter sweep, always regular at eight o'clock. Our peasant arrived with a bottle of wine and informed us that it was Sunday and I listened to the sound of feet pattering along the road below as the people returned from early church. Twelve o'clock. The relief nurse arrived but there was still no sign of Antonio. I had only eight days left. Time was running out and we still lay there.

Antonio arrived soon after dusk. The moment I saw his face, I knew he had good news. . .

'You must be ready at dawn tomorrow morning. An ambulance will take you into the mountains and you will not be stopped at the check points.'

I wrote two letters: first a short note to Roy telling him our plans. I asked him to wireless base to tell them that we were going to the Ranzano area and ask them to arrange a plane in three days time. The other letter I wrote to the officer at Ranzano, recounting what had happened and asking him to get the airfield ready. Antonio took the letters and promised to get them off by courier at once.

I was awakened by the noise of footsteps on the stairs. It was still dark outside but a candle spluttered beside my bed. The door opened softly and someone came into the room. . .

'Who is that?' I asked suspiciously.

For answer the visitor moved into the circle of light thrown by the candle. It was a soldier dressed in the grey uniform of the German army.

As I reached for the automatic under my pillow, I heard a soft laugh and he pushed the peaked cap up from his forehead. It was Antonio!

'Your ambulance is ready, sir.'

*

I lay on a stretcher at the edge of a small field in the mountains near Ranzano. Two lines of white parachutes were laid out along the field which formed a small ledge in the mountain side a hundred yards long by thirty broad. A group of men stood around watching the sky to the south. Phil sat on the ground beside me.

'It won't be long now,' he said. 'They're due soon after ten. In three hours' times you'll be in liberated territory. How are you feeling?'

'Not too bad thanks. My leg hurts like hell of course but if all goes well, that'll be fixed by tonight. Give me a hand to sit up, will you?'

Phil put his arms around my shoulders gently and helped me into a sitting position so that I could look at the country around me. It was a glorious morning. The new grass, damp from a heavy dew, flickered and sparkled in the warm sunlight. Far to the north, a valley curved down to the plains which were still curtained by the morning haze. To the south, ten miles away, lay the long hunched back of Cusna, its brilliant white peak reaching to the sky in lofty splendour. In the woods all around, patches of colour showed where the primrose and crocus pushed up their heads and birds sang merrily, heralding the spring. At that moment I loved the mountains more than ever before and how I hated to leave them. The glorious air, the open spaces, the free adventurous life which was soon to be just an episode of the past, a memory of the perfect world.

In liberated territory! What a contradiction of terms! Liberated but annexed. In three hours' time, I thought, I shall be liberated, in body – yes, but my spirit will be locked behind bars, escaping only during fleeting dreams. I thought back over the last three months –

the happiest of my life. The debacle in January, running like rabbits frightened by a stoat. The return to Secchio and those long weeks of tedious preparation building an army from a rabble – that stirring Garibaldini attack across the Secchia, confirmation that my work had been worthwhile – then, on the crest of the wave, the advent of the parachutists and our attack on Botteghe. The wild music of those pipes and that terrible moment when I found I could not walk, then those anxious days hiding in the plains, for the first time in my life helpless and relying on others. . .

I thought of Antonio and the ambulance in which we had driven past enemy sentries who smiled and waved their hands in greeting, little knowing the reward which was theirs if they apprehended the men who lay inside! Then the last three days: a blurred memory of pain, turning to agony and then to moments of oblivion as, with Gordon groaning in unison with me, we had bumped across the mountains, lying on a straw-covered bullock cart – that terrifying second crawling into the ditch when, close to journey's end, the lunatic pilot of a Thunderbolt had roared down upon our little farm wagon, emptying his guns for amusement near us, in the absence of a better target. And now, lying waiting for the aeroplane which would take me away. Not just away from that area to return again somewhere else, as I had done twice before, but away from the Partisans for ever – into another life.

From Cairo to Oruglica, from Kraljevo to Pino, from Mt. Grammondo to Bari, from Florence to Secchio. A long trail, always moving, always alert, attacking, escaping, but always preparing, waiting for that day, the *Ustanak* to the Yugoslavs when, guided by a few British officers, the Partisans all over Europe would rise against the enemy. Two years I had worked, two years I had waited and, on the eve of that day, crippled and useless, I had to withdraw from the game. Hard justice indeed. . . but the mountains are cruel though fair and a wounded man is of no use to them. In a month, I thought, in a week perhaps, the flame which smoulders now in these hills and valleys will burst ablaze and arm in arm with their allies in the south the Partisans, strong and united, will advance from their stronghold to drive the Germans out. Soon the Reggiani will be marching across the plains; soon they will be in Reggio dancing in the streets, exuberant with the joys of liberation. I shall be far away that day but perhaps, just for a moment, my spirit will join the throng and once again I shall be with the guerillas of all nations praising, cursing and encouraging them.

Phil, who had marched with Kiss from Secchio the previous night, roused me from my reverie...

'There it is!' he exclaimed.

He pointed to the south where, high above Cusna, a tiny speck hung in the sky. Seemingly motionless; slowly, ever so slowly, it grew larger. A murmur of engines reached me from the distance and two more planes came into view. Mustang fighters, approaching and receding as they circled above the tiny rescue plane.

We waited anxiously. Would they find our field or pass us by? Was the field long enough? Was the wind too strong? A mass of worries, ridiculous and otherwise, engulfed my mind.

The plane was low now. It was a German Fieseler Storch which, I was told, had been captured some months previously. It had a short stocky body, between two ridiculously large curved wings and its tiny engine puttered like a motor cycle as it circled over the field. One wing tip cleared the ground by inches as, in a vertical bank, she swung round and away. I held my breath. I had seen the pilot's face frowning as he examined the ground. It was rough, yes, and very, very small. Had he decided that it was too risky to land? The plane was below us now, turning in the valley out of sight beneath the shelf on which I lay. I heard the engine's murmur change to a roar and with nose well up and huge flaps down, the Storch appeared five feet above the end of the strip, hovered motionless for a second and, like a great bird, settled upon the ground, drawing to a halt in less than twenty yards.

I was carried to the door of the plane. Struggling and straining, I pulled myself inside. The pilot, a young Italian, strapped a parachute around my body which was naked but for a blanket. The Partisans crowded around the doorway to wish me good luck.

'Bye bye, Phil. My love to everybody and a kiss for Don Pedro's mother. Tell Bert not to bust himself.'

The fighters were roaring overhead now, dipping their noses and rolling their wings as they urged us to make haste. The pilot turned and smiled at me. Then, as the assembled Partisans held on to the wings and lifted the tail, he roared the engine to full power. A second's pause for the propeller to bite, his hand dropped, and we bumped slowly forward across the field. There was one agonising moment as the valley rushed up to meet us and I thought she would never lift. Then the nose swung violently upwards, throwing me back into my seat. As in a dream of the past, I watched those ragged figures waving hysterically at us till they receded into the distance and we settled on a steady course over Cusna to the south.

Index

Personal names, rank, title, decorations etc. are given as I knew them at the time and recollected them when I wrote this book in 1949/50 without the benefit of notes or diary. Apologies are extended to those whom I have slighted in error and to the many, indeed most, who have of course, acquired additional appendages since 1944/45.

Alexander, King, 31
Andrejević, Lt later Capt Miroslav (Mile), 70, 71, 75, 84, 85, 87, 88, 89, 95, 101, 102, 106, 107, 110, 112, 113, 116, 118, 120, 121, 123, 130, 135, 136, 147
Andrew, *see* Capt Arne Flygt
Anne St Paul Butler FANY, *see* Butler, Anne
Antonio, Major, (Piedmont), 164-167, 169, 172, 194
Antonio (in Reggio), 266-273

'Biagio', W/T Sgt Secondo Balestri, 197, 198, 205, 215
Bert, *see* Corporal Farrimond
'Black Marco', 110, 120, 122
Blackmore, Sgt, 65, 66, 68, 69, 146
Bogdan, 124
Bolden, Corporal SAS, 13
Butler, Anne St Paul FANY, 153, 154
Butler, Phil, 246-250, 259, 260, 272, 274

'Carlo, Don' (Don Domenico Orlandini), 13, 228, 230, 232, 235-239, 245, 246
Carter, Sgt, 36, 37, 38, 39, 155
Churchill, Mr W. S., 28
Čikabuda, 49-51, 53, 74, 75
Cosa, Capt, 189, 190
Crni Marko, *see* Black Marco

Davidson, Maj Basil, 11, 24-27, 34, 57
Davoli, Giulio, *see* 'Kiss'
Dicky, *see* Maj Richard Lonsdale
Djurić, Maj Radislav, 33, 34, 43-45, 53, 54, 56-64, 66, 67, 69, 86, 100, 140
Dobson, Fred, 198, 201, 203, 205, 209, 210, 215
'Don Carlo' *see* Carlo, Don
'Dragan', 118, 121, 122, 136

'Eros', 13, 223, 228

Faithful, Sgt 'Red', 99, 102, 124
Farran, Maj Roy DSO MC, 15-16, 253-256, 259, 260, 269, 270, 271
Farrimond, Corporal Bert, 5, 190, 191, 216-218, 221-225, 233, 238, 241, 243, 244, 247, 257, 270, 272
Feuerstein, General, 244, 252, 253, 254
Flygt, Capt Arne Andrew, 152, 154, 155, 156, 159, 188
Frits, Lt Snapper, *see* Snapper
Geoffrey, *see* Capt Long
'Gianni' Farri, 15, 266, 268
Giorgio (Reinert), 249
Glenconner, Lord Christopher, 25
'Gordon' *see* Monducci, Glauco
Graziani, Marshal, 244
Guscott, Sgt SAS, 13
Gwen *see* Lt Johnson FANY

Hackett, Brig John, 25
Hans, 16, 243, 257
Harvey, Sgt NZ Forces, 63, 69, 70, 76-78, 81, 82, 84-86, 92, 95
Hauk, General, 253, 254, 270
Jimmy, Frenchman on Villa Rossi attack, 167-174, 176, 185
Jimmy, Frenchman in Piedmont, 16
Joe, Shepheard's bartender, 17
John *see* Col Lonsdale
John *see* Maj Sehmer
Johnson, Lt Gwen FANY, 153-157, 159, 162, 188, 192, 270
Johnson, Sgt, 99, 101, 116, 124, 131, 132, 135, 139
Joško (in Serbia), 64
Joško (in Cairo), 27, 28, 30, 31, 32
Jovo *see* Capt Stefanović

'Kiss', Davoli Giulio, 233, 234, 236, 238, 241, 243, 244, 247, 251, 252, 254, 256, 274

Lazarević, Capt Stan, 63
Leban, Sgt, 59, 60, 63, 68, 69, 70, 75, 82, 83, 85, 86, 89, 92, 93, 94, 96, 97, 107, 124
Lees, Gwen *see* Johnson
Lesar, Sgt Harry, 111, 113, 114, 124, 139, 140
Lindstrom, 66
Lizza, Corporal Peter, 219, 221, 224, 246
Long, Capt Geoffrey, 160, 161, 163-166, 170, 172, 174, 182, 184, 186, 188, 191, 193, 194, 196, 199, 216
Lonsdale, Col John, 19-22
Lonsdale, Maj Richard, 19, 20
'Luigi', 236, 237, 245, 246, 270
McClellend, William, 175-178, 180-183, 188, 193, 197, 198, 199
Manić, Capt Bora, 70, 71, 75, 83-92, 95-102, 109-110, 116-118, 121
Marconi, Dr, 228

Marko *see* Black Marco
Mauri, Major Enrico, 160, 165, 166, 168, 176, 178, 179, 181, 184, 185, 186, 188, 189, 192, 216
Micky *see* Major Thomas
Mihailović, General Draža, 11, 29, 30, 32, 34, 54-57, 70-73, 84, 85, 86, 88, 92, 95, 96, 100, 101, 111, 113, 117, 118, 120, 123, 131, 133-140, 145-148, 151, 212
Mile *see* Capt Miroslav Andrejević
Mile, Orderly, 136
'Miro', 228, 233
'Modena', 15, 16
Monducci, Glauco ('Gordon'), 15, 16, 233, 235, 236, 238, 240, 243, 246, 248-250, 255-257, 260, 264-266, 268-270, 274
'Monti' (Col Augusto Berti), 223, 225, 227, 230-233, 235, 237, 239, 240
Morton, Capt Paul, 160, 161, 165-168, 174, 175, 182, 191, 193-196, 199, 200, 205, 212, 216
Mussolini, 200

'Nani', 164, 165, 168, 169, 175-181, 185
Nedić, General, 31, 32, 56, 70, 147
Neville *see* 'Maj Temple' (Darewski)

Paul *see* Capt Morton
Paul, Prince Regent of Yugoslavia, 28
Pavelić, Ante, 31
Pećanac, Kosta, 30
'Pedro', Don Pietro Rivi, 238, 252, 254, 256-258, 270, 274
Pešić, 103-107, 112-115, 130, 135, 136, 138
Peter, King of Yugoslavia, 28, 29, 30, 32, 56, 57, 86
Peter *see* Maj Solly-Flood
Petro, 228
Piva AVV, 192
Popović, Lt, 97, 98

'Ramis', 237
Riccomini, Lt SAS, 13
Richard *see* Maj Lonsdale
Roberto, 160, 161, 165-170, 172, 174, 176
Roy *see* Maj Farran DSO MC
Rubens, 235

'Salvi', Prof Giovanni Bessone, 192, 201, 202 203, 205, 209, 210, 211, 212, 215
Scalabrini, Ettore, 240, 253
Sehmer, Maj John, 33, 34, 43, 44, 45, 46, 48, 54-59, 62, 63, 65-69, 86, 99, 124, 125, 131, 133, 139, 140, 146
Siciliano, 263, 267
Smith, Lt (in Serbia), 34, 36, 40, 41, 49, 53, 55, 59, 65-67, 87, 146
Smith, Lt (in Italy), 250, 253
Snapper, Lt Frits, 237, 241, 242, 252, 255
Solly-Flood, Maj Peter, 133-145, 149, 150, 151
Stan *see* Capt Lazarević
Stefanović, Capt Jovo, 70-92, 95, 100-102, 109, 110, 116, 123, 125-130, 147

'Temple' (Maj Neville Darewski), 156, 158, 160, 162, 165, 184, 186-193, 198, 212, 213, 215-217
Thomas, Maj Micky, 26
Thompson, LAC, 34, 40-43, 49, 53, 55, 58, 59, 65, 66, 68
Tito, Marshal, 86, 96, 117, 118, 120, 121, 146, 147, 148, 190
Tomlinson, Lt Tommy, 34, 36, 38, 40-42, 46, 49, 51, 59, 60, 68, 69, 86, 87, 89-92, 94, 95, 97, 98, 101, 102, 104-108, 113, 116, 121, 136, 139
Trbić, 33, 34, 45, 55, 58, 59, 68

Vasco, Don, 239
Vlada (Orderly with Mile Andrejević), 63, 64
Vlada (Sgt Maj with Jovo Stefanović), 63, 64, 113, 114, 115
Vuk, 125, 126, 129, 130

Wilcockson, Maj Ernest, 222-224, 230